# A New Heaven

# A New Heaven

## Death, Human Destiny, and the Kingdom of God

Harvey Cox

ORBIS BOOKS
Maryknoll, New York 10545

ORBIS BOOKS
**Maryknoll, New York 10545**

Founded in 1970, Orbis Books endeavors to publish works that enlighten the mind, nourish the spirit, and challenge the conscience. The publishing arm of the Maryknoll Fathers and Brothers, Orbis seeks to explore the global dimensions of the Christian faith and mission, to invite dialogue with diverse cultures and religious traditions, and to serve the cause of reconciliation and peace. The books published reflect the views of their authors and do not represent the official position of the Maryknoll Society. To learn more about Maryknoll and Orbis Books, please visit our website at www.orbisbooks.com.

Manufactured in the United States of America

Library of Congress Cataloging-in-Publication Data

Names: Cox, Harvey, 1929- author.
Title: A new heaven : death, human destiny, and the kingdom of God / Harvey Cox.
Description: Maryknoll, NY : Orbis Books, [2022] | Includes bibliographical references and index. | Summary: "A survey of theological, cultural, and historical perspectives on heaven, the afterlife, and the 'kingdom of God.'"— Provided by publisher.
Identifiers: LCCN 2021047415 (print) | LCCN 2021047416 (ebook) | ISBN 9781626984585 (cloth) | ISBN 9781608339211 (epub)
Subjects: LCSH: Heaven—Christianity. | Future life—Christianity. | Kingdom of God.
Classification: LCC BT846.3 .C69 2022 (print) | LCC BT846.3 (ebook) | DDC 236/.24—dc23/eng/20211005
LC record available at https://lccn.loc.gov/2021047415
LC ebook record available at https://lccn.loc.gov/2021047416

We are still trying to work out a theory of love, . . . so that the revolution of love instead of that of hate may come about and we will have a new heaven and a new earth wherein justice dwelleth.

Dorothy Day
*The Catholic Worker*

*I dedicate this book to my son,*
*Nicholas Tumarkin Cox*

I was present at his birth thirty-five years ago and the physician even handed me scissors so I could cut the umbilical cord and introduce him into a personal human existence. Except for his college years, we have never been very far from each other. We built enormous sand castles on various beaches and took bike rides along the Minute Man trail. His performances in musicals like *Man of La Mancha* sent me home warmed and whistling. His decision to major in religion at Princeton pleased me, and initiated years of animated intellectual and personal conversations. When I taught a semester at Arizona State University, he joined me for part of the time. We walked in the mountains, and then took an overnight sleeper together home.

Two years ago, I officiated at his marriage to Valerie Lute in our sunlit side yard. The couple now lives only a few blocks away. We see them often, and they join us every Friday for Sabbath prayers, candles, and dinner, which Nicholas, now a skilled professional cook, prepares.

Nicholas, from the first moment of your life, when I took those scissors in my hand, we have been close, and I am endlessly grateful for the love, delight, and companionship with which you continue to shower me in my twilight years. Shalom!

# *Contents*

# Why We Need a New Heaven

*Then I saw a new heaven and a new earth, for the first heaven and the first earth had passed away, and there was no longer any sea.* (Revelation 21:1)

I had recently turned ninety when I started writing this book. Consequently, when friends asked me what I was currently working on, and I told them, they smiled knowingly. They were sure they knew why I had seized on this topic. Entering my sunset years, they thought, it was only natural that my thoughts would turn to what might or might not come next. The curtain was about to go up on my last act, so a book about the "hereafter" was just what everyone would expect. It would be my swan song, my last hurrah.

But my friends were mistaken. I did not undertake this project because of a sharpened sense of my mortality. I had other reasons. However, my friends were not entirely wrong. The reader will see that as I wrote, my awareness of my finitudes did become increasingly significant to me, making the book more personal than I first intended.

When I was fourteen, I thought about death and the afterlife a lot. I think most kids do at that age. But I did not worry about heaven or hell. I could not imagine that God, whom I pictured as a kindly old man, could possibly dispatch me, or anyone else, to eternal torment. As for heaven, I was not sure whether there was such a place, but I had my doubts. At that age, neither possibility bothered me much. What did unsettle me, however, was the prospect of nonexistence. Imagining a universe spinning on for millennia, its stars and planets heedlessly orbiting, but without me, made my stomach tighten. When I learned that our solar system and eventually the universe itself would also eventually expire, it did not seem alarming. It was the nonexistence of my own self that seemed so unthinkable. As I left my early teen years, this jumble of horror and the emptiness gradually faded, and for decades I rarely thought about any hereafter. Then why this book?

It is the product of a combination of personal, spiritual, and intellectual experiences. First, for several years I had been meeting in my home now and then with some of my former students to sip beer and soft drinks, munch cookies, and discuss current theological, political, and religious issues. At one of these informal seminars, one of these ex-students, the Rev. Rebecca Pugh, the minister of a thriving congregation in Salem, Massachusetts, suddenly told me that I should "write a book about heaven." I looked at her in disbelief. I told her that I had little intellectual interest and no direct experience with whatever lay beyond "this mortal coil." I reminded her that my first major book had been *The Secular City*, not "the celestial garden." I said that for years I had focused my teaching and writing on the role religion plays in this life, and that Jesus constantly urged his listeners to stop their persistent staring upward and to pay attention to what was happening within and around them: "Behold, the kingdom of God is in the midst of you."

I thought this would settle the matter. But it did not. The next time we met, Rebecca persisted. The members of her congregation, she said, were baffled and frustrated by the contradictory claims about the "hereafter" they heard, mostly but not exclusively, at funerals. She warned me that she would continue to pester me until I agreed to write the book. Still, I temporized. I had no appetite to rake over the coals of a subject that had been fought about so fruitlessly for so many centuries. I even remarked, maybe a little tastelessly, that Jesus had once said, "Let the dead bury the dead" (Luke 9:60).

Then, however, in quick succession I attended the funerals of two old friends, one in St. Luke's Roman Catholic Church, the other in a funeral home. Fresh from my recent debates with Rebecca, I listened to what was being said with more than usual attention. Rebecca was right. In the prayers and hymns, and in the words of the priest and the minister, a cascade of inconsistent images and phrases flowed into the congregation's ears (or maybe over their heads). We heard both that the deceased was now in the merciful presence of God, but also that at the final resurrection he would be "carried into that presence." But why should someone be carried to where he already was? One prayer referred to his grave as a "final resting place," but also that what we were participating in today was not final. We were urged to comfort those he had left behind in their sorrow, but also to celebrate the joyous welcome he was even now receiving from the heavenly host. At the graveside we heard "ashes to ashes and dust to dust" but also that this earthly body would one day be "clothed in an eternal raiment, and a new and glorified body." No wonder Rebecca's church members were bewildered.

Attending these funerals brought back to my mind the dozens I attended when, as a teenager, I worked part time with my Uncle Frank, the undertaker in our little hometown. (I will return to that formative episode in a later chapter.) I had heard these funereal phrases many times then, but never noticed any incongruity. After all, death itself is the ultimate contradiction. Maybe, I thought, given its intractable incomprehensibility, people simply have learned not to hear the contradictions. I will return to this issue later.

In any case, after the home seminars and the funerals, I started to ponder more often about death and the afterlife. I decided it was time for me to engage in some serious study, observation, and reflection on this old but new mystery. I thought that I might even eventually attempt to write a book on it. I knew this would be an arduous voyage. But it might make Rev. Rebecca Pugh a little quieter, at least for a while. What follows then in these pages is a kind of logbook of my journey through a universe of heavenly signs and symbols, of fervent beliefs and equally potent doubt and disbelief.

As the reader will see, my travels carried me to a rich range of sites. My travels landed me in Kursk, in the limitless steppes of Russia, where one of the biggest battles of World War II took place. It is the area to which hundreds of devoted Russian young people hike along muddy paths each year to carefully disinter the skeletal remains of some of the thousands of soldiers who died there but whose bodies were never formally buried. Motivated by a blending of reverence and patriotism, the youngsters undertake this task to give these long-neglected defenders of the fatherland a proper funeral.

My travel also allowed me to go back in memory to the desert in northern Mexico where I had once passed an unforgettable night with some Huichole Indians, who, for generations, have respectfully eaten peyote in their sacred ceremonies, and who believe that heaven is not far away. It is a present reality, though it can only be visited temporarily on special occasions.

Also, through intriguing research and conversations with faculty colleagues in archaeology, anthropology, and ancient history, I learned about a thirty-thousand-year-old human burial pit. Later, I found out about the different, even contrasting opinions the early Christians held about the hereafter. Finally, my long trek also took me back to my small hometown in Pennsylvania to revisit the funeral parlor where I worked when I was sixteen, and to the cemetery near my home where I played hide-and-seek among the tombstones but now returned to see what I could find out about evolving views of the hereafter from the fading epitaphs carved on those granite slabs.

During the long mission I sometimes thought about my favorite traveler, Odysseus, whose brief visit to Hades we will return to later. Unlike him, I never had to contend with a Cyclops or a Circe, but like him I did hope to drop anchor finally in a home port that, after a prolonged absence, would feel familiar and welcoming, which is what actually happened.

To embark on any expedition, one needs some basic navigational instruments like a compass, a quadrant, and a chart. One of my teachers, theologian Paul Tillich (1886–1965), has provided the theological equivalents of these necessities for me. Tillich developed an approach he called "the method of correlation," which I have applied in this book. The process begins with recognizing that the word "theology" has two parts. The first is *theos* and the second is *logos*; and "theology" means relating the divine or eternal (the *theos*), on the one hand, and, on the other, the human quest for meaning as it is expressed in a given culture, its symbolic self-understanding (*logos*). This method produces the following procedure: The theologian begins by analyzing the symbols through which a culture expresses its existential questions, what Tillich called its "deepest concerns." Then he or she searches the religious tradition to locate the symbols that attempt to respond to these questions. Theology thus pursues a pattern of question and response and becomes a process of "correlation." Tillich suggested this tactic because, as he put it, "for too long theology has served up answers to questions no one was asking, so we must begin with the questions." His point brings to mind a story told of Gertrude Stein as she was dying, when one of the friends by her bedside asked, "Gertrude, tell us, what is the answer?" Stein opened her eyes and replied, "No! What is the *question?*" In one sense then, this logbook is not just the record of assorted answers but also a quest for "the questions."

But since any question or answer invariably raises other questions, theology is not an enterprise that is ever finished. Why? Because cultures are constantly changing, and because a religion is not a closed and inert collection of doctrines but an ongoing practice. As Pastor Robinson told his fellow passengers on the *Mayflower* as they set sail, "For I am very confident the Lord hath more truth and light yet to break forth out of His holy Word."

In this extended journey through cultures and eons, the *logos* will be what we learn about the quest for meaning that animates the many visions of heaven we encounter. The *theos* will be drawn from the Judeo-Christian tradition, the one I know best, particularly what it says about death and human destiny. I choose this tradition not to advocate its superiority but for two other reasons. First, because it is the one most familiar to me and probably to many readers. Second, it is a living and changing tradition that has absorbed vital elements from others, and still does. For example, during the last century, nonviolence, which Martin Luther King Jr. derived both from Gandhi and from the Sermon on the Mount, has become integral to many Christians, who have also learned various forms of meditation derived from Asian faiths. At the same time, some other religions have adopted the idea of an ultimate victory of peace and justice, the equivalent of a kingdom of God, such as the "Buddha realm." This is such a widespread tendency that some religious scholars believe that studying these visions has become the most fruitful way to compare faith traditions today.

Thus, since my starting point is my own spiritual tradition, my travel diary also reflects a subtle change that took place within me, one that I will return to in the last chapter. In brief, my thinking gradually became not just an effort to respond to other people's questions but also to my own. Like the specialist in Aleksandr Solzhenitsyn's novel *The Cancer Ward* who discovers he has the disease himself, my orientation toward my subject became more "existential," not just reportorial. But an even more profound insight surfaced.

The word "death" is prominent in my subtitle. But I quickly noticed that it is not death itself that distressed our ancestors and still vexes us, if not continuously, then periodically. But what is it? "It" assumes an array of forms and has many names, and they all fuel the anxiety that gnaws at us, especially in certain circumstances.

I once worked as a chaplain in a hospital for what the staff called "terminal patients," with whom I had memorable conversations. These talks taught me that for many people today it was not the "dread of death" or of "something *after* death" that disturbed them. It was the process of dying. It was the prospect of lying encased by tubes and gauges while modern medical science squeezes out a few more days or hours of something that is hardly life. But even more fundamental than the fear of death or dying are the misgivings about whether our brief lives have any meaning beyond what we try to fashion for ourselves: "What is this really all about?"

As Tillich puts it, it is not the fear of death that unnerves us, as it did the ancients, who hungered for immortality; nor is it the dread of punishment after death, which caused people in the age of the Reformation to slaughter one another over how to be justified before God's judgment. In this era, Tillich says, our characteristic anxiety is that our lives, and maybe even the whole of earthly and cosmic history, are devoid of significance. This does not mean that we fret about the meaning of life all the time. And doubtless some people might claim that the issue never bothers them at all. But I think Tillich is right in identifying the "quest for meaning" as the underlying spiritual question of our time. And what compounds this civilizational malaise is  that the language in which we once thought about either death or the meaning of life no longer works for many people. Maybe this explains why the profoundly enigmatic symbol of "a new heaven" seemed so apt to me for a title.

This is where the word "new" comes in. It refers to two sources. One is the *logos* side of our method of correlation; the other from the *theos* side. From the first side, the obvious fact is that much of the language in which we have traditionally expressed the hope for heaven no longer seems plausible for many people. The symbol is broken. A new language is needed. But it must be one that preserves the reality of what the older language pointed to. A recognizable continuity with the past is  necessary. The "new heaven" must be a new *heaven*, not a new something else.

But the "new" also comes from the *theos* side. As the vision from Revelation quoted at the head of this chapter makes clear, "heaven," however we may conceive it, is not eternal. Like the earth, it "passes away." But it is not replaced by nothing. It is replaced by a "*new* heaven." As I will suggest later, this confirmation of the significance of heaven correlates with the physical resurrection of Christ, which, as Reinhold Niebuhr writes in *The Nature and Destiny of Man*, is the Christian hope (against the idea of the immortality of the soul) that all history, and  not just certain individuals, is being redeemed. There is a new heaven and also "a new earth."

In light of this understanding of a "new heaven," as I will suggest in this book, the ideas about heaven that informed our *forebears* were not just about "what happens next." They were also, and more importantly, responses to the question of how we should live here and now, about the purpose of our lives. Yes, earlier generations lived under different circumstances, so some of their concerns are no longer ours. But they were also human beings like us, so some of their deepest concerns are still with us. And our existential question about the meaning, if any, of life was their question as well, although they asked it in different ways. This is why the "answers" they generated in myths, dreams, philosophies, and depictions of heaven are still invaluable for us. The idea that "everything changes" has some truth, but anyone who reads Sophocles or Shakespeare or the Bible knows there are also some things that do not.

Clearly then, this is not a book "*about heaven.*" To claim that would surely be presumptuous. Rather, this book is my effort to render a faithful account of what some of our fellow human beings, in an assortment of cultures, and in our own, have thought both about life after death and what such a life means for life on earth. Also, when I write about "what they thought," I use the word "thought" in an expanded sense. More than thinking about heaven, human beings have more often sung, danced, chanted, dreamed, and envisioned it. Therefore, the present book is not an intellectual history. The most revealing images of the next world are found not in formal theological treatises. They are passed on through the customs, ballads, anecdotes, jokes, folk sayings, legends, myths, and fantasies of ordinary people. They are "in the midst of you."

But this is too much for any one book. And when you add the memories that I have recovered from my own nearly forgotten past, it amounts to even more. Then when you stir into this mixture of the inner and the outer the question of how the two cohere or conflict with each other, a new picture comes into focus. The plot thickens, but this is just the beginning. My overall goal is both to see how humanity's visions of the next or other worlds are shaped by their terrestrial *civilizations* and how much these visions in turn impact their birthing societies. Traffic on Jacob's ladder goes both ways.

This is hardly a new issue: How do the City of God and the City of Man interact? It is a perennial preoccupation. No theologian from St. Augustine to Reinhold Niebuhr has been able to avoid it. It is the meta-question that lurks behind all the others. The way we think about it defines how we think about much else, and this intricate dance has played out over the entire course of human history. It is a chronicle so massive as to defy exploration. Consequently, for this, in addition to the nautical equipment and the chart already mentioned, we need to have some idea of just what, amidst the welter of possibilities open to us, we are looking for. How can this be done?

For reasons I will explain in the next chapter, I will concentrate at first on *ritual* as the phenomenon most likely to expedite our search. The word "ritual" is usually linked to formal religion. But this is not true. There are secular as well as religious rituals. A ritual is a repeated and patterned form of behavior that conveys a distinct meaning, one that is larger than itself. There are family rituals and national rituals, rituals associated with sports and with politics. Individuals evolve their own personal rituals. My interest in rituals here is that, however simple or complex, if carefully examined, they express a vital element of the larger worldview of which they are a part. Think, for example, of the wealth of connotations implied in crossing oneself or shaking someone's hand.

National and religious rituals encapsulate whole worldviews and can be fully understood only in light of these larger canvasses. And as we will now see, the most promising rituals for understanding ideas of another world or an afterlife are the ones that represent the "gates of heaven": initiation and death rituals. We will turn to them in succeeding chapters.

# 1

# *Gates of Heaven*

*Lift up your heads, O gates! And be lifted up, O ancient
doors, that the King of glory may come in. Who is this King
of glory? The Lord, strong and mighty, the Lord, mighty
in battle! Lift up your heads, O gates! And lift them up, O
ancient doors, that the King of glory may come in. Who is
this King of glory? The Lord of hosts, he is the King of glory!
Selah.* (Psalm 24:7–10 ESV)

Many is the explorer who starts out on an expedition without out a clear idea of what he or she is looking for. Some of
them stumble onto important discoveries they could not have
anticipated. These are the pioneers whose names appear in the
history books. Others set out knowing exactly what they are
looking for and either find it or do not. Those who do join the
other "discoverers." Those who do not eventually become frustrated and embittered. These we rarely hear about. Others still,
maybe most, begin with a clear idea of what they want to find
but are uncertain about where to search.

In looking for views of heaven, I was in the third category.
Where should I look? One easy answer would be to examine the
explicit doctrinal teachings about heaven taught in the different
spiritual traditions. But this would be insufficient. Since conceptions of the afterlife are not restricted to doctrines but are

widely dispersed throughout the cultures in which they exist, this approach would not do. We would miss some of the richest material. Consequently, the hard questions remain: if we are looking for ideas about heaven, where should we begin?

Clearly, we need some way to facilitate our understanding of the countless visions of the hereafter. But if a culture or a religion is like a constellation, we need a way to investigate without getting "lost in the stars." If we cannot explore the whole, then what element, or "keystone," within it might best help us? As I puzzled over what this keystone might be, I thought of the funerals I had recently attended, and it occurred to me that what I was looking for was right in front of me. It was *rituals*.

All religions, from the simplest to the most complex, have rituals. They usually consist of a combination of words and actions, repeated on special occasions. In catechisms they are sometimes referred to as "an outward and visible sign of an inward and invisible grace." This means that rituals are empirical. They can be seen and heard, and in many cases, tasted, smelled, and felt. But they are intended to point beyond themselves to something more ultimate.

Most critically, for our purposes as we survey conceptions of the afterlife, scholars view rituals as a particularly revelatory component of any religion. Not quite perhaps the proverbial grain of sand that contains the whole universe, nonetheless rituals usually reveal the essential contours of a religion in a compressed form. Among rituals, there are two that are particularly helpful sources in a search like this one: rituals of *initiation* and rituals of *death*. During all rituals, but especially these two, elements that are normally diffused in various ceremonies and doctrines become concentrated—a small-scale model of the vital rudiments of this religion: its origin, its salient beliefs, its worldview, and its vision of the ultimate. Especially in initiation and death rituals, elements that remain implicit at other times, become explicit. A ritual is not only a keystone, it is a compact index of the faith of which it is a quintessential component.

As we begin the formidable task of thinking about "heaven," it is important to recognize that *the concept of heaven is not universal.* Heaven is not nirvana. It is not Valhalla. It is not the Isles of the Blessed. There may be similarities among all these conceptions, but there are also radical differences. Heaven is not even the same for all Christians, who, for twenty centuries, have held dramatically contrasting views, as we will see in this book. The descriptions of heaven in the writings of Christians in the first centuries after Christ differ from the ones we read in the Reformation and Counter-Reformation eras. And these differ from the ones that arose in the nineteenth and twentieth centuries.

Epitaphs in old cemeteries trace these changes. The words on the tombstones in the oldest parts tell us that the deceased looked forward to enjoying intimate, uninterrupted communion with God and Jesus: "Leaning on the Everlasting Arms." The stones in the more recent sections voice a different hope. They speak of being restored to previously lost friends and relatives: "Will the Circle Be Unbroken?" Whatever one's conception of heaven today, whether one believes in it or not, it is one way of thinking about a range of disparate conceptions that have all been called "heaven."

Not all religions have an equivalent of the Christian heaven, but all point beyond themselves to something much more complete and more inclusive, even though what this is may not always be made explicit. This "something" is what students of religion, in a noble effort to find a common denominator that makes room for everyone, have sometimes called *"ultimate human destiny."* A gallant attempt, but even this endeavor to shape a far-reaching capaciousness turns out to be more parochial than it sounds. Why?

It is the word "destiny" that consigns this phrase to a much less than universal status. "Destiny" is related to "destination," which suggests purposeful movement toward a goal. But there are significant traditions that view the whole idea of a destination as a misleading one. Most Buddhists teach that we are where we are at this present moment, and we should learn to be at home in it. Buddhist meditation practice requires sitting quietly for as long as it takes to leave behind our nagging aspirations to be somewhere else or to be someone better. One may think that the grass must be greener on the other side of the stream. But it is not; and this is an insight that is a maxim almost impossible for most Americans even to grasp, let alone to believe, and one can see why. Freeing oneself of goals and destinations is not an idea or a theory. It is a way of seeing life, one that is realized not by concentrated thinking but by "awakening." Indeed, for Buddhists, the attempt to resolve problems by concentrating on them results only in our becoming further "attached" or enmeshed in them. The answer to this is the most essential of all qualities, and the basis of the Buddha's teaching: "detachment." In this view, the effort of many Christians and others to "get to heaven" is tragically misplaced. It will not only not "get" us anywhere; it will cripple us by binding us to more attachment.

I got a hint of this the first time I walked into the meditation room in a local Buddhist center. I had a clear "goal." That was to master the Buddhist meditation practice and thereby perhaps become a calmer, more centered, better person. I naively asked the instructor how I should begin. He said nothing, but just smiled and pointed to some other guests who were sitting silently on flat cushions. "You mean I should just sit?" I asked. Again, he smiled and nodded. So, I sat, and sat, and sat. I sat for over two uncomfortable hours until the "ping" of a miniscule bell announced a short break. Only after this somewhat frustrating period did the instructor offer some advice. He had wanted me to feel this exercise directly in my body before introducing words and concepts, which, like most Buddhists, he regarded as secondary. Once, it is said, the Buddha was seated in the grass with his disciple on a hillside. One of his followers begged him to tell them the secret of existence. The Enlightened One said nothing. He picked a wildflower growing near him and looked at it in silence.

Of course, on other occasions, the Buddha did speak and teach. But the incident on the hillside with the flower made a real point. Likewise, my instructor knew that verbal instructions would be wasted on me before I had a direct encounter with that which language can touch only indirectly. I think his approach was the right one. When he advised me about how I should learn to step back from the constant flow of thoughts that coursed through my mind and simply observe them, neither rejecting nor welcoming them, I got the message. Doing otherwise, one is sure to be caught up in them, while escaping such attachment is the way to freedom. The point is to free ourselves from our exclusively conceptual style of thinking. This does not mean discarding it altogether. Rather, it means viewing it as just one among other ways of thinking. But how do we learn to do this? That is exactly the significance of the "sitting" practice I have described above.

Still, for the present book, this primal Buddhist ritual raises some cautionary signals we must take into consideration. First it underlines a question about the word "ultimate." Does this word, like "destination," not imply something ahead of us, something we may eventually "get to" after a sequence that includes the "penultimate"? This is indeed one definition of "ultimate," and one that is flatly contradicted by the Buddhist teaching that it is just this kind of future-directed thinking that prevents us from being content with being "where we are." But this teaching also has, as I have written above, far-reaching consequences for thinking about "heaven." Can we think about heaven in terms that are not futuristic, or mostly futuristic? I remember when I was a child hearing someone criticize a person considered "too religious" by saying, "He is so intent on heaven, he is no earthly good." This was sometimes a harsh dismissal, but beneath it there is an insight that is both Buddhist and Christian. Looking elsewhere, above, or in the future for human fulfillment can make it hard for us to see the grace around and within us. Could it be that the "new heaven" foreseen in the Book of Revelation will not impose this dichotomy but instead introduce us into a unity we now experience only sporadically? This would make what sometimes seem to be contradictory statements by Jesus describing the kingdom of God as both already here and yet to come more understandable.

Still, I am glad Jesus did not settle the "now or later" question but left us to struggle with the tension. And Buddhists have had to contend with the same tension. In view of the rejection of a futuristic orientation, it is significant that within the larger Buddhist tradition there emerged an important movement called Pure Land Buddhism in which that "land" has some of the qualities of a heaven. But the Buddhist teachers have continued to insist that the Pure Land is not some future realm but is available to us in the here and now, making it similar in this respect to the way Jesus described the kingdom of heaven. But any attachment, whether to a "now" or to a "later," is still attachment. Maybe we need to mix a little of each of these traditions. In any case, it seems that "ultimate destiny" is not the universal keystone we need.

And yet the dictionary lists another equally valid usage of "ultimate" when it is not wedded to "destiny." This second definition is "the best achievable or imaginable of its kind, a fundamental fact or principle." For this chapter I will use "ultimate" in its second sense. As we have just seen, a sense of "destiny" is common in many, but not all, religions. Still, all religions do have some idea of an "ultimate," in its second sense, the "best imaginable of its kind." Even the Buddhist sage who has escaped thinking about goals and who rejects the notion of a "destiny" believes that where he "is now" is better than where he was before his enlightenment, even though it is not his destination. Of course religions differ widely about what the "best imaginable is," yet this fundamental principle is something they do have in common. The sense of the "ultimate" can be uncovered in various elements of a religion. It is expressed in its liturgies, art, music, doctrines, and sacred calendar and in innumerable other features. For example, its vision of "the ultimate" is often displayed in its architecture.

According to an old Slavic Chronicle, in 1000 CE the Russian pilgrims who had been engaged in a long search for a faith for their country, which was still "pagan," had not been satisfied, even though they had considered Islam and Judaism. Tired from their travels, again according to the Chronicle, they had recoiled at the Muslim prohibition of alcohol. A life without vodka would be unacceptable. In Judaism, they gasped at the idea of a God who punished his own people. Discouraged, they finally stepped inside the Hagia Sophia in Constantinople, and "knew not if we were in heaven or on earth."

One can appreciate their reaction. Today, visitors to an Orthodox Easter service, with its flickering candles and gold-framed icons, often mention the plaintive chants that explode into jubilant alleluias at midnight, and report feeling as if they had been transported temporarily into paradise.

The "ultimate" can also be portrayed in a quite different architectural mode, including the landscape. Beside a Buddhist shrine near the Japanese city of Kyoto there is a trail, understood to be an integral part of the holy place, that leads into the surrounding forest. As it meanders among the trees and bushes, it gradually becomes increasingly narrow, until finally it disappears entirely. It does not really "end," and it leads nowhere. The whole complex, with both the shrine and the trail, is an eloquent statement of the Zen Buddhist sense of ultimate destiny—or perhaps more correctly, non-destiny.

Compare this with the grand Hassan II (Muslim) Mosque in Casablanca, which I have visited more than once. When no prayers are being recited, the visitor finds himself in a vast indoor space devoid of any statues or paintings, with nothing to look at except the "minbar," the pulpit where the imam reads from the Holy Qur'an. Just outside, a stately, vertical minaret, with no steps or gradations, points toward the sky. During prayers, every person in the mosque is kneeling and facing in the same direction. There is no hierarchical seating. Everyone is radically equal. Everything combines to provide a visual reminder that there is "no God but Allah."

At the Sree Padmanabhaswamy (Hindu) Temple in South India, the visitor, after entering, walks through a series of rooms that become progressively smaller, ending in a tiny windowless chamber with no outside lighting. One is alone with oneself, with only inner resources to draw on. Whatever ultimate there is must be found within.

On the other hand, the (Roman Catholic) Basilica of the Shrine of the Immaculate Conception in Washington, DC, projects a different vision of the ultimate. It is flooded with light through multicolored stained-glass windows. The visitor's eye moves in stages to an ornate main altar and step by step upward to the gold-sheathed cupola. We are reminded by every step that we live in a hierarchical universe in which one approaches the Holy by degrees. Returning to floor level, one's eyes can roam around magnificent paintings and statuary, much of it placed in several "national chapels" that ring the entire interior, each one representing a different country with its own apparition of the Mother of God. This, we are reminded, is a "national basilica" with a special relationship to America, but it is also part of a "universal, catholic" church made up of many nations. The basilica itself is an eloquent statement of the essence of the Catholic faith.

What do these architectural creations tell us about the concept or concepts of heaven in each tradition? This is a very large question. Many prayers and hymns speak of heaven as a kind of temple, but the details are rarely explicit. Some works of art depicting aspects of heaven make it appear similar to a site of worship. But other artistic allusions to heaven are filled with flowers and trees and flowing streams. We get no consistent image.

Also, we should be careful not to generalize. The examples mentioned above are all drawn from one branch of a religion. There are expressions of Buddhism and Hinduism, for example, with wholly different ideas of the ultimate. But the examples I have mentioned illustrate both the universality and the comparability of symbols of "the ultimate," and in some cases, the ultimate destiny of ourselves and of all things. Again, these structures differ radically from one another. But insofar as they all bear witness to the "ultimate," we can learn from them how to think about our ideas of heaven in a larger context.

Psychologists who study how people learn agree that one of the most elemental ways we do so is by seeing the similarities and differences between things. Infants learn how to cope with what William James called the "great blooming, buzzing confusion" of seeing the difference between a chair and a table or hot and cold. As adults learning about varying worldviews or conceptions of the hereafter, we also learn by comparing. We learn not to confuse surface similarities with deeper differences.

And we learn not to confuse surface differences with essential similarities.

One of the reasons why examining rituals is a promising way to organize our search is that they lend themselves to comparison. Like a temple or a path in the forest, a ritual is also something that can be compared, albeit on a smaller scale. What gives them this quality of comparability is their underlying organizational similarity to the rituals of other religions. Not only are rituals found in all religions, but despite the obvious differences among them, they are structurally analogous, and therefore comparable.

One of the first scholars to call attention to this commonality among rituals was the French anthropologist Claude Lévi-Strauss, who died at the age of one hundred in 2009. He did his original research in Brazil, but soon became recognized as the world's leading expert on myth and ritual. He rejected the idea that differences between societies were of no consequence, but he still focused on the common aspects of humanity's attempts to understand the world. Thus, regarding rituals, he recognized their rich variability but also noticed that they had a common framework, which he called a "structure." Thus, Lévi-Strauss's work is indispensable in trying to appreciate how rituals of initiation and death, for example, can be keystones in thinking about the "ultimate." This is one reason why the next two chapters of this book will highlight initiation and death rituals.

Lévi-Strauss never claimed to be a theologian, but his observations show how rituals point to more comprehensive symbols of something ultimate. His approach allows us to compare, for example, such seemingly incomparable ideas as nirvana, the bardo, purgatory, limbo, "the Isles of the Blessed," Hades, heaven, Gehenna, perdition, the inferno, the bosom of Abraham, among others. Does the "kingdom of God" belong in this list?

Yes, but only with caution. As we will see in another chapter, the idea of God's kingdom appears throughout the Bible, but its meaning varies, and in the New Testament it is sometimes rendered as synonymous with heaven. But this is confusing. The kingdom of God is a far more comprehensive term than "heaven." The kingdom of God is the symbol for what has been called the culmination or climax, not only of individual human beings, but of the entire course of history and of the entire cosmos. But this raises a crucial question. Religious language is always symbolic, so is it possible for people like us, living in what someone has called "a world of broken symbols," to grasp the meaning of these terms?

I think it is possible. First, we need to remember what we mean by "symbolic." Symbols speak to us at the cognitive, pre-cognitive, and emotional level. They link the conscious and the subconscious. They both *point* to a reality beyond themselves and *participate* in that reality. We can grasp the significance of symbols only by avoiding a literal reading, by letting them "speak" to us, and insofar as we can, by participating in them ourselves. Only then can we begin the necessary task of asking more analytical questions about their context and intended audience.

Finally, we also need to pose this question: what does the symbolic way of using ordinary language to convey something transcending the ordinary tell us? For one thing, it tells us that to grasp the meaning of what we call "reality," we need to recognize that reality consists both of what is "there" and what we bring to what is there. Both Einstein's discoveries and recent cognitive theory underscore this, rejecting the mistaken idea that reality is an inert object, finished and complete, that we merely register and record. Perception, it turns out, is a much more active process, more like reading a poem than reading a street sign, more like looking at a Jackson Pollock abstract painting than at a realistic photograph. Likewise, to grasp a symbol (which includes all religious language), we need to forgo a strictly objective stance and allow ourselves to be drawn into the delicate dance of interpreting without slipping back into a tone-deaf literalism. This is what I will try to do (not, I fear, with complete success) in this book.

There was another important reason for me to open with rituals in the early chapters. That is the *personal connection*. I knew that what I would write might sound like lifeless second-hand reporting unless I could draw on memories of the rituals I have experienced. If I could, it would invite readers to do the same, making a connection possible. I would need to revisit the hopes and fears about death and what, if anything, might come later that I have harbored at times. But I knew this would not be enough. I would also have to be as honest as I could about how I feel today, this minute, about the theme of the book. But, as has been said, a man cannot think for very long about his own death any more than he can stare for long at the sun. I agree with this warning. But I also take seriously the philosopher Martin Heidegger's observation that we should not look away from the certainty of our own death too quickly, lest we miss the full reality of our own finitude.

As I turned to the personal, I was also aware that memory is one of the first elements in our cognitive apparatus to decline. Still, when I started what I thought might be a taxing and possibly fruitless search in the attic and basement of my mind, I found that it was not as difficult or as painful as I had feared. Maybe, at my age, I had grown more accepting of my own mortality. Maybe, too, the effort to dust off old memories, some of which I had not thought about for decades, was not all that grueling after all. The memories were alive and seemingly waiting to be summoned. When I mentioned this to a psychologist colleague, she did not seem impressed. Many older people, she said, remembered events and people from their earliest years. "What they forget," she added, "is what they had for breakfast a few hours ago."

But once jogged to life, I quickly discovered, memory can recuperate. As I wrote about bygone episodes, recalling them became easier. They also became more alive. I could not only think about them; I also felt some of the same exhilaration, anxiety, awe, pain, and pleasure that I had originally experienced. The most important contribution psychoanalysis has made is its unearthing of both the images and the feelings of these "lost memories," and then drawing on them to contribute to the healing process. For this memory recovery phase of my "research expedition" I found a guide and exemplar in St. Augustine. Remember that the bishop of Hippo (354–430 CE) wrote his classic *Confessions* thirty years after the recorded events took place. And he demonstrated for succeeding generations that he could now see meanings in them that he had not noticed at the time. The youthful prank of stealing pears from a neighbor's tree came back to his consciousness after decades, but laden now with new layers of meaning. He proved that the meaning past experiences have for us now is often more insightful than what they meant the first time. There is no such thing as a "dead" memory. Memories are not like butterflies fixed in a glass case. They grow and deepen as we return to them. They continue to affect who we are and how we perceive reality. Given what I have learned from him, I would not be displeased if some readers describe this book as "Augustinian."

With this objective in mind, the chapters with which I begin this book combine the personal with a wider horizon. The first of these chapters spotlights the ritual of *initiation*, a rite that sometimes reveals more about the faith of which it is a part than any other and is found in one way or another in almost every culture. I will discuss this universal practice as it is exemplified by my own potent initiation rite, baptism by immersion, a death-and-life drama, at the age of fourteen.

The next chapter turns the page toward the end of the life cycle, to death and burial ceremonies, which like initiation reveal more about a religion's understanding of the "hereafter," and therefore of its view of "the ultimate," than the other rites. Here also I will be drawing on my personal experience of working as a teenager in a funeral parlor, where I heard more eulogies in a few months than most people do in a lifetime.

So here we set sail, hoping that we will discover perhaps not the "undiscovered country" itself but a little about the vast role it has played in so many people's lives.

# 2

# *Rituals of Initiation*

*There was a man of the Pharisees, named Nicodemus, a
ruler of the Jews:*

*The same came to Jesus by night, and said unto him,
Rabbi, we know that thou art a teacher come from God:
for no man can do these miracles that thou doest, except
God be with him.*

*Jesus answered and said unto him, Verily, verily, I say
unto thee, Except a man be born again, he cannot see the
kingdom of God.*

*Nicodemus saith unto him, How can a man be born
when he is old? can he enter the second time into his
mother's womb, and be born?*

*Jesus answered, Verily, verily, I say unto thee, Except
a man be born of water and of the Spirit, he cannot enter
into the kingdom of God.*

*That which is born of the flesh is flesh; and that which is
born of the Spirit is spirit.* (John 3:1–6 KJV)

Among some of the indigenous peoples of Central Austra-
lia, when boys reach puberty, they undergo an initiation
ceremony that is almost a paradigm for that universal practice.
The boys are placed, naked, inside a dark tent heated by steam
for twenty-four hours with only water but no food while their

elders sing and chant around the outside, recounting the stories of their people. After this the boys emerge one by one from the front of the tent and crawl headfirst between the legs of one of the elders. As the head appears, another elder pulls it vigorously until the boy is out. He is then bathed, given a blanket to wear and some soft food. In this reenactment of childbirth, the youth has been "born again." He is now fed and handed a carving tool used only by adult males. He has become a full member of the tribe.

Evangelical Christians do not hold a monopoly on being born again. Even the staid *Book of Common Prayer* contains this passage in its baptismal ceremony: *Let us now pray for these persons who are to receive the Sacrament of new birth [and for those (this person) who have renewed their commitment to Christ].* Ceremonies of rebirth can be found all over the world. Why is this practice so widespread? In his suggestive but controversial book *Symbolic Wounds,* Bruno Bettelheim proposes an explanation derived from psychoanalytic theory. Drawing on his own clinical practice, his work with children between eight and twelve, and his investigations of preliterate peoples, he suggests that just as women are said to have "penis envy," males have something analogous he calls "vagina envy," which takes the form of jealousy of women's ability to bear children. I have never met a man who admits to harboring this kind of envy. But this does not count against Bettelheim's thesis. True to the psychoanalytic tradition, he grants that for most people this inner motivation remains mostly unconscious but that it explains the near universality of rebirth rituals as a societally sanctioned compensation strategy. Bettelheim subtitled his book *Puberty Rites and the Envious Male.*

I do not want to criticize or endorse Bettelheim's theory here, but I suspect that we should see such a psychoanalytic perspective as one among many ways of understanding rites of rebirth. There are other ways to look at the same phenomena. Even within the psychoanalytic frame, another explanation is the mixture of fascination and anxiety with which we view death. From yet another field, there is the continuing need of any group to replenish its membership and to create occasions at which its basic worldview can be restated and reenacted.

At another level, initiations take place in a myriad of institutions. Fraternal lodges like the Elks and the Lions practice them. Boy Scouts and Cub Scouts have them. Most of these are harmless and serve a useful purpose for those who use them. But it must also be recognized that initiations can be cruel and even sadistic. The military has long practiced purposely humiliating initiations on new recruits, even as their top authorities have sometimes taken measures to restrict them. Yet such measures were not wholly successful, in part because painful initiation is seen as integral to the rigorous training soldiers are expected to undergo. Recently we have seen reports of students injured or even killed while they were being initiated into college fraternities. Again, college officials have tried to reign in these customs, but are notoriously hard to control. It appears that initiations are an element of social reality and probably will be so in the future. It is imperative to distinguish between good and bad forms of initiation. But on whatever side of that calculation an initiation falls, they all reveal something important about the institution that observes them. In some cases, this includes its larger worldview or overall purpose. But before I discuss any of these, I want to start with a brief account of my own experience of two initiations: baptism by immersion and marriage.

Raised in a Baptist family I was not sprinkled as an infant. Instead, I was fully immersed at fourteen, which our tradition recognizes as the age of accountability, the age when a young person is old enough to make such an important decision. Baptists first appeared among the other reforming movements

in sixteenth-century Europe. But they were harassed and persecuted by Lutherans and Calvinists and Roman Catholics.
They were proscribed as heretics, "Anabaptists" (re-baptizers);
and their punishment often took the form of being drowned,
which their irate persecutors, with a surly sense of humor, saw
as appropriate. In the early years of their settlement of New
England, the Puritans, who are often celebrated for champi-
oning religious freedom, did not think it applied to Baptists.
Roger Williams, the founder of the first Baptist church in the
New World, was driven out of Massachusetts. After living for
a time in the forest and then with the Indians, he finally settled in Rhode Island, where he founded the city of Providence.
Chastened by his own experience with religious persecution,
Williams welcomed other "heretics," including Catholics and
Quakers, to the colony. The first Jewish synagogue in America
was also founded there. In fact, so many of these theologically
incorrect people relocated there that the established church
advocates took to calling it "the cesspool of New England."

The small church my family attended was not a cesspool. An
impressive brown sandstone edifice, it was topped by the highest steeple in town, several feet taller than that of St. Patrick's
Catholic Church just down the block. With my brothers and sister, I was taken to Sunday school there as a toddler. Eventually I
started to attend church there, sitting in my grandmother's pew
with her. Later, I sang in the choir, helped take up the collection, and joined the youth group. It was always a pleasant time
for me. I never heard any hellfire preaching, and I liked being
appreciated, even loved.

When at fourteen the minister asked me, along with four
other boys in my age cohort, if we were ready to "accept Christ,"
be baptized, and become members of the congregation, I did
not hesitate. From my pew I had seen several baptisms in the
pool just behind the pulpit and Communion table. It seemed

only natural to follow suit. So, five of us met with the pastor every Tuesday evening for five weeks to learn the basic tenets of Christianity. We read and discussed passages from the Bible, especially the life of Jesus. More than once the pastor told us that being baptized was to "die with Christ, be buried, and be raised to newness of life." It sounded daunting, and a bit scary, but we had already watched people being baptized and surviving it. No one dropped out of our little class.

On the Sunday set for our baptisms we appeared at church in clean white shirts and slacks. We assembled a little nervously in a back room, where the pastor led us in a brief prayer. Then, one by one, we climbed a dusty staircase and emerged next to the pool. It was about seven feet long and three feet wide. It had been filled earlier that morning to about four feet deep with lukewarm water. When I got there the pastor was already standing in the water facing the congregation with his Bible open in his hands. He helped me slide in, then stood beside me, still facing the congregation, and read the verses from the Gospel of John cited above. When he finished, the congregation began singing,

> *Just as I am*
> *Without One plea, but that*
> *Thy blood was shed for me . . .*

Then the minister placed his Bible on the edge of the pool, turned to me and asked me if I had accepted Christ as my personal savior and if I would endeavor to follow Him and seek to advance the cause of His kingdom. I answered with a firm "yes" to both questions. The congregation continued,

> *And that Thou biddest me*
> *Come to Thee,*
> *O Lamb of God, I come, I come.*

Then the pastor put his arm around my shoulders and said, "I baptize you in the name of the Father and of the Son and of the Holy Spirit," and lowered me fully below the water. After only a couple seconds, he pulled me back up, placing a dry towel over my face as he did so. When I was back on my feet and wading toward the steps out of the pool, I did not know what I was supposed to be feeling. I was not aware of any throb of ecstasy or exhilaration. I felt very much the same as I did before I entered those waters. And I was disappointed. But I was not done with my baptism, or maybe my baptism was not done with me.

I learned later that the phrase the pastor had enunciated to me about seeking "to advance the cause of His kingdom" was not used in all baptisms. It occurred in mine because of the unusual nature of our little congregation. Because we did not have much money, we usually relied on young ministers who had just graduated from seminary. These novice preachers were therefore eager to try out the latest theology, which varied over the years. In the Baptist denomination, which has no bishops, the members of a local church select their own pastors by a majority vote through what is sometimes a prolonged process of interviews and trial guest sermons, to which the members often listen with great attention.

At the time of my baptism, the main theological tendencies were a kind of individualistic pietism, which explains the phrase "personal" savior, and what was called the "Social Gospel." The latter was introduced in the early twentieth century by Walter Rauschenbusch, an American Baptist theologian who taught at Colgate-Rochester Divinity School, one of the seminaries in which our young ministers were trained at the time. Rauschenbusch came from a conservative pietistic Baptist family of German immigrants. After seminary he assumed pastoral duties in the Hell's Kitchen section of New York City but soon decided that an individualistic approach to the gospel was irrelevant to the people he served who were suffering from the poverty, hunger, and unemployment that originated in corporate and institutional injustice. What was needed, he decided, was a gospel that would address corporate sin. And he believed that this is just what the message of Jesus, with its emphasis on the kingdom of God, was originally about. In 1907, he published the book *Christianity and the Social Crisis.* His book kicked off the Social Gospel movement, which spread rapidly among Protestant churches, including Baptists. It has also informed my own theological writing throughout my life.

The Social Gospel never displaced the old pietism completely. The two coexisted in many churches, even though their interpretations of heaven and other doctrines differed. Pietists thought of heaven as the place you go to (if you are saved) after death. Advocates of the Social Gospel saw it as synonymous with the kingdom of God, which was coming to earth but required our efforts to actualize it. There were other differences, but the two theologies usually lived side by side, and songs expressing both can be found in the hymnbooks of the time. In *Favorite Hymns of Praise*, published in many editions for decades by the Tabernacle Publishing Company, and the one used by our congregation, one could find such gems of pietism as "Washed in the Blood of the Lamb" and "Leaning on the Everlasting Arms" but also the Social Gospel favorite "Where Cross the Crowded Ways of Life." This admixture of theologies lasted until both components were threatened by the growth of fundamentalism in the 1920s and 1930s, which strongly opposed both. It assailed the Social Gospel for its alleged lack of attention to personal sin and the need for individual repentance. But it also castigated pietism for its tendency to make a warm personal relationship with Jesus more important than doctrinal correctness.

But since the members of our church were not attuned to what they considered theological niceties, they were more interested in a pastor's personal qualities (should be warm and friendly, but at least somewhat dignified), and his ability to deliver interesting sermons that were neither too short nor too long. Thus, as it happened, the young pastor who baptized me mentioned "the kingdom of God," the favored biblical idea of the Social Gospel, in my ceremony. I am glad he did. As I have said, the Social Gospel greatly affected my own thought, and it prepared me for what became the most significant theological movement I participated in, liberation theology, which seemed to encapsulate what Jesus taught and demonstrated.

In trying to "follow Jesus," I have discovered a direct connection between him and liberation theology. It is a connection that begins with Jesus's own baptism by John in the Jordan River. Through this ceremony, Jesus aligned himself with a protest movement, one that had both a political and a religious dimension. It was a liberation movement. Its very existence threatened the established religious leaders, who ruled the temple and who were sycophants of Roman imperial rule. And why not? After all, it was the Romans who had appointed them to their lucrative posts. John's preaching promised God's coming judgment on them and on an unrighteous society: "The ax is laid at the root of the tree." The baptisms John administered were derived from the Jewish *mikvah*, the ceremonial bath. But in John's hands it signaled a rejection of the temple's politically compromised religion.

There is little wonder that Herod Antipas had John arrested and eventually beheaded. Like Jesus after him, John had become a clear and present danger to the alliance of Rome and Jerusalem's priestly elite. Unfortunately, the significance of John's officially sanctioned murder has been obscured by the juicy stories about Herod's mother and Salome's salacious dance: "Bring me the head of John the Baptist on a platter." John's killing was not a crime of passion fired by lust or jealousy. It was a tyrannical political act, an assassination; and although Jesus eventually left John to start his own movement, clear traces of his predecessor are evident in the rest of his life. He began his mission by announcing in his hometown of Nazareth that his purpose was to "free the captives and bring good news to the poor." And, like John, he died a state-sanctioned death by torture.

There was another facet of my baptism that I also gradually came to appreciate. By the time I was in college, and later in seminary, I began to learn about rituals and rites of passage in different religions, including death and rebirth symbolism. I noticed that some of my fellow students, lacking any personal memory they could refer to, were puzzled. But I was not. I could see that my immersion and surfacing, spitting water and wiping my eyes in that little pool, were not just a feature of my religion. I shared it with adherents of many other faiths but also with thousands of people, living and dead. Émile Durkheim once said that "man is a ritual animal." He was right, and perhaps the most fundamental ritual is a rite of death and new life. But almost as important are the rituals in which new people are made members of the community. These "initiation" rituals reveal the tradition because they almost always include rehearsals of a religion's myths of origin and destiny. Initiation rites differ from one tradition to another, but they all expose striking structural similarities, a "universal grammar." From then on, I knew I had a touchstone memory to refer to as I studied the religions of the world.

By the time I first visited Rome, having become more interested in initiation practices, I was eager to visit a temple of Mithra, whose devotees had a particularly dramatic death/ rebirth ritual. In 1961, at the age of thirty-two, I made that visit, and I recall it here as a sort of case study in comparative initiations. When, after anticipating such a visit for some years, I finally stepped inside a Mithraic temple near the Colosseum, dating back to the third century CE, I had to stop and catch my breath. I felt that I was back in about 200 CE. It was strange, but at the same time familiar. The Mithraic religion was one of the many Eastern "mystery cults" that migrated into Rome as its empire expanded. It first appeared in Rome about 200 CE but spread throughout the empire from Britain to Syria. Over two hundred Mithraic temples have been discovered, of which only a handful are open to visitors. Mithraism appealed especially to soldiers, and no women were admitted. Its adherents, unlike the Christians who were often seen as their rivals, Mithraists strongly supported imperial rule and were therefore seldom persecuted. The question of why they died out while Christianity flourished is one that historians still debate.

The central figure in this fascinating cult was a young Persian man who is painted or sculpted in all the temples in the act of slaying a bull by wrestling it down and slitting its throat. As the blood gushes from the bull's throat, a snake and a dog drink it, while a scorpion chews at its scrotum. Fortunately, we can learn a lot about the adherents of Mithraism from the detailed observations of the contemporary Christian theologian Tertullian in his treatise *De corona militis.* Because of the subject of this book, however, I will touch only on their initiation rituals and what they tell us about their beliefs about death and the afterlife.

Since their temples were in caves and hollows hewn out of rocks, the new initiates to Mithraism, after instruction and fasting, were stripped naked and led down to the cave's thick darkness. It must have seemed like the bowels of the earth. There a prescribed drama was enacted. The initiate was offered a crown, which he refused, stating, "Mithra is my only Lord." He then lay on his stomach, stretched out on the floor, and was ritually slain. As he "came back to life" he was assured by those in charge that he had now been infused with the qualities of Mithra, which were strength and fecundity from the snake and the dog, and immortality from the scorpion.

Obviously, the symbols in the initiation to the Mithraic religion were different from the ones in my baptism. Although an occasional dog wandered into church in the summer when the doors were open, there were no snakes. Still, the *structure* of the two initiations is evident. In my baptism I was not offered a crown, but I did confess that Jesus was my Lord. As I sank into the pool, I was identifying with Christ's dying. And when I came up from the water, symbolizing both cleansing and death, I was entering a new life or at least a new chapter. Baptism encompasses both death and rebirth. Now, years after that moment in my own life, I do not feel that my baptism separated me from other people. Given the near universality of initiation rites and their profound roots in human history, I feel a sense of solidarity across borders.

Still, while appreciating the structural similarities of widely various initiation rites, I do not want to forget the singularities. It is often forgotten that by his own baptism by John in the Jordan, Jesus aligned himself not with the "establishment religion" but with a suspect dissident movement. This is not something that candidates for baptism or confirmation are often told, but it is nonetheless supported both by the biblical accounts and by history. As a follower of John's faction, Jesus soon fell under suspicion and left the area, while John himself was arrested and beheaded. This is a crucial, albeit frequently overlooked, part of the baptism I hope not to forget. And it has critical implications for the promise to "follow Jesus and to work for the cause of his kingdom."

In sum, what we have today are two contending interpretations of baptism. In effect, the tension between "heaven" and the kingdom of God is playing out around the meaning of this ritual. For many, perhaps most people, being baptized has become a kind of admission ticket into social and religious respectability. Parents are often eager to have their infant children baptized, based on a half-believed conviction that if a child dies before being baptized, he or she is in a less favorable position vis-à-vis heaven or eternal life. It is like a spiritual vaccination, and there are many parents who never appear in church except for this visit to the font.

But baptism as demonstrated by John and Jesus in the Jordan River was not any of these things. The central motif was the imminent arrival on earth of God's new age, in which those who have been pushed down will be exalted and those on top will be cast down. What was coming was something for which one had to prepare by changing one's life. "Repent," Jesus said, "for the kingdom of God is at hand," and the death-and-resurrection action made it clear that the change would have to be a radical one. Therefore, baptism was originally itself a radical act. But what has happened over the centuries is that baptism has been deradicalized, turned into a social convention with religious décor.

I admit that this indictment of the way baptisms are usually practiced now may sound harsh. The baptism of a child has become, after all, a joyful occasion that often brings parents and grandparents and other family members together. In some traditions, godparents are selected, enlarging the circle of intimacy. There are often gifts, and sometimes a reception. Only a prune-faced Scrooge would want to label this "humbug," and this is not my intention. But somehow the original intent of Christian baptism needs to be recovered. The "kingdom of God" message needs to be rescued from its present distortion, and this is not an impossible thing to do.

Along with baptism, the marriage ceremony is a classic initiation ritual. Two people are entering a new phase of their lives, joining a new community of married people. The traditional

Christian service has all the elements of ritual. It is a reenactment of something that has happened millions of times before. The costuming may vary a bit, but within certain established parameters. The action proceeds like a choreographed ballet, with each dancer performing the moves that thousands of people have performed before them. The words of the service invoke the larger tradition by rehearsing a history, sometimes beginning with our earliest (biblical) forebears and mentioning how Christ himself sanctified the rite at the marriage in Cana, where he saved the host from acute embarrassment by turning water into wine. The service then moves from past to present, underlying the continuity. The couple exchange vows, scripted words that have been repeated by other couples, countless times. In traditional prayers, God is invoked to bless the couple and sometimes (with the couple's permission) for the gift of children. As the ceremony ends, the minister or other presiding person moves the focus to the future: ("I declare that x and y are husband and wife [or wife and husband, or both]." A kiss then symbolizes the new intimacy the two persons may now enjoy.

Such a ritual might seem very far from the theme of this book. But when we begin to compare the marriage ceremonies in different traditions, some dramatic differences emerge. Not many years ago, the couple were to say the words "until death do us part." But because some people expressed their dislike of mentioning "death" on such a supposedly happy occasion, the phrase became "so long as we both shall live." But that did not end the squeamishness about mentioning the dark angel in the bright sunlight of connubial light. Even toned down, "so long as we both shall live" seemed to some people to cast a dark, unwelcome shadow over the proceedings. Now, sometimes little or nothing is said about how long the vows just exchanged are supposed to obtain.

But here a pronounced contrast enters. In the Church of Jesus Christ of Latter-Day Saints (Mormons), when people marry each other and are "sealed" under the auspices of the church, they are not married either until death or so long as they live. They are married *for eternity.* Mormons of course are aware of the verse in Matthew 22:30, in which Jesus says that in heaven there is neither marrying nor giving in marriage. But since in addition to the Bible they also have *The Book of Mormon,* which they believe contains a later revelation, they see no problem. There is of course no problem at all with polygamy, which the Mormons practiced until the church ended it in 1890. After all, there appears to be no scriptural warrant against it, and the Old Testament patriarchs often had more than one wife, as well as concubines. Nonetheless, some critics claim that although polygamy is banned in practice, it has not been officially expunged as doctrine, and there are some Mormons who claim that it continues in heaven. I will have more to say about the Mormons in my chapter on American heavens.

Initiations, including baptism and marriages, are meant to signal that something is being left behind and something new is beginning. Like all rituals, they also reveal a more ample overview of the meaning of human life and of history, and often glimpses of what some ultimate consummation of both might promise.

In the next chapter we will explore a parallel but equally illuminating range of rituals, those that mark the transition from this life to what comes next, namely, funerals.

# 3

# *Death and Burial*

*Verily, verily, I say unto you, except a corn of wheat fall into the ground and die, it abideth alone: but if it die, it bringeth forth much fruit.* (John 12:24 KJV)

*O death, where is thy sting? O grave, where is thy victory?* (1 Corinthians 15:55–56 KJV)

In addition to initiation, another ritual that provides valuable insights into a religion's vision of the ultimate is the funeral. Death-and-burial rites are often considered a form of initiation, in this case initiation into the next life. It should not be surprising, therefore, that so many initiation rituals include death-and-rebirth motifs. When we compare the rites among different religions it offers us a particularly rich insight into the various views of the "next world" that these traditions teach.

Human beings have been burying, cremating, or otherwise intentionally disposing of the dead bodies of their fellow human beings for a very long time. The first example of such an interment for which we have any evidence took place between 80,000 and 50,000 BCE. But what does this practice signify? What does it mean that "grave goods" such as tools and cooking utensils were found among the bodies? Did anyone think the dead might need them in some other life? No one knows for sure. For many of us today the biggest question is: do the burials and the grave goods suggest that the survivors who interred the bodies were aware that one day they too would die? Did they have the *conscientia mortalis*? To me and to many other scholars it seems probable that they did have some awareness of their own finitude. But who is to know for sure?

Some people claim that such perception exists only in human beings and that this sets us apart from our fellow creatures. But this argument can sound like yet another device to assert not just a difference but a superiority. For some, this assertion of human uniqueness/superiority became more important after we seemed to lose our sense of difference after Darwin and Freud reminded us of our similarity to other animals. But since we are not privy to the inner thoughts of chimps or dolphins, thought to be our closest relatives, there is no way of knowing if they have any sense of their inevitable mortality. Remember that in T. S. Eliot's poem "On the Naming of Cats," in addition to all his other names, the cat has one that he alone knows, and is telling no one.

There is another question about these prehistoric burials: what if anything was said (or sung, danced, or chanted) during the interments? Archaeology can help, but only up to a point. It is a "hard" science, at least in one sense. It concerns itself only with the "hard" evidence found in these sites. We have, alas, no films or tapes of what was going on. Stone chisels and the shards of utensils can tell only a part of the story, certainly not what they thought about an afterlife. But still, we must proceed on the basis of what we know to try to find out what we can, which may also turn out to be very little.

My personal introduction to such persistent questions began early, and it took place in the context of bodies and burials. It started when I was fifteen with what I now see as a crash course in what might be thought of as "comparative eschatology." In the small town in Pennsylvania where I grew up, my Uncle

Frank was the undertaker, or "mortician" as he preferred. And he was the only one, so he handled all sorts of funerals. Methodists and Catholics, Black and White, wealthy people and those of limited means all sought his services. A friendly, genial man with a prominent bald head, he was always well dressed, but not overdressed, with polished black shoes and a conservative tie. His funeral home, a tasteful gray stone edifice, stood next to his home on a street lined with stately maple trees. He had the reputation in our town as someone who could manage the complicated arrangements for a funeral calmly and discreetly. When I was fifteen, Uncle Frank offered me a part-time job working for him. I gratefully accepted. And now, looking back, I see how that position became a turning point in my life. It stoked a growing interest I already had and that I have never lost in theology and comparative religion. And it is, even after so many years, one of the sources for this book.

It was not an easy job, but it was endlessly fascinating. Uncle Frank already had a small staff, but I was a favorite nephew and he brought me in as a kind of personal assistant. I gladly undertook all the tasks the assignment entailed. I sat in the front seat beside him when he drove to pick up bodies at someone's crepe-decked home, or at the chilly morgue of a hospital, or at the scene of an accident where a coroner had just declared a victim dead. In all these cases the corpse had usually been placed in a body bag. But it was quite different on the day when my uncle asked me to join him in the small room where he did the embalming.

When we entered, the body of a middle-aged man was stretched out on a glistening white table. He did not look like the dead bodies of the bandits or cattle rustlers I had seen in westerns at the local theater. He appeared so colorless, rigid, and inflexible that my first thought was, "Boy, that man is really dead." His clothes had been removed so he could be washed, but his hips and private parts were discreetly covered with a towel. The table had long, narrow grooves on either side that came together at the base in an opening drain. My uncle hesitated only briefly. Then, using a small knife, he cut a slit just under the armpit on each side. I immediately saw what the grooves were for. As the blood flowed out of the incisions, it ran into them. A handle on either side allowed the end where the head lay to be raised or lowered. Since blood tends to accumulate in the lower parts of the body, tilting it facilitated its flow toward the grooves and the container suspended under the drain. It would later be burned in a fireplace behind the house, tastefully surrounded by high bushes. After the blood was drained, my uncle attached a bottle of formaldehyde to an artery. It found its way through the veins and arteries to the whole body. This took about twenty minutes. Then he dressed the body for the viewing and funeral, unless it was a female, in which case he left this to an older woman assistant.

Uncle Frank assigned me several tasks at the funeral parlor. I unloaded delivery trucks, helped haul heavy caskets to the display room where they would be sold to patrons, swept and vacuumed the halls and rugs, washed the windows, mowed the lawns, and clipped the bushes. I set out chairs for the funerals and folded them when it was over. But my most memorable assignment was to stand at the door as the guests arrived, greet them, assist them with their coats, guide them to where the casket, either open or closed, stood, where some would pause, some would pray, and some would move away quickly. Then I would show them to their seats.

Uncle Frank coached me on how to be friendly but dignified during this procedure, neither morose nor cheery, serious but not solemn. Meanwhile, soft recorded organ music played through the sound system. It was usually "The Old Rugged Cross" or "Abide with Me." But if the family made suggestions

Uncle Frank had an extensive library of discs to draw on. Some were only musical, but some featured choirs or even soloists. Most of these, of course, made some mention of heaven, and I continue to believe that many people, especially Protestant Christians, derive whatever concept of heaven they have from songs and hymns. The hymnbook most widely used at that time had a "topical index," in which the section on heaven contained thirty-four entries, such as "Beulah Land," "Beyond the Sunset," and "When the Roll Is Called Up Yonder."

This part of the funeral usually went very smoothly. But not always. Once a disagreement among the members of the deceased's family temporarily disrupted the tranquility. It seems that a few years back the man lying in the casket, who had been a Methodist, married a Roman Catholic woman. Contradictory stories circulated about whether he had converted or not. The wife's family claimed he had, but his own denied it. Tempers flared. When he had been asked, he contrived different ways to avoid answering. After a while, people stopped asking. Rumors multiplied. It was widely known, in the kind of small town where nearly everyone knew nearly everything about everybody, that maybe in an effort to reduce the chance of a blood feud, he did not attend any church at all.

But this did not head off all the friction, and when heaven is involved, tempers can flare. At the open-casket funeral, as the mourners filed by, a woman who was a member of the wife's family quietly placed a crucifix on his chest and folded his hands around it. However, when the dead man's brother, who had already been seated, noticed what had happened, he walked up to the casket, whisked the crucifix away and returned to his seat, whereupon the woman who had put it there walked over to him and demanded he give it back. He refused, clutching it closely to his own chest. The woman then strode to where Uncle Frank stood watching all this and asserted that the crucifix was *her* property. Frank respectfully invited both parties to go into an adjoining room, where, after he had exercised some skilled diplomacy, the contenders agreed that the crucifix would be given back, but it would not be placed in the coffin. I was surprised at this agreement, and I suspected that Frank had somehow quietly promised the woman that at some unspecified point, he would make sure the contentious crucifix accompanied the man to his next destination. Thus was an impending conflict over the hereafter avoided by a diplomatic funeral director whose talents might have been useful in the settlement of boundary disputes in the Middle East.

The short-lived crisis of the crucifix seemed like a minor incident at the time, but in retrospect it taught me a couple of noteworthy things. First, it demonstrated that many people are anxious to make sure a burial ceremony is done "properly." There is ample evidence in folklore, superstition, and classical literature of the dire consequences of improper burial. Stories abound about the not-quite-dead whose restless ghosts roam the world haunting the living because they have not been properly buried. The chilling film *Night of the Living Dead* terrified me when I saw it first as a kid, and still does when it returns on television. When the cadaverous zombies, their rotting flesh hanging from their bones, swarm around the besieged house and climb through the windows, I want to cover my eyes. Yet I admit that at some level I enjoy being terrified now and then. I think most people do; otherwise the audience for horror films would disappear. And this tells us something about the ambivalence we all feel about death. Freud spoke of the "death wish," which he claimed existed in a discordant but creative tension with our persistent drive to stay alive.

How does one relate this tension to the cold depository in Scottsdale, Arizona, where the bodies of dozens of people are stored? These folks were quick-frozen after death to wait quietly for a future cure for whatever disease felled them, then to be thawed and, they hope, healed. The process is called "Cryonics." A pamphlet states that it uses temperatures below −130°C, to attempt to preserve brain information for an eventual revival. Those of us who are Boston Red Sox fans were treated to a memorable version of this procedure when the team's star slugger, Ted Williams, died in 2002 and an argument broke out in his family. It seems that Ted had wanted to be cremated, but some members of his family wanted the body frozen. Finally, one sports magazine reported that his head had been removed from his body, but accurate details of what happened to the two parts are not publicly available.

On a more elevated level, in Sophocles's *Antigone* the heroine is determined that her dead brother must be buried with the "proper" rites. But, since he died in a rebellion against Thebes, the family's native city, he is considered a traitor, so the authorities will not allow his body to be buried. Refusing to accept this judgment, Antigone insists. She will see to it that her brother has a proper burial, or die in the attempt, which is what happens. She proceeds with the burial anyway but is killed in the process. Is a proper burial more important than one human life? The importance of a proper burial is still with us today. In Russia, every summer hundreds of youthful volunteers travel to the sites of battles fought over half a century ago during World War II. There they camp in tents while they dig up the remains, now only skeletons, of the soldiers who died there but were never "properly buried." Then they carry the bones to a nearby village where an Orthodox priest conducts a funeral. It is nearly impossible to identify them because Russian soldiers, who believed name tags brought bad luck, often threw them away. When a historian who was camping with these volunteers asked how, with no name tags and only the rotted tatters of uniform, they could be sure they were Russians, they answered right away that it did not matter. The Germans, one young man said, "Well yes, they were our enemies, but they also deserve a proper burial." The crucifix-in-the-casket case was both a question of proper burial and about the afterlife. The two are not easily separable. The woman who put it there obviously believed that to send her relative to the next world without it would be improper. But the man's kinsmen thought the opposite. Only my uncle's skilled diplomacy prevented an escalation of this eschatological impasse.

Sometimes the need for diplomacy was felt long before the actual funeral. One day Uncle Frank asked me to take his place at something he usually attended himself but could not on this occasion. It was the routine meeting that family members held with the minister who was to preside to go over the details of the funeral service and the interment. I had accompanied him to one such meeting and apparently he felt this was sufficient preparation to go it alone. I need not, perhaps should not, say anything, he advised, but just listen carefully to what was decided and quietly answer any questions that might arise. He said it would be a useful education for me, and so it was.

Two days later, in my clean white shirt, black suit, sober and polished shoes I was seated in the office of the local Presbyterian minister along with the minister himself and a couple I did not know, Ken and Alice, who nodded as I arrived. They were seated on a sofa in the book-lined study. The young minister, whom everyone called Bob, stepped out from behind his neat maple desk to welcome me. I slipped into a chair across from the couple. The minister told the couple that I was "from Mauger's," which they already knew.

Satisfied that the little circle was now complete, the minister reminded us that we were here to discuss the arrangements for Alice's sister, who had just died of a heart attack at the age of fifty-six, as well as "whatever else" might be on our minds. I got out my little notebook and looked attentive. The three of them talked quietly about a date, what hymns and prayers to include, and who the pallbearers should be. So far, everything went smoothly. But then a disagreement, quietly bubbling between Ken and Alice, came to the surface. It seems they did not agree on the question of burial or cremation.

Ken looked askance at what he considered a waste of good money on expensive metal caskets. Besides, he had attended two cremations, which, he said, were carried on with impressive dignity and simplicity. But Alice opposed cremation. She strongly preferred a traditional burial in a casket, one that should be "not fancy but of good quality." It seems they had already talked about this at length, but just could not agree, though they realized that the matter had to be settled quickly before the funeral plans could proceed. Alice raised her eyebrows and looked at me as though maybe I could cut through this knot. I looked thoughtful and nodded to both but said nothing. Uncle Frank had not prepared me for this.

After an awkward pause, Alice turned to the pastor. "Don't we as Christians believe in the resurrection of the *body*?" she asked. "That is what the Creed says. Right?"

At first the pastor said nothing. But Ken did. As Alice was speaking, he had been looking at the floor and shaking his head very slightly. Apparently, he had heard Alice's view before, maybe more than once. Then, in a very subdued voice, he said, "Yes, but the Bible does not make any distinction between ashes and dust. It says 'ashes to ashes and dust to dust.' Besides," he added, "as a matter of fact, a hundred years from now there won't be much difference between what is left of the body, no matter how watertight the casket is." Then he also glanced at me, the mortician's assistant, as though hoping for some confirmation of his observation from someone who should know something about such things. But I once again carefully avoided responding.

Clearly sensing that this exchange had probably gone as far as it should for the moment, the minister stepped in. "Well," he offered, "you are both right, in a way. So, this is something you two will have to sort out between yourselves. Did your sister express any preference?" They both shook their heads, and feeling that my prolonged non-intervention might be making me appear unprofessional, I cleared my throat. "Well," I said, "both things are done nowadays, though burials are more frequent. We do both, and I am sure that whatever you decide, we can handle it. Either way is fine with us."

Now Ken, getting a little edgy, looked at me with a stiff smile. "I know enough about your business to know that you make your real profits by selling caskets, not just from funerals, and not for sure from those little boxes they put the ashes in. Can you really be neutral about this?"

Once again, I thought that a slight smile and silence were my best tactic. But the minister, sensing what might become an escalation in the rhetoric, said, "Well, I don't think the economic part of this is the most important. What *is* most important is how you and her other loved ones feel about it."

But Alice moved nervously on the sofa. She was not satisfied with this answer. "Yes, Bob," she said, "but you have not really answered our question about the body. How can there be a resurrection of the body, if it has gone up in smoke, or don't you really believe in what the Creed says? After his own resurrection, didn't Christ have a body . . . hands and feet, and didn't he even eat broiled fish with his disciples? And doesn't the Bible say we will be raised 'like him'?"

The minister was not happy with the direction this was taking. "Well," he said, "the Bible is not entirely consistent about these things, and Christians have thought about them for a long time, but we have never reached a clear consensus. Some believe that when we die, our souls go immediately to be with God, and that our bodies are reunited to them later, at what is called the Last Judgment, but I don't know many people who believe this today. Others, as you know from the words 'rest in peace' carved onto so many tombstones, believe that the departed are in a peaceful sleeping state, and will awaken in God's good time to be in his presence for eternity."

"For eternity?" Ken interjected. "Like *forever*? But what does that mean?" He had just remembered singing words like these when his college chorus performed Handel's *Messiah*. But he had never thought about their implications for funerals. The minister, visibly tiring from being caught in this theological crossfire, decided not to get into a discussion about the meaning of "forever." Instead, he tried to steer the conversation back to the decisions that had to be made. He asked Ken and Alice to think about their decision some more, pray, and perhaps talk with friends. He stood up and smiled weakly. Then the couple also stood up, thanked him, shook his hand and mine, fumbled for their coats, and slipped out.

Following them to the door, I asked them kindly to call when they had decided so that my coworkers and I could make the appropriate preparations. When they were gone, I stepped back into the study, but the minister did not appear to want any further conversation for the moment. I left feeling that the quantity of questions that had assailed me since I first started working for Uncle Frank had suddenly taken a quantum leap, and I wanted to think about them some more. But what was said during the funerals themselves only raised further questions.

Funerals at Uncle Frank's generally began with a viewing of the body in the casket. Afterward came a part of the funeral that contributed substantially to my life's work as a theologian and student of comparative religion. In retrospect, it also provided memories I have drawn on for this book. The minister the family had asked to officiate now stepped up to the movable pulpit Uncle Frank supplied and started the service. Admittedly, the scope of religious traditions in our small town was not very wide, nothing like the differences among Buddhists, Hindus, Muslims, and Christians I would eventually learn about. But to me at the time, the variety looked rich indeed. The Methodists sang loudest, the Baptists read more biblical passages. The Black Baptists took more creative liberties with the rhythm and the chords. The Quakers did not have a leader behind the pulpit. They did not sing at all but sat in silence until someone felt moved by the Spirit to speak. Now and then one of the Methodists or Black Baptists would sob or cry. The Quakers never did.

The Catholics always held their funerals in St. Patrick's, their local parish church. The Mass lasted about thirty-five minutes, and while it continued Uncle Frank and one or two of his staff passed the time at a nearby restaurant drinking coffee. Then they returned to the church to help the pallbearers carry the coffin out, put it in the hearse, and drive to the cemetery. But I did attend the funeral Mass. Frank realized it would be awkward for him and his men to go back into the church while the Mass was still continuing, but also if the priest finished a little early, and they were not on hand. This is where I came in. My uncle stationed me just outside the big red Catholic Church doors and, when I heard the ceremony ending, I would hurry down the street and fetch him. However, after a few of these funerals, intrigued by the chants and the Latin phrases emanating from the darkened interior, so different from the gospel hymns I was used to, I began slipping inside and sitting in the last pew. This added another example of comparative ritual to my growing inventory. I did not hear much of what the priest said in his eulogy. It was usually very short, much shorter than Protestant ones; and since I sat in the back, I could not hear it well. When I tell Catholic friends about this they say, "Don't worry. You didn't miss much." I concluded from this that for Catholics the question of "what comes next" was already settled, and that talking about it at a funeral was unnecessary and maybe even inappropriate.

Back at the funerals in Uncle Frank's, however, I did hear most of the eulogies (although they were not usually called that). They were usually delivered by the minister the family had invited to preside. The Quakers did not have this since at least in our town they had no ordained clergy. Still, this was the part I looked forward to. It provided me with my first lesson in comparative theology. The messages were usually short and simple. There were exceptions. But if one went on too long, Frank, standing in the back, would sometimes raise the wrist with his watch on it so the speaker could see it, and the conclusion followed quickly. True, some of the ministers managed to avoid the "what next?" question. They spoke about the "loved one," the exemplary life they had lived and how sorely they would be missed. But with the most skilled circumlocution, the subject was difficult to avoid completely. If the person being buried had undergone a painful illness the speaker usually suggested that they were "now freed from their suffering." Others affirmed that they would now be reunited with family and friends who had gone before. Sometimes it was underlined that the departed one was now in the immediate presence of God or Jesus. But I noticed it was the older clergy who spoke about being in the presence of God. It was the younger ones who favored the reuniting theme.

In Carol and Philip Zaleski's fine anthology *The Book of Heaven,* they point out that this transition from divine presence to familial restoration took place in the nineteenth century, when society was becoming more family centered and the "home" was becoming a warm place to retreat to, away from the harshness of an increasingly urbanizing world. This insight strengthened my opinion that changing images of heaven so often reflect changes in the earthly cultures.

After the ministers had spoken, they would sometimes ask if anyone had something they would like to say. This was always a little risky. Depending on how many guests wanted to speak, and for how long, the schedule could get out of hand; and since we were to arrive at the cemetery at a specified time to avoid traffic jams with other funerals, we wanted to stay on schedule. Also, the mood and tone of the ceremony might be upset by an unscripted guest. Once when the invitation to "say something" was given, a man from out of town walked to the open coffin and took the dead man's hand in his. The guest was not wearing a black suit. He had on a pair of wrinkled khaki slacks and a sport jacket with two buttons missing. Gazing at the body, he said, "Freddie, we've known each other for a long time. You were a good friend and a *good* man, Freddie. I am going to miss you, and all of us, I mean ALL of us (here he gestured at the other guests) are sure going to miss you." He paused, blew his nose with a loud snort, and wiped his eyes. "And listen, Freddie, we know what some people have said about you. But Freddie," he went on, "we all know that you were a good man, a *good* man, and we know you are in good hands." I glanced at Uncle Frank, who as usual was standing in the back, but he remained completely calm and unperturbed. He did not even glance at his watch. The guest then stood in silence with his hand on Freddie's shoulder. After a minute or two he returned to his seat.

Later I realized that although the demonstrative guest had spoken in rough-hewn language, he had touched on the themes that those attending the funeral wanted to hear. They expected to hear a voicing of the sadness they were feeling and of appreciation of the virtues of the departed. The guests also listened for some words of reassurance about what would now happen to the deceased. A couple words hinted at a side of Freddie the Lord might have to overlook, but they were coupled with an implied belief that he surely would. In his own way, the demonstrative mourner had covered all the bases. And by walking up, standing by the coffin, and holding Freddie's hand, he had even introduced an element of ritual action into what can often be an inert ceremony.

Some years after I worked with Uncle Frank, when I attended seminary, I took a course on myth and ritual, and I learned that anthropologists claim that in the history of rituals, bodily movement (mimesis) appeared before words, not vice versa. Religion is embodied before it is spoken. For that reason, I regret that so much worship today leaves the body out almost completely. We stand or kneel and walk to the altar, but most of the time we sit. Quakers, in their early history, were given that nickname because they shook and trembled when they prayed. Now, however, they have become ever so sedate. But most Black churches still nourish an embodied worship style: they and Pentecostals ("Holy Rollers"), who come in all skin colors, sway and wave their arms, and sometimes collapse on the floor in what they call being "slain in the Lord." All have demonstrated the continuing importance of the body in worship. I think those of us who hold to the traditional Christian doctrine of the resurrection of the body (not the immortality of the Spirit) should appreciate this welcoming of flesh and blood in worship.

After Freddie's friend seated himself, the funeral moved ahead in its normal way. After the benediction, our staff had the solemn responsibility of doing something that seemed very painful for many of the guests, closing the coffin. I could understand why. Closing that cumbersome lid signaled a certain finality. It would not be opened again. Now the pallbearers with assistance from our staff trundled the coffin to the spotless black hearse. The family members and guests climbed into their waiting cars, and we started for the cemetery.

After any service at the funeral home, our hearse carried the body to the cemetery or, on rare occasions, to the crematorium.

The pallbearers, with the sometimes awkward help of our staff, then slowly lowered the casket into the grave, using a portable metal frame with strong leather straps that we had brought from the mortuary. But they lowered it only part way, not the whole six feet to the bottom. It would only be lowered to the bottom after the graveside ceremony was over and the guests had left. I wondered for a while why it was done this way, but when I asked, my wise Uncle Frank told me that suddenly seeing the casket on the bottom might be too jarring for the mourners. He had seen it done that way, he said, but the crunching thud the metal sometimes made when it hit the earth could also upset the guests. Frank tried to do everything quietly and smoothly, and he usually succeeded, and his style was an accurate reflection of much of the modern American attitude toward death. Try not to make a fuss about it. Mourn, but not for too long. When you think of the departed one, imagine them in a good place, but without much detail.

During the graveside ceremony, our mortuary staff, having driven the hearse close to the grave, discreetly withdrew. They now stood back in respect for the mourners. The minister then led a brief graveside service. Since I had also been instructed to stand at a short distance out of respect for the family while the final rites were being enacted, I never heard much of what was being said. But one day, after the discussion about burial and cremation in the minister's study, I decided to edge a little closer when I was at a burial, to hear what the minister was saying. I still did not hear everything. An added problem was that at this stage, the ministers spoke more softly, and a car or truck often drove by. Consequently, what I overheard were isolated snatches. Over the mounds and gravestones drifted phrases like: "We commit this body to the earth. Ashes to ashes, dust to dust." But I also heard, "clothed in a new and spiritual body," and "angels escort him on his way." Almost always came the words "in the sure and certain faith in the resurrection. . . ." Who, I wondered, was so "sure and certain"? I did not think it was I.

If it was a grave, mourners usually dropped clumps of earth into it, then began to leave. When they had left, we gathered whatever equipment we had brought along, like ropes and tarpaulin and some folding chairs, then drove slowly away, this time with no body in the hearse, but with the truncated expressions I had just heard repeating themselves in my head.

The fragments continued to roll around in my memory, disconnected and incoherent. Only later did I learn that the words were usually taken from the liturgies the ministers read from at the graveside. Still, as I write this book, I am grateful that for so long these condensed sentences hovered in my mind, if only as a disconnected hodgepodge. I am glad because a jumble is precisely the way they exist in the minds of most people today. Neither our culture nor our religion possesses a coherent view of what happens to us after death. In fact, it never has. What we have inherited is a conglomeration of fragments haphazardly patched together in such a way that they throw their contradictions into stark relief. Why do we talk about "his final resting place" and murmur, "rest in peace," and in the next breath summon angels to escort the departed into the immediate presence of God? What connection, if any, does the "new spiritual body" have with the body we are committing to the earth? The list could go on.

It may well be that this glaring lack of consistency is, on balance, not a wholly negative thing. At least it does not invent a consistency where none exists or is likely to. Life itself is not consistent, and since death remains, as Shakespeare wrote, an "undiscovered country, and no traveler has returned," it may be better not to draw a coherent map. Collectively our picture of the hereafter is more like a Jackson Pollock canvas than a Raphael. We need to bring something of ourselves to either one to grasp its meaning, but the Pollock one demands more of us. In any case, I do not intend in this book to try to reconcile these real or apparent contradictions. Rather, I will explore why we have them, and ask what, in various times and climes, such images have meant to people, what role they once played and may still play in our worldview, and what effect they had and still have on how people lived or live.

Years after I worked with Uncle Frank, he died at eighty-eight. I attended his funeral, which took place in his family's church, The Church of the Good Samaritan, in Paoli, the next town to Malvern. He was a well-known figure, and a throng of people attended. The service followed the *Book of Common Prayer*. The coffin, as expected, was "good but not fancy." When we left the cemetery, I had a deep sense of gratitude for the brief time I served as his assistant. People write and speak about "near-death" experiences. And that is what working with him gave me, if in a different sense. Surrounded by coffins, flowers, and graves, I still did not face the nearness of my own death. But on the other hand, exposed as I was every day to hearses, bodies, graves, and mourners, the actuality of death was never very far from me. All this helped me grow up a little more quickly than I might have, and it opened the door on many questions I have pursued for years, and which have fed into the present book.

# 4

# *Jesus and Heaven*

*For if we have been united with him in a death like his, we will certainly be united with him in a resurrection like his.*
(Romans 6:5 ESV)

*Beloved, now are we the sons of God, and it doth not yet appear what we shall be: but we know that, when he shall appear, we shall be like him; for we shall see him as he is.*
(1 John 3:2 KJV)

What did Jesus say about heaven? The answer is, very little. The leitmotif of his teaching was the kingdom of God, which is something quite different. When he was asked questions about heaven, he almost always responded, rabbi-like, with another question, or he changed the subject. His purpose was to turn people's attention away from their preoccupation with rewards and punishments after death and toward the reigning of God that was already appearing in their midst. For this reason, when anyone asks what Jesus taught on death, resurrection, and heaven, it is important to remember that he rarely mentioned these subjects. When on a few occasions he did speak about them, he spoke as a Jewish teacher to a Jewish audience. Throughout his ministry, his disciples called him "rabbi." As a Jew living in a Jewish religious culture, Jesus inherited the unsettled disputes about life after death that were still being disputed among his people. But since he had a different agenda, he took little interest in them. The result is a scarcity of evidence on what he thought.

There were, however, a few times when Jesus did touch upon heaven. For example, when one of his disciples asked him to teach them to pray, he tells them to say, "Our Father, who art in heaven" (Luke 11:2). Again, remember that here Jesus was conversing with a group of first-century Jews. Just as Christians (Protestants beginning with the Reformation and Catholics since Vatican II) have wanted to use a vernacular language whenever possible, so did Jesus. His message was radical, but he delivered it in the idiom of the day. Consequently, the prayer he taught them was not made up on the spot. It is an adaptation of a familiar Jewish prayer of the time, one that is still used today: "May he establish his kingdom during our life and during our days." By "your kingdom come," Jesus was referring to the *malkuth* of God, not a place but the active reigning of God. And in speaking of "heaven," he was using vernacular language to designate both God and those people in whom the reigning of God had begun to take root. Saint Augustine puts it this way: *"'Heaven' . . . in this context means that God dwells 'in the hearts of the righteous, as it were in his holy temple.'"*

Thus, in responding to the disciple's request, Jesus, as he always did, affirmed both the present and the coming reigning of God, which is what we do today when we pray "The Lord's Prayer."

The almost universal use of this prayer by Christians of all denominations for centuries and all over the world has had both beneficial and negative effects. Some have said correctly that this prayer sums up the entire gospel, but how many people are aware of this? Others say that it is very significant that despite all their differences, it is so rudimentary that all Christians can affirm it. The difficulty, however, is that because the concept of "heaven" has been so thoroughly distorted, the word inevitably invokes a distant place or a postmortem condition, both of which are contrary to Jesus's meaning. By teaching a prayer that uses the vernacular name for "father" (it means something closer to "Daddy"), Jesus intended to enable his followers to feel close to God. But instead, whatever else "heaven" means, for most people it means "not here," and so the opposite of what Jesus meant. Even the sign language gesture for "heaven" is hands piling on top of each other in an upward direction. Also, some of the vernacular resonance of the prayer has been dissipated by the way it is so often repeated in antiquated language, using "which art" and "thou," whereas this archaic idiom is not used in other prayers. Still, when Jesus taught his followers this prayer, not only was it an exception to his usual habit, but he said nothing at all *about* heaven. Therefore, when we look for what Jesus thought about the afterlife, we can rely on only a handful of clusters of verses. In this chapter I will discuss these clusters and a couple of shorter references to heaven. I will not include the passages in Matthew in which he substitutes the phrase "kingdom of heaven" as a way of avoiding the not-to-be-spoken word "God" in deference to the Jewish readers for whom his Gospel was intended.

The *first cluster* of verses is a brief account in the Gospel of Luke (20:27–39) of how some of his critics tried—unsuccessfully—to draw Jesus into an argument then going on among his fellow Jews about life after death. The *second cluster* (Luke 24) describes Jesus's activities after his resurrection, which are thought to be relevant because of St. Paul's statement in Romans 6:5 (quoted at the head of this chapter) and the verse in 1 John that after their own resurrections human beings will be *"like him."* In this discussion, we will first recall how Jesus responded to the argument among his people about the "resurrection life." Then, trying to understand what "like him" might mean, we will turn to the account in Luke of Jesus's "resurrection appearances." Finally, we will examine Jesus's words in Matthew about the "keys of the kingdom of heaven."

First, according to Luke 20, Jesus is questioned, as rabbis often were, by a group identified as Sadducees with a case for his decision. This one concerns a woman whose husband dies, and she is then married, one by one, to seven of his brothers, in keeping with a Mosaic law stating that when a husband dies, his brother should marry the widow and raise the children as his own. As it happens, all six of the surviving brothers marry the widow in sequence, and each eventually dies, as does the woman who has been widowed seven times. "Now," the questioners slyly chortled, "to which of the brothers will she be married in heaven?"

I have sometimes mused that an apt response to this riddle would have been to ask what on earth could possibly motivate one of these brothers to marry a woman whose spouses died with such predictable regularity. But this was not, of course, a genuine case being brought to the rabbi for a just decision. It was a *reductio ad absurdum*, a hyperbolic conundrum thrown out to expose the absurdity of the view of heaven they thought Jesus held. If we listen, we can almost hear the inquisitors tittering as they poke each other in the ribs. "Well, let's see how this 'great teacher' squirms out of this one!" The question to Jesus was merely a gimmick designed to force him to take sides in a debate or to expose him as a fraudulent rabbi. But the quarrel they tried to lure him into was not a fake. It was a real one, and it was not about a merry widow, but about life after death, which was called the "resurrection life" by those who looked forward to it.

In Jesus's time, there were two rival religious parties, each advocating dramatically different views of death and the afterlife. The first were the Sadducees, some of whom, in this incident, were trying to trap Jesus. The second party was the Pharisees. The Sadducees constituted the aristocratic elite. They filled key positions in the sacrificial cult of the temple, including the office of the high priest. Since the Romans, who occupied the area at that time, preferred to rule their conquered provinces through their existing local governing institutions, and since Judah was considered a theocracy, they tried to work through the Sadducees, whom the Romans saw as the theocrats of a theocratic state. The arrangement never worked entirely smoothly for either side. The Sadducees wanted to be left alone without too much oversight from beyond the Tiber. But the Romans, who constantly pushed them to be more subservient, kept forcing out one high priest after another. The historian Josephus writes that in one eighteen-year period, no fewer than thirty high priests came and went.

But the Sadducees hung on stubbornly. They flaunted their venerable name, which derived from Zadok, the chief priest under Solomon, and they based their claims to authority on being experts in ritual exactitude. It may be surprising to learn that the Sadducees were skeptical, even disdainful, of belief in the afterlife. Not only did they not believe in the resurrection of the body, which they considered to be a crude innovation, but they also rejected belief in angels and spirits. They claimed that they trusted in the mercy and goodness of God. Anything more than that seemed presumptuous, even idolatrous.

In response to these theological tricksters Jesus must have weighed his answer carefully. He did not allow himself to be traduced into either side of this doctrinal competition. In offering one of his few comments on heaven or the "resurrection life," he said, "they neither marry nor are given in marriage, but they are like angels in heaven." These words were meant to be a retort to an impossible question, but they raise more questions than they answer. What is "like the angels" supposed to mean since human beings know so little about how the seraphs and the archangels live? Clearly, it was Jesus's signal that he did not want to pursue the debate, but to move on to something else. (Because angels are such fixtures in our mental images of heaven, we will return to them later.)

Also, if ideas of heaven so often serve as normative models of how we should live on earth, what implication does the absence of marriage in the resurrection life have for earthly conjugal life? There have been a wide variety of answers to this question. Two examples will illustrate the disparity among readings of the text. On the one hand, the American Shakers took it to mean that the only faithful Christian life must be one of celibacy, a predictable result of which is that the childless Shakers have disappeared. On the opposite end of the interpretive spectrum, I once visited a Christian community in Colorado whose members believed that "no marriage" meant that it was just wedlock that was prohibited, but not sex, and they enjoyed following this divine approval of their unfettered style of life. The Catholic Church has tried to make room for both interpretations by stressing at times the special sanctity of the celibate life but also encouraging large families. My own view is that Jesus's riposte should not be read as a guidepost for marriage or its absence on earth. Nor did Jesus intend it as a description of life in heaven, a subject he generally avoided so that his listeners could open their eyes and ears to the dawning kingdom on earth and prepare themselves to live in it. Jesus's response to his interrogators was not to answer them at all, probably because he wanted them to become aware of something far more important, the active presence in their world of the kingdom of God.

After Jesus's crucifixion, the internal row among the Jews over the qualities of the resurrection life continued. But when the Romans destroyed the temple in Jerusalem in 70 CE the sacrifices had to stop, and the Sadducees, who had supervised them, were out of work. They soon disappeared. A new form of Judaism under rabbinical leadership emerged and is still with us today. But it is interesting how the skepticism of the ancient Sadducees resembles that of some of today's humanists or liberal Unitarians. When I described the Sadducees to a Unitarian acquaintance, she said, "Hey, these guys sound like us." She was right, but only in part. The difference between the metaphysical skepticism of the Sadducees and that of modern religious skeptics is that the former based theirs on a radical theism, while the latter is derived from the methodological skepticism of science and from a larger culture-wide skeptical mood.

In the centuries before Jesus, the Sadducees did not have a monopoly on spiritual leadership. In the first century CE their rival party were the Pharisees, whose base was not in the temple in Jerusalem but in the synagogues scattered throughout the country where they had become recognized teachers of the Torah. Even though in the Gospels Jesus is often depicted as engaging in disputes with the Pharisees he was closer to them than he was to the Sadducees. The arguments between Jesus and the Pharisees were intraparty affairs, and despite their differences, the Pharisees apparently accepted him as almost one of their own. He is often described as speaking and teaching in synagogues and even gave his first sermon in the synagogue in his hometown of Nazareth.

The story of Jesus's exchange with the Sadducees is important, however, because it clearly reveals that at this time there was no consensus about the afterlife among his fellow Jews. Widely conflicting ideas coexisted, and still do. The rabbis have never laid down an authoritative doctrine on the subject (or many other subjects as well). There is still room for much disagreement within the big tent. There is an anecdote about a young Jewish student who asked a wise rabbi what the Gentiles would have to do to be in God's favor. Did they need to get circumcised, avoid eating pork, and observe the Sabbath? "No, none of these," the rabbi replied, "all they need to do is not worship idols." The rabbi's response was acutely appropriate. In the Jewish faith, a certain element of skepticism, or "holy disbelief," is not denigrated but welcomed.

To understand what the early followers of Jesus thought about the afterlife, one must take two things into consideration. First, these followers were Jews, among whom there was no single conviction that they all held. Second, because these first Christians were convinced that in Christ God's kingdom had begun to appear, it was not worth wasting time speculating—much less arguing—about any next life. Christians did, however, find time to argue about certain things, and echoes of these quarrels can be found in the Gospels, as well as in the Epistles of Paul, and the Book of Revelation (in which the Christians who do not agree with the writer are strongly condemned). Hence, inconsistencies in the New Testament, including on the subject of heaven, should not be surprising. The documents we now find in it were just being written during the first centuries of the "Jesus movement," before there were any settled creeds or even any agreement about which books, out of the sea of Gospels and Epistles available, should be regarded as authoritative and which ones discarded.

Today, as we try to understand what was going on in these early years, we are fortunate that not all the rejects were consigned to the ash heap. As in the case of the Dead Sea Scrolls, some were hidden in caves only to be discovered in 1947, nearly two thousand years later. These scrolls, however, posed a delicate test for scholars. First, many were found in hundreds of small fragments that had to be pieced together like a jigsaw puzzle. Others had been wound so tightly and then stuck together for so long that opening them was a formidable challenge. To damage them would have been unforgiveable, but not to open them would have been unthinkable. Finally, the biblical researchers huddled with faculty members in chemistry departments, and eventually a liquid mixture was concocted into which the scrolls could be immersed for a time, then slowly pried apart, a procedure that took years. When I began my doctoral studies, this sensitive operation was still under way, and I sometimes watched as an excited gaggle of scholars leaned breathlessly over the table as the chemists worked, waiting to scan words that had been written twenty centuries before. Their waiting was not unrewarded. The scrolls, in Hebrew, contained parts of the Old Testament, some law codes, and assorted bits of information that painted a picture of the world into which Christianity was born.

Another stash of scrolls had been found two years later in a place called Nag Hammadi, in Egypt. These documents, written in Coptic during the first centuries after Christ, proved to be much more valuable and informative than the Dead Sea Scrolls, which gave us a picture of the religious and political landscape into which Jesus was born. The Nag Hammadi texts, in contrast, allow us to catch a glimpse of the first decades of the Christian movement itself. The picture they present overturned many inherited assumptions about that era, including the differing ideas Christians had about the afterlife.

Interestingly, although the scrolls reveal many unresolved questions among the followers of Jesus, it appears that these divergences did not cause deep splits. So long as these early followers were loyal to Jesus as Lord and tried to follow him, they could practice their own forms of worship and organize their congregations as they chose. If differences came up, the people often asked one of the apostles, or their successors, to settle the dispute. We can also see this procedure in operation in the Epistles.

For example, in the small congregation in the city of Rome some had come from Jewish backgrounds and some had not. The former wanted to continue to celebrate the Sabbath, but the others did not. Unable to agree, they wrote to St. Paul. The Apostle told them that it did not really matter. Sadly, to a much later generation of Christians, it *did* matter, so much so that it precipitated painful schisms and divisions. Today's Seventh-Day Adventists remind us that for some people the question has still not been settled. It appears also that differences of opinion on death and the afterlife existed within some congregations. But when they asked St. Paul about this disagreement, he wrote rather testily that it was "foolish" to worry or speculate or to argue about such questions. He appears to have thought that there were some matters about which we could now know little or nothing, and that therefore peering into them was both unproductive and inappropriate. As he puts it in another passage, now we can only "know in part."

Recent historical research brings to light just how diverse the Christian communities were prior to Emperor Constantine's forced unification in the fourth century. It should not come as a surprise that their beliefs about the afterlife differed. One such difference, which is closely related to their ideas about heaven, was the dispute among the early Christians about whether it was appropriate to baptize their dead friends and relatives who had not been baptized before they died. We will return to this issue in the chapter on "American heavens," since a very American denomination, the Church of Jesus Christ of Latter-Day Saints, still practices baptizing the deceased. Here I only want to allude to this practice because it is another example of how the earliest Christians differed with one another.

About the year 50 CE, St. Paul wrote a letter to the tiny Christian congregation in Corinth. It has come down to us in the New Testament as First Corinthians. Apparently, some members were being baptized on behalf of deceased relatives and friends, but although we might expect the Apostle to have condemned this practice, he does not. Instead he cites the practice in support of a long argument against some skeptics in the church, insisting that the coming bodily resurrection of Christ's followers will be real. "What do people mean by being baptized on behalf of the dead? If the dead are not raised at all, then why are people baptized on their behalf?" (1 Corinthians 15:29). True, a dispute has continued for centuries about what the Apostle "really meant," and some have claimed this was a backhanded way of condemning postmortem baptism, but the text speaks for itself. He not only does not question baptizing the dead, but he uses it to make his own case. Also, although there is ample evidence that the same thing was done in other congregations at the time, he does not condemn it in any of his other Epistles either. But what did the practice mean to the Christians who did it? Did they think it was indispensable? Did they think not being baptized endangered their relatives' salvation? Did it have any bearing on whether they "went to heaven"? We will never know the answers to these questions, but it is remarkable that these clashing views on the afterlife did not cause major splits or schisms. This makes them, in this respect, more like most twenty-first-century Christians, who can agree on the core tenet of the faith ("Jesus Christ is Lord") but are willing to permit a range of views about heaven.

The argument about heaven between the Sadducees and the Pharisees that was seething in Jesus's time is over. But the Sadducees remain a fascinating chapter in the story of Jewish faith. Their opinions originated not in theology but in ethics. Again, like many modern religious and nonreligious people, and like the classical ethical sages, the Sadducees insisted that one should lead a virtuous life not in anticipation of rewards for one's good deeds but because virtue is its own reward. Therefore, they reasoned, since the afterlife is so often held to be a time of punishment and reward, it was not only not needed, but morally misleading, even perverse. Thus, the Sadducees who confronted

Jesus with the shaggy-dog yarn about the widow and the seven brothers undoubtedly thought they were performing an important moral service. In so doing, however, they also unknowingly illustrated why the Bible contains such a wide-ranging assortment of views of the afterlife, and why even the most persevering searchers are unable to find a consensus.

The second cluster of verses that give us a hint of what a resurrection "like his" means is in the descriptions of Jesus's postresurrection appearances. When St. Paul and St. John used these two words to describe the "resurrection life," they did not supply any details. And since, like Jesus, neither says much about heaven, we are left only with the brief accounts of Jesus's own life after his resurrection to suggest what "like his" might mean.

To look at these postresurrection appearances we begin here with the account in the Gospel of Luke, chapter 24. It comes just after descriptions of the empty tomb and of the troubled state of the disciples as they gathered in a room puzzling over what had happened, when suddenly Jesus appears to them:

> *He said to them, "Why are you troubled, and why do doubts rise in your minds? Look at my hands and my feet. It is I myself! Touch me and see; a ghost does not have flesh and bones, as you see I have."*
>
> *When he had said this, he showed them his hands and feet. And while they still did not believe it because of joy and amazement, he asked them, "Do you have anything here to eat?" They gave him a piece of broiled fish, and he took it and ate it in their presence.* (Luke 24:39–43 NKJV)

Admittedly, this is only one short passage, and its significance should not be exaggerated. Still, it affords one of the few pointers to the nature of the "resurrection life," so in a book on heaven and the kingdom of God we need to try to understand it. First, it is noteworthy that, after Jesus has shown his skeptical followers his hands and feet, and assures them that he is not a ghost, he goes a step further. He asks them for something to eat. This might not seem surprising at first. After all, it has been three days since his execution. He has been dead all that time and has obviously not eaten anything. But some early readers of the Gospel were fascinated with the question of what the "resurrection life" will be like, especially if we all rise "like him." Naturally, impressed by Jesus's eating the broiled fish, these early followers went on to surmise that, in order to eat the fish, he must then have had not only the "flesh and bones" he mentions, but teeth, a throat, and an entire digestive system. They never said much about resurrection of the excretory organs, but this must have seemed plausible, even though unmentioned. From hands and feet to digestive tract it is an easy step to asking about the other organs and systems that human beings need in the earthly life. And this is just what the earlier students of the Bible did. If a large and small intestine, liver, and pancreas are required to eat broiled fish, then what about lungs, arteries, glands, and all the rest?

Notably, the first interpreters stopped short of asking about gonads, testicles, and the other reproductive organs. This subject was left to be examined by later theologians, such as Augustine and Aquinas, and we will turn to them shortly. But why were these early exegetes so reticent about sexual organs, an important part of a human being? Did they labor under a touch of Victorian prudery *avant la lettre*? Maybe they reasoned that since Jesus had said there would be "no marriage or giving in marriage" in the kingdom of God, sex organs were not all that important. In any case, their rather truncated view of the human body after the resurrection did not prevent them from speculating about other aspects of the hereafter in considerable detail. We will return to this shortly.

The other salient point to notice about his passage and what follows it immediately in Luke is how it will carry us briefly into the documentary history of the Gospel itself. Here is the following text from Luke:

> *Then he [Jesus] led them out as far as Bethany, and then, lifting up his hands, he blessed them. While he was blessing them, he withdrew from them* and was carried up into heaven, *and they worshiped him, and returned to Jerusalem with great joy; and they were continually in the Temple, blessing God.* (Luke 24:50–53)

I have emphasized "and was carried up into heaven" because there is an ongoing dispute among biblical scholars about whether these words appeared in the original Gospel as Luke wrote it or were added later. Clearly, for anyone interested in a biblical perspective on heaven or life after death this is a question of paramount significance, and it does not help to ask, "But what does the Bible *say*?" The earliest written versions of the Gospels are based both on oral traditions and on even earlier documents of those Gospels available to them at that time. But the difficulty is that there were often several copies of any one of these sources, and they did not always agree with each other. Sometimes the differences were on small details, but they often disagreed with each other on more basic matters. Some had passages that others did not, and the wording of a single passage differed from one source document to another. What is a poor copyist and, later, a poor translator to do?

In the twentieth century the editors of the Revised Standard Version of the Bible confronted and even debated this question: What to do with passages about which the early manuscripts differ from each other? Should they just vote on which to base their new translation (and so what to exclude)? That seemed arbitrary. Should they simply follow the translators/editors of the King James edition first published in 1611? But that seemed irresponsible. Those translators lived in the seventeenth century. They had used the best tools at their disposal and had produced a literary masterpiece. But there have been many advances in biblical scholarship since then, both in our understanding of ancient languages and in the discovery by archaeologists of other texts of the Bible, some of them just as old as the ones used in our current Bibles. The Dead Sea Scrolls and the so-called Nag Hammadi texts are good examples. The RSV editors asked themselves how their new translation for modern readers could indicate the translation issue. They finally decided to try to inform current Bible readers that variant versions of the sources they had drawn upon existed and, at some points, differed from each other. In the biblical text itself, these RSV translators did this by marking some words, phrases, and even larger passages with a small letter, directing readers to a footnote on the same page. In this way the flow of the translated text was not interrupted, but the reader was made aware of the differing sources.

This procedure has a crucial bearing on our questions about the biblical picture of heaven. It brings us back to Luke 24:50–53 in which, as I have indicated, the words "and was carried up into heaven" are marked with the tiny letter "m." And we are informed by the footnote that these words—hardly trivial ones—are not to be found in some of the other early manuscripts of Luke on which our current renderings of the Gospel, including the RSV, are based.

This is not just a petty dispute among esoteric specialists poring over dusty manuscripts. Many branches of Christianity have made the ascension ("and was carried up into heaven") a central doctrine, and created a Holy Day dedicated to it. The idea of the ascension is also a major matter in a book such as this one, on the idea of heaven. The vexing question is this: Did the original writer of Luke know the narratives circulating among at least some of the early Christians, about Jesus's ascension into heaven after his resurrection? Did he include a description of the ascension in his original text, or did he not know about it, or did he include a description that was deleted by subsequent editors in some editions but not in others? And if so, why? Or, could it possibly be that Luke did not know about accounts of the ascension, or had heard them but did not believe them? The whole question makes the mind scurry, and we do not intend to answer it here. But we can surmise why we have this seemingly contradictory account within the New Testament itself. It is because different clusters of early Christians held differing beliefs, sometimes about what we might consider very important questions.

Stepping ahead into history, remember that for the first three centuries of its life, Christianity was anything but unified. It spread across the Mediterranean basin mainly in small congregations, only sporadically in touch with each other. There was no single creed, no hierarchy, no standard worship service. And, important for our purposes, there was no single view on what books should be included in the Bible. These Christians were united in their determination to follow Jesus, whom they understood in somewhat different ways. This multiplicity suggests that there were probably congregations that used the versions of Luke that include "ascended into heaven" and others used versions that did not include these words.

But this raises an even more basic question: How important was the idea of heaven and of ascending to it after death to early Christians? More exactly, was it important to some but not to others? Did their expectation of the imminent arrival of the full kingdom of God render ideas about going to heaven when they died unimportant? Our image of the early Christians is that they bravely died as martyrs torn apart by lions in the Roman arena, secure in the conviction that they would enter heaven. But was that true of all, or even of most of these Christians? Current historical research indicates that the actual number of martyrs has been exaggerated. Some undoubtedly died that ghastly death. But many did not. They made peace with the Roman authorities one way or another and were grudgingly tolerated.

Recent historical research also demonstrates just how diverse the early Christian communities were. It should not come as a surprise that their beliefs about many things, including the afterlife, differed. I am grateful that, even within my lifetime, the depiction of an originally unified Christianity, only later split by schisms and heresies, has been discarded. The Christian movement from its outset has never been unified. We have just discussed the diversity that obtained during the first years. But in the later age of the church councils, more separations occurred as some branches, often for reasons more political than theological, refused to accept the council decrees. Nevertheless, later historians obscured this multiplicity by classifying these separated sections as "heretics" or "schismatics," while the true church remained undivided. Even the division between the Eastern and Western churches in 1054 and the Protestant Reformation of the sixteenth century failed to dislodge the fiction of unity. Meanwhile, how many thousands of people have suffered and even feared they might not "go to heaven" because they belonged to the wrong church? When I was a child, the Catholic children we played with and who lived across the street sometimes took the opportunity to forewarn my younger brother and me that we were not going to make it into heaven because we did not belong to the "true church." Fortunately, after a reassuring conversation with my father, I never believed my playmates' admonitions, and they soon stopped issuing them.

One rarely hears the words "true church" nowadays. But my childhood occurred before the Second Vatican Council, when most Catholic theologians hesitated to use the word "church" in reference to any Protestant denomination: there was, after all, only *one* "Church" and the rest were something else. Remembering those days now, I am still surprised and gratified by how quickly this triumphalism has been left behind. But that fruitless discussion takes us to another passage in which Jesus does, despite his usual reluctance, use the word "heaven" twice. It occurs in the sixteenth chapter of the Gospel of Matthew, in which Jesus asks his disciples who people say that he is. They proffer various answers: Elijah? John the Baptist? Jeremiah? Maybe one of the prophets? At first these answers sound odd to the modern reader. Did the disciples believe in reincarnation? But we are not left to puzzle long before Jesus makes the question personal. He asks the disciples, "Who do *you* say that I am?" and Peter answers, "You are Messiah, the Son of the Living God." Then Jesus tells Peter that he did not get this answer from "flesh and blood," but it must have been revealed to him by "my father who is in heaven." Then, however, Jesus goes on to add some words that have become perhaps the most argued over in the entire Bible:

> *And I say also unto thee, That thou art Peter, and upon this rock I will build my church; and the gates of hell shall not prevail against it. I will give you the keys of the kingdom of heaven. Whatever you bind on earth will be bound in heaven, and whatever you loose on earth will be loosed in heaven.* (Matthew 16:18–19)

This much-disputed text is crucially pertinent to a discussion of heaven. First, it provides the basis for centuries of Roman Catholic claims: if Christ himself appointed Peter as the gate-keeper, and the pope is Peter's successor, anyone who wants to approach God must go "through Peter to God." We rarely hear this formula in the post–Vatican II era. But the concept lives on in all the jokes about arriving at the gates of heaven and being questioned by St. Peter before gaining entrance. He holds the keys to the kingdom.

The passage is disputed for different reasons. The first has to do with the text itself. Did Jesus really say this, or was it added by Matthew to bolster the bishop of Rome's attempts to solidify his growing authority? Why would Jesus choose the notoriously wavering and undependable Peter (who had vociferously denied him) for this responsibility instead of, for example, John, to whom he later entrusted the care of his mother? If an event of this import happened, why don't any of the other Gospel writers mention it? Why does Paul seem not to have heard of it? How could Jesus have mentioned his "church" when it did not yet exist but came into being only after his death? The list goes on.

But it may be the "keys" that have stirred up the most controversy. What does Jesus mean when he tells Peter that he is giving him "the keys of the kingdom of heaven"? In the area where Jesus lived at the time, the owner of an estate or household would customarily hand his keys to his most trusted servant when the owner left on a trip. Keys symbolize both authority and power. But in the case of Jesus and Peter, what authority over what? And what kind of power? This handing over has played such a big role in Christian history that it has become iconic; Catholics have said that the keys handed over to Peter were then handed on to his successors as bishop of Rome and all the popes that followed him. At times in history this investiture has meant authority over all Christians. At other times it has meant authority over Catholics. At still other times it has meant authority over the entire world, not just *urbs* (the city of Rome) but also *orbis* (the world).

But in this passage the "keys of the kingdom" include far more: the power "to loose and to bind," both on earth and in heaven. In the past, popes have used this power to excommunicate (interdict) whole cities or countries. One of them inflicted this punishment on Venice and on England because he deemed Elizabeth I a heretic. This meant no Masses, baptisms, or church weddings or funerals. But these were all, in a sense, still religious measures. Still, there have been times, ultimately unsuccessful, when popes have tried to actualize this authority and power not just religiously but in earthly political rule. In 1302 Pope Boniface VIII issued a "bull," an official statement, entitled *Unam Sanctum,* declaring that the pope possessed authority over both the church and all earthly realms. Popes initiated Crusades, arranged and dissolved marriages, accumulated vast stretches of property, and some even rode into battle at the head of armies of papal troops. But after Boniface the secular power of the papacy declined; and in recent years, especially after the loss of the Papal States in 1870, the popes have interpreted this authority and power as spiritual. But "spiritual power" is still real power, despite Stalin's notorious sneer: "How many divisions does the pope have?"

What do this ascent and descent of papal authority have to do with heaven? For some people, very little. But for others, mainly in past centuries, quite a lot. If you believe that in order to get to heaven, you need to be baptized, sustained by the sacraments (which were once called "the medicine of immortality"), assured of forgiveness of sin, and buried with the proper rites, then being deprived of all these would put you in a desperate situation. But this is just what excommunication and interdiction did. Also, a schism in the church can cause other anxieties. In order to benefit from these requisite sacraments, you have to trust that the church that is administering them to you has the authority to do so.

But the other reason these verses have been the subject of such venomous conflict is that the Roman Catholic Church has made them the basis for its authority. They are its Magna Carta. For many years the church has taught that, by means of the apostolic succession since Peter, it has inherited Peter's power "to bind and to loose" both on earth and in heaven. The exercise of this pontifical authority became one of the principal causes of the Protestant Reformation in the sixteenth century when some ecclesial authorities asserted that the pope had delegated this awesome authority, and therefore, often for a price, they could "loose" the souls of one's deceased relatives who were now suffering the pains of purgatory. Luther and the other reformers began by questioning this claim but went on to reject the entire edifice of papal authority.

During the centuries after the rupture, Protestants advanced a cascade of assaults on the doctrines and practices of the "Roman" Church, but nothing quite matched the energy, even venom, with which they attacked papal power. They declared it not only erroneous but blasphemous. Since only Christ is the head of the church, to invest the pope with this title was not only pretentious but sacrilegious. Protestants said the church of Rome was sinful and fallen, and that the fall dated from the rise of the papacy. For years, the favorite Protestant term of opprobrium for Catholics was "papists." When the Ku Klux Klan launched its nefarious crusade in the nineteenth century, its declared enemies were "niggers, Jews, and papists." But this animosity was not restricted to the South. In 1834, an anti-Catholic mob burned down an Ursuline convent in the Charlestown section of Boston. The stubborn continuity of antipapist sentiment was clearly demonstrated in the presidential election of 1928 when Herbert Hoover defeated Al Smith, in large part because of Smith's Catholicism, even though Smith was no hardline papalist. It has been reported that when a questioner asked him whether he would obey the pope's encyclicals, Smith answered, "What is an encyclical?"

It is sometimes hard for me to believe how much has changed in my own lifetime. Cardinal Newman writes that on the days he made the decision to join the Catholic Church, he walked into the office of a priest he knew and said, "Please accept me into the one true church." It is hard to imagine anyone using that language today. But we should remember that it was in the twentieth century that Catholic, Protestant, and Orthodox churches have begun to envision Christian unity not as something they once possessed but which was destroyed by the disruptive actions of one of the other branches but rather as a gift of God which is still to be realized. After the transformative papacy of John XXIII (1958–1963) and the Second Vatican Council (1962–1965) the Catholic Church publicly recognized Protestant churches and began to hold dialogues with them. The phrase "*the* true church" virtually disappeared.

Why is this important to notice in a book on heaven? For one thing, it presumably means that St. Peter, if indeed he is still gatekeeper, will not be denying entrance to Methodists or Pentecostals because they do not hold valid membership cards in the "true church." Of course, for a while recalcitrant voices in the Catholic Church clung fiercely to a narrow reading of the doctrine *Extra ecclesiam nulla salus* ("outside the church there is no salvation"). But that interpretation has few defenders today. When John F. Kennedy ran for president in 1960, his opponents, including some prominent Protestant ministers, tried to use his Catholicism against him, but the effort failed. Then when Joe Biden, also a Catholic, ran in 2020, his "religious affiliation" was hardly mentioned. But the *nulla salus* formulation had a long life, and still has an afterlife. The first thing a visitor sees upon entering St. Peter's Basilica in Rome are the Latin words, "You are Peter and upon this rock I will build my church," inscribed in a huge circle inside the circular dome over the high altar. These are reputed to be the very words of Christ, but what do they mean to Catholics today, or to non-Catholics?

I got a rather authoritative answer to this question in the summer of 1984. I was teaching at the small Evangelical (Protestant) seminary in Rome. The students included both Americans and

Europeans. At lunch one day, a messenger rushed in and told us that the pope (John Paul II) was inviting us to come to the basilica at 2:30 for a special audience. It seems that the Holy Father had just returned from a trip that had taken him by car through Czechoslovakia, where he noticed a roadside memorial. When he asked what it was, his Czech guide told him with some embarrassment that it was in memory of a group of Protestants who had been killed by Catholics in the sixteenth century. The pope ordered the driver to stop, got out, approached the monument, and knelt to pray. When he returned to Rome a few days later, he told his appointment secretary that he wanted to invite any Protestants who were now in Rome to an audience where he could express his penitence.

A few moments later, some fifteen students and faculty from our group were shuffling along the pathway by the Tiber that leads from the seminary to Vatican City. We were quickly ushered inside and asked to stand in a circle just in front of the high altar of St. Peter's. The Holy Father, the Vatican host informed us, would be here in a few minutes. While we waited, my eyes strayed up to the inside of the cupola and to the words I have just been discussing ("I will give you the keys of the kingdom") emblazoned there. One would be hard put to find a more prominent place for these words anywhere in the church. But before I could think about that, the pope entered in a white cassock and a fringed white fascia with the papal coat of arms picturing the keys of the kingdom embroidered on it. Standing just in front of the altar, his pectoral cross around his neck, he greeted us in English, then proceeded to tell us about his recent trip, the monument, and the sadness that seeing it had caused him. "It is time," he said, "to move beyond the petty differences that have divided us and to emphasize what we have in common." Then he walked around our circle shaking hands with each of us. This could have created an awkward moment because the first student in the line had seen people on television kissing the pope's ring, and apparently thought he should do so too. But the pope quickly thrust his right hand to him and to each of us, and we all shook hands while he smiled, nodded his head, and asked where were from. Having completed the circle, he turned to leave. But an aide whispered in his ear. The pope turned toward us, raised both arms, made the signs of the cross, and said in what appeared to be an afterthought, "All sacred items are hereby blessed," and walked out.

I was pleased he had done that. In my pocket I had a small medallion of St. Francis I had just purchased the day before. After I got home, I gave it to the woman who, as a little girl across the street, had told me I was not going to heaven. She was now grown up, mellowed, and a family friend. Still a faithful Catholic, she had never been to Rome or even seen a pope. She was obviously thrilled with the gift, blessed by none other than the pope himself. And I, as the childhood friend she had once said did not belong to the true church, took special pleasure in presenting it to her. I resisted the temptation to ask her if she still thought I would not get to heaven. She had probably long since forgotten that childhood conversation anyway.

In summary, what Jesus said about heaven was very little. His message proclaimed the presence and imminent coming of the reigning of God, which we discuss in the next chapter. It was not about heaven. If, over many years, for many people, heaven has displaced the kingdom of God as the essence of the gospel, this constitutes a severe loss. But if St. John's words in Revelation can be trusted, a "new heaven" is now appearing, and in the meantime, Jesus has asked us to pray, not that we "go to heaven" but that God's kingdom should come on earth.

# 5

# *Heaven and the Kingdom of God*

*Seek ye first the kingdom of God, and his righteousness; and all these things shall be added unto you.* (Matthew 6:33 KJV)

The Roman Catholic theologian Alfred Loisy (1857–1940) is said to have quipped, "Jesus came preaching the kingdom of God, but what happened was the church." A quip it may have been, but nonetheless there can be no doubt that his message about the "kingdom of God" constituted the core of Jesus's message. Further, Jesus derived this idea from his own Jewish tradition, so the kingdom of God is the theme that links the two parts of the Judeo-Christian tradition together. But, if we count on this primal concept in looking for insights about the "next life," we are headed for disappointment because in neither the Old Testament nor the New Testament does the concept of the kingdom of God provide any description of a hereafter. However carefully we read both testaments searching for portrayals of the "next life" or about heaven or hell, we will be dissatisfied. The more one learns about the Bible as a whole and the kingdom of God in particular, the clearer it becomes that the Good Book is not primarily about our next lives. Rather it is about what God has been doing in history, is doing in the present world, and what he can be expected to do in the future.

This helps explain why Jesus says so little about the next life. He has other, more pressing concerns. He wants those who hear his message to be awake to the opening stages of the coming of God's reign now in this life and in this world. Repeatedly he resists being lured into discussions about a next life and directs people's attention to what is happening under their noses. About the kingdom of God, he says, in effect, "Just look and listen," it is "in the midst of you." When, after his resurrection, Jesus sees his disciples staring upward as he is ascending, a voice from heaven says, "Ye men of Galilee, why stand ye here staring upward?" then goes on to tell them that Jesus will return but that in the meantime they should return to where they had worked with him and carry on the work he had started (Acts 1:11).

In short, the reason the Bible can disappoint those who expect to uncover in its pages satisfying depictions of heaven is that this is not its primary concern. With the exception of the Book of Revelation the biblical writers explicitly discourage curiosity about celestial matters. Jesus instructs his followers to stop staring up into heaven. Saint Paul dismisses this curiosity as "foolish." Jesus typically retorts to such inquiries as "Who will sit at your right hand?" not with an answer but with a rabbinical counterquestion. The Book of Revelation, which unfolds a turbulent scenario about the end of this world/age, is painted in such technicolor symbolism that we are left to wonder just what it is symbolizing. The result is that anyone who searches the Scriptures to find out "what the Bible says" about reward and punishment after death will find only scanty references.

And yet, it is from the Book of Revelation that I discovered the Rosetta Stone that helped me grasp the significance of the other reference to heaven and to the kingdom of God.

> *Then I saw a new heaven and a new earth, for the first heaven and the first earth had passed away, and there was no longer any sea.* (Revelation 21:1 KJV)

This is a remarkable passage, which, rather than making heaven eternal, positions it along with the earth and the sea as an element of the created world. And this is a world in which the kingdom of God is now taking shape, an eternal kingdom in which these elements are being transformed and, in biblical language, "glorified." This is a sweeping cosmic vision that dwarfs the minimalist idea of individuals entering one by one through St. Peter's Gate into an ethereal sanctuary isolated from all the bruises and defeats of history. It is important to notice that in his appearances after the resurrection, Jesus still bears the wounds on his hands and feet. The audacious promise of the kingdom of God is not that single persons will be plucked out of this vale of tears, but that history itself, with its laughter and tears, and the individual lives that have existed within it, will be redeemed. Although some have objected that this hope does not make enough room for the individual, we should remember that a *person* (as opposed to an "individual") is nothing without the worldly collectivities of family, friends, neighborhood, community, and nation within which he or she becomes a person. In this respect, the persistent human hope that in eternity the "circle" will not be broken is an authentic one. The problem is that its scope is too narrow. It usually centers only on the immediate family and leaves out the larger "circles" within which the family lives.

True, postbiblical preaching and teaching brim with portrayals of the bliss or torment that await the dead, but in marked contrast, the Bible itself mainly avoids any descriptions. And in those rare instances where these depictions do appear, they turn out to be an assortment of seemingly contradictory ideas. This apparent evasiveness is not an attempt to keep the reader in ignorance. It is grounded in the nature of the biblical God, and it has a long history in the Jewish faith, one that Jesus, a trained rabbi, continued. Nonetheless, this very reticence tells us something important that we will be exploring in subsequent chapters. But why such reticence?

Starting in the earliest centuries of their lengthy saga, the Hebrews were loath to say much about the Holy One, who was, in any case, so ineffable that any attempt to describe him in human language could diminish his awesome grandeur, at least in the view of human beings. Theologically, to talk about God was to imply that one knew something that only God himself knew, and this was tantamount to idolatry, worshiping something less than God instead of God. God's indescribability was an essential quality of his holy otherness. Consequently, the Hebrews never pronounced his name. They believed their mission was to follow his commandments, and to serve his purpose in the world, not to talk about him. Likewise, they were hesitant to talk about a possible life after death. To "sleep among their fathers" or to "rest in the bosom of Abraham" was as much as they would say.

However, if they avoided speaking about God, what the writers of both testaments were willing to discuss was the "kingdom of God," which is not the same as heaven, even though the two are sometimes misleadingly equated, leading to much misunderstanding. The confusion is understandable. Both in Jesus's time and in our own, many people have thought of "heaven" as the place you may eventually go to or attain. But that was not how Jesus spoke of "heaven." In the prayer he taught his disciples, he told them to pray for the kingdom to "come on earth," that is, to take shape in human history as it already exists in the mind and will of God ("in heaven"). For Jesus, this new era has now begun to break through into our confused and broken world. This kingdom is a fresh new reality, one now dawning on the current outmoded and decaying one. It is a "new being," one where God's original intention (his "will") permeates everything; everyone receives their daily bread, and debts are forgiven. If, for some people, heaven was or is a place you may go to after death, Jesus turns that formula upside down by highlighting the kingdom of God, which is not a distant Elysian Fields we may get to. It is a radical renewal of our present reality, and it is both already present, like the aperitif at the beginning of a feast, and is also coming to us in its fullness when the banquet is served.

Still, the confusing of heaven with the kingdom of God persists for many people, and this suggests that we cannot just drop the subject. When and why did the misguided identification of the two begin? Does it do any harm? Why has it been so enduring? These are questions that deserve to be considered. And in considering them, it might help to compare popular Christianity's blending of heaven with the kingdom of God with similar patterns in other traditions. But to make such a comparison, we will begin with a brief glance at the circuitous history of these two terms—heaven and the kingdom of God—in Judeo-Christian history.

As we have just said, the seemingly paradoxical idea of the kingdom of God, as both present now and as coming soon, was central to Jesus's message. It begins in the opening verses of the Gospels and continues in his principal mode of teaching, the parables. They all feature either the presence or the impending arrival of the kingdom, the overlapping "now" and the "not yet." In fact, it was the tension between these two that lent the kingdom of God its dynamic quality; an overemphasis on the "now" or the "not yet" side always weakened that creative tension. But, what did the ancient Jews and Jesus have in mind when they talked about the "kingdom of God"?

First, the kingdom of God does not mean a domain, the joyous abode of the blessed dead. It is not the polar opposite of a Sheol or Hades. It is not a place or a quality some people may get to and others miss out on after they die. In the Jewish Scriptures the Hebrew expression for "kingdom of God" is *malkuth Yahweh*. In the Greek New Testament, it is *basileia tou theou*. But, while in neither case do these original terms shed much light on their content, it is important to notice one crucial fact: neither for the Hebrews nor for the New Testament does the term "kingdom" mean, as it does in English, a "realm," a territory ruled over by a sovereign. Some scholars suggest that "kingly rule" is a better translation than "kingdom" with its strong implication of a place. But others, considering the dynamic quality of the phrase, consider "kingly rule" too static. They prefer the gerund form, "reigning of God," to suggest a moving, ongoing, recreating, or transfiguring process. I favor "reigning." Not only does it come closest to catching the full import of the original words, it casts a light on all the references to God's kingdom in both testaments as "dawning" or "appearing" or "promised" or "coming to be," a reality in motion. This way of thinking about "God's reigning" helps focus the question, but it does not answer it. Rather, it raises other questions to which we now will turn.

Jesus made known what the here-and-arriving reigning of God means in a number of ways: his parables, the "signs" he enacted (often called his "miracles"), his Sermon on the Mount as a snapshot of life in God's reigning, and the events of his passion. Here, we will look briefly at each of these.

First, parables were Jesus's favorite way of teaching. Fifty-five are recorded in the Gospels, some of which are duplicates. When he tells a parable he frequently begins with "The kingdom of God is like. . . ." Then, however, he rarely mentions "God" but instead he directs the hearers' attention, not to another life, but to this present world, to the kinds of events his listeners would have experienced themselves or heard about. However, in many of these anecdotes he adds an unexpected radical twist that must have shocked and angered many of those listening, such as when he makes the member of a despised minority, a Samaritan, the unlikely hero in the rescue of a Jew who has been beaten and robbed. He tells about a man who prepares a magnificent banquet, but none of the people he invited come, so he drags in surprised pedestrians from the streets and seats them at his table. He talks about a family rift that happened when one son stayed at home and worked on the farm while the other took his inheritance early and then spent it in "riotous living." Everyone knows such a family, or is a member of one. But then comes the twist: when the profligate decides to creep back home the father races out to meet him and then throws a welcome-home party, which infuriates the older brother who has stayed home. This parable is known as "The Prodigal Son," but some prefer to call it "The Forgiving Father." That, however, is just the point. Different people can identify with different characters. When I was talking about this story to a class of undergraduates, and asked them with which character they identified, fully a fourth said "the older brother."

Like the other things Jesus said and did, his parables do not give us a seamless picture of the reigning of God. Certain tensions remain in the picture. On the one hand, the kingdom comes slowly, like a seed growing. On the other, it comes as an unexpected surprise, a thief in the night. The entrance is narrow, but it includes many of those who are excluded or forgotten, even the wastrel self-indulgent son, even the workers in the fields who did not show up until late in the day. In fact, God does not wait for these marginated people to come so they can be welcomed. Like the shepherd's lost sheep or the woman's lost coin, God does not wait for them to appear on their own, but actively searches for them and celebrates their return.

The Gospels also offer narratives about Jesus's actions in what are usually called "miracles." Jesus enables a blind man to see, a cripple to walk, and restores a demon-possessed boy to sanity. He walks on the water of the Sea of Galilee and later is awakened from a nap by his companions so he can quiet the turbulent waves. He feeds large numbers of hungry people with extremely scarce resources. To my regret, much of the discussion about these incidents has been wasted arguing about whether they really happened. Some misguided Christians have even insisted that the miracles are a proof of Jesus's divinity. The Greek word that is usually translated "miracle" in the New Testament is *sēmeion*, which scholars say can also mean "sign" or "portent." I strongly prefer this translation, in part because it helps us escape from the useless argument of whether it really happened. The narratives in the New Testament come from an age when people believed in signs, and would probably not have thought of them as miracles in the modern sense of the word. Of course, the substance of each of Jesus's healings was to enable individuals to walk and see so they could take their places in the common life. But they also had a larger purpose. Jesus offered them as a sign, a foretaste of the nature of the reigning of God.

The third window into what Jesus meant when he talked about the kingdom (reigning) of God is in the Sermon on the Mount, which includes the Beatitudes, in Matthew chapters 5, 6, and 7. Some have called this collection of teachings the "charter" or "constitution" of God's commonwealth. But like many other charters and constitutions, this one has been the subject of endless debates and conflicting interpretations. Much hinges on whether Jesus was describing how it will be when the reigning of God on earth is fully accomplished or whether he intends his followers to strive to love their enemies and turn the other cheek even before his kingdom comes in its fullness. In the earliest years of Christianity many believed that even the most difficult demands should be obeyed, but later church leaders began to call these demands "counsels of perfection," intended only for an elite, required of some but not all Christians. There was also a disagreement, which was never settled, over whether he meant his demanding ethical dicta for everyone or just for his disciples. The argument went on.

In the nineteenth century many suggested that Jesus did intend them for everyone, but not literally. They were meant to instill a set of moral dispositions that could be flexible, depending on the situation, a predecessor of what in the twentieth century became known as "situation ethics." One of the severest critics of this position was Albert Schweitzer, who said it reduced Christianity to artillery shells from which the explosive core has been removed. He insisted that Jesus be taken seriously or not at all, and he exemplified this in his own life by leaving his career as a prominent theologian and world-class organist to move to the Belgian Congo to serve as a physician to the poor. In more recent years, hundreds of young men, many motivated by a Christian or other religious perspective, have chosen to go to prison rather than take up arms.

I do not expect this old argument to be settled soon. But if, as we have argued in this book, the kingdom of God is both here now and arriving, then we are free to live by the life models it announces before it appears in its fullness. And if heaven is both aspirational and normative, then its core moral imperatives are plain enough. Its radical inclusiveness subverts the norms by which we customarily judge ourselves and each other. It welcomes both the workers who toiled all day and the ones who showed up late, the self-satisfied moral majority and those who fall below their moralistic standard, the pious and the impious. Despite the disparate readings to which it has been subjected, there are more than enough gems in the Sermon on the Mount to inspire and sustain us without achieving a final consensus on exactly what it means. It means different things to different people, and that will not change.

Jesus derived the idea of the "kingdom" or "reigning of God" from the Jewish Torah, thus linking the two testaments. Some have even called the Sermon on the Mount "the new Torah," but that designation was sharply and correctly disputed. I do not believe the Nazarene rabbi wanted to impose a New Law. Jesus says that "until heaven and earth shall pass away," not a jot or tittle of the Law should be ignored "until all is fulfilled" (Matthew 5:18). He did not want to abolish the Law or impose a new one, but to affirm the original intention of the Law, and to celebrate it as a gift of ("amazing") grace rather than a constraining yoke. A better analogy than a New Law or Torah would be a declaration of human rights and freedoms. Jesus wanted his listeners to realize that they were free now to exercise the freedoms enunciated on that mountain.

But this was only the beginning of the history of the idea of the kingdom of God. As the "Jesus movement" grew, the idea was carried forward in a variety of often conflicting ways. After the age of Constantine, Catholics often identified the kingdom of God with the church. But this diminished the hope-inspired, future-oriented power of the yet-to-come aspect of the kingdom. One way or another, the idea of the kingdom of God, often in highly distorted ways, exerted an enormous influence as Christianity spread around the world. Sometimes the kingdom idea was deployed in destructive and inhumane ways, involving the enslavement, forced relocation, and murder of thousands of indigenous peoples. It was a paramount motivation in the minds of the European conquerors of both North and South America. Those who dropped anchor off Cape Cod were convinced that they were building the kingdom in the wilderness of what they described as a "virgin continent." The Europeans who overran South America announced that in conquering and converting "heathen" peoples they were winning souls for the true church, the earthly embodiment of God's kingdom. But, to relate these conquests to the central topic of this book, in both cases, the conquerors believed, or said they believed, they were not only civilizing the unwashed, they were also paving their way to heaven. The Europeans did not always keep these two goals separate. As Hernán Cortés said, as his armored horsemen overwhelmed Mexico, "We have come here to add souls to our Holy Mother, the Church, and to get much gold." One could therefore amend Loisy's remark by adding that after Jesus preached the kingdom of God, "what happened" was not only the church. It was the dogma of Christian civilization and Christian empire, neither of which comports with what Jesus taught about the kingdom of God.

On the other hand, a vision of the kingdom of God, closer to its original meaning as a here-but-coming world-age characterized by peace, mercy, and equality, also motivated many people such as St. Francis, Mother Teresa, Dorothy Day, Martin Luther King Jr., and others. This include those who founded hospitals, built shelters for the poor, cared for the sick and the wounded in wartime, and visited prisoners. Since Jesus had instructed his followers to pursue such "acts of mercy" and engaged in them himself, those who follow this interpretation are convinced that these acts of mercy are an accurate expression of the kingdom Jesus was speaking about and demonstrating. A central tenet in Martin Luther King's theology was the combination of freedom and equality, which he identified with the kingdom of God. As the present-and-coming epitome of justice and dignity, this kingdom was one source of inspiration for the anticolonial rebellions of Africa and Asia. Historians have documented how several of the leaders of these revolutionary rebellions, such as Jomo Kenyatta, Kwame Nkrumah, and Julius Nyerere, attended missionary schools.

The history of the global spread of the idea of the "kingdom of God" is a mixed one. But whether positive or negative, the

idea has had unparalleled power. It has exercised enormous
influence on how we have thought about both the City of God
and the City of Man, about what life on earth should be like,
and what heaven could be like, and how the latter might shape
the former. As the starting point for the inquiry we are pursu-
ing in this book, the kingdom/reigning of God is the nucleus
around which everything else rotates.

If the kingdom, or reigning of God, is central to both the
Old and the New Testaments, then where does heaven come
in? It can be surprising to anyone who reads the passages in
the Bible on the relationship of heaven to death and the afterlife
to find out how little is said. The words for heaven and heavens have several meanings, but hardly any connect it with the
hereafter. "Heaven" refers to the curtain that separates the earth
from the next layers up. Sometimes the curtain is of cloth, like
a cape. Sometimes it is made of a metal strip. Sometimes the
Bible speaks of the "pillars" of heaven, which support the curtain, whose main function is to separate the earth from what
lies beyond (which is never described). But only in a couple rare
verses does the Bible refer to heaven as a place or an abode. And
these references appear when the writers are making use of colloquial beliefs for other purposes, just as Jesus, who wanted
ordinary people to understand him, sometimes does in his
parables. In two of these parables he mentions "heaven" in its
colloquial sense.

Given this paucity of biblical grounding for heaven as a destination for those who are "saved" or found worthy, it seems
amazing that this conception has achieved such widespread
acceptance, especially when many of those who hold to this
view claim to be "Bible believing." But it becomes more com-
prehensible from the perspective we are following in this book.
When we understand that views of heaven serve as reflections of

earthly concerns and aspirations and that the kingdom of God does not erase history but transforms it, then we can understand that ideas of heaven, however transient, like the cultures in which they appear, are essential to human history. Maybe this is why Revelation speaks of a "new heaven" and a "new earth." But, just as with the old heaven and earth that have passed away, no descriptions are given.

Finally, a compelling reason why the "kingdom of God," despite its ambiguous history, is the most appropriate category to undergird this book is its massive significance for America, both in the past and for the future. The European settlers who arrived here in the early seventeenth century had mixed motives, among them greed, the desire for adventure, the desire to escape military recruiters, and the chance to start a new life. But for some it was the conviction that they were building God's kingdom in what they were told was a virgin continent, beyond the reach of the tyrants who ruled both church and state in Europe. Those who landed on the shores of the Massachusetts Bay borrowed a phrase from the Sermon on the Mount and declared they were building a "City on a Hill" whose light would illuminate the whole world. William Penn called his colony a "Holy Experiment." Roger Williams named the first city in Rhode Island, the colony he organized, "Providence," and made it a haven of religious tolerance that welcomed persecuted minorities. Go where you will in America today, it is hard to travel many miles without passing through a town named Goshen, Bethesda, Canaan, Bethany, Mount Hermon, or one of dozens of place names drawn from the Bible. Sometimes the idea of the kingdom of God was openly proclaimed; sometimes it was implicit. But it was always present, coursing just below the streams and counterstreams of political waves but breaking to the surface in sermons, songs, and battle cries. But it always reminded Americans that their nation, like Israel, had been given a mission by God, what some called an "errand in the wilderness."

From the time they built their first log cabins, it was never far from the minds of these settlers that they had a righteous purpose to fulfill, not just as individuals but as a nation, and sometimes this idea had lethal implications. Even before they achieved independence from their motherland, many believed they had the responsibility to Christianize or civilize the indigenous peoples, or—failing that—to expel or eliminate them. They could build schools, like Dartmouth, for the enlightenment of the Indians, and at the same time dispatch the cavalry to massacre them. The moral is that the concept of the kingdom of God is such a potent one that it can be deployed for contradictory causes, and its misuse must be constantly countered by remembering what it originally meant. When the struggle for independence began, for some of its advocates it was a fight to escape British misrule, especially in its power of taxation. Others, particularly among the Baptists and other sectarians, saw it as a continuation of their battle for "soul liberty." As the Civil War approached, both sides were convinced that God was on their side. The South viewed it as another chapter in the national fight for freedom under God that had begun in Concord, and Robert E. Lee was revered as a model of the Christian gentleman soldier, bravely contending against formidable odds. The North rallied to the strains of Julia Ward Howe's "Battle Hymn of the Republic" with its apocalyptic imagery. Not just an intersectional conflict, it signaled the "coming of the Lord," as God "loosed the fateful lightning of his terrible swift sword." Historians of the Civil War have written that thousands of fatally wounded soldiers, both Union and Confederate, were assured on their deathbeds by their caregivers that they would soon be in the presence of Jesus.

In the decades after the war, America's empire builders announced that the nation had a "manifest destiny" to bestride the entire continent from sea to shining sea. In the twentieth century, President Woodrow Wilson, the son of a Presbyterian minister, or, as he called himself, "a child of the manse," instructed Americans that they were called to win a war to end wars and to make the world safe for democracy. After that war, Wilson urged his countrymen to join a "League of Nations," which would be united not by a mere treaty but by a "covenant," the biblical term for God's pact with his chosen people. The failure of his fellow Americans to adopt his visionary plan broke Wilson's heart. But the idea of the kingdom of God, albeit sometimes in modified language, lived on. Religious rhetoric continued to color American political projects at home and abroad. When Dwight D. Eisenhower wrote the history of his successful military campaign in World War II, he entitled it *Crusade in Europe* (1949), framing it as another episode in a centuries-old confrontation between the legions of light and the hosts of darkness, dating back to the Christian reconquest of the Holy Land in 1099. But "Ike" obviously liked the historical metaphor. When he ran for president in 1952, he called his electoral campaign a "moral crusade."

It is never easy to separate the effort to "build the kingdom of God in America" from a self-righteous patriotism ("My country, right or wrong") or chauvinism. But it is not impossible, as can be seen in the abolitionist movement in the nineteenth century, peace organizations like the early League of Women Voters, and the civil rights movement of the 1960s. But perhaps the best example of how the kingdom of God can be a critical force occurred in the early years of the twentieth century in the Social Gospel, described in a previous chapter. Its founder was a Baptist pastor, Walter Rauschenbusch, a minister in the crowded Hell's Kitchen section of New York City. After struggling futilely on the individual and family level with the hunger, poverty, sickness, and unemployment that his people experienced, he decided that the Christian message had to engage the larger social structures that created their pain. He published in 1907 a widely read book entitled *Christianity and the Social Crisis.*

The Social Gospel soon became one of the most influential currents in theology. Many understood it as a Protestant parallel to the social encyclicals of the popes that defended the rights of workers. The nationally known New York preacher Harry Emerson Fosdick wrote about it, the book "struck home so poignantly on the intelligence and conscience . . . that it ushered in a new era in Christian thought and action." It is worth noting that the word "heaven" is hardly mentioned in this book. The biblical basis for the Social Gospel was the kingdom of God, which Rauschenbusch once described in a phrase that captures his thinking as "always present, always arriving."

But as America edged closer to war in 1914 and 1915, Rauschenbusch and the Social Gospel movement found themselves under siege. Rauschenbusch held that the gospel called for a peaceful resolution of international disputes, not war. He publicly opposed a war with Germany. But, given his own German family background, his critics accused him of disloyalty, and maybe even treason. Given that he considered himself to be both a true patriot and a faithful Christian, such charges broke Rauschenbusch's spirit. A depressed man, he died in 1918, before the war he had opposed ended. Yet the voice of Rauschenbusch reached into the next generation. "His writings," said Martin Luther King Jr., "left an indelible imprint on my thinking, and his understanding of the kingdom of God continues to appeal to those who want to combine evangelical passion with social justice."

After the war, opponents of the Social Gospel accused it of being socialistic or communistic. At the same time a strident fundamentalism was gaining ground among American Protestants. Among the "fundamentals" it defended were the literal inerrancy of the Bible, opposition to ecumenical or interfaith cooperation, and a staunch opposition to the Social Gospel. Although it is sometimes mistakenly interpreted as a rural or small-town movement, fundamentalism was based largely in cities, and its principal theological hub was Princeton Theological Seminary. It was an emphatically individualist theology. "There is NO Social Gospel," their preachers constantly reiterated; through Christ, God saves people from hell and welcomes them to heaven "one by one," as their favorite song made clear. This individualism has shown a remarkable persistence in conventional American Christianity, both Catholic and Protestant. *Our* hope for the kingdom of God on earth was overshadowed by *my* hope of getting to heaven.

But the fundamentalists did have their own version of a Social Gospel. It was Christian Americanism. After World War II, as the Soviet Union became our nation's rival in the Cold War, and domestic conservatives saw atheistic communism as a mortal threat to our faith, fundamentalism shed its earlier exclusively transcendental emphasis and became deeply involved in partisan politics. Groups emerged like the "Moral Majority," led by fundamentalist minister Jerry Falwell. He began his career with a popular radio program called *The Old Time Gospel Hour*, which patterned itself on a traditional how-to-get-to-heaven revival, but evolved into a highly conservative bulwark. The Pentecostal TV preacher Pat Robertson entered presidential primaries in 1988, and competed in early primaries before dropping out. By the early twenty-first century, politically conservative religious movements had cemented an alliance with the Republican Party. By the second decade of this century they had lost their independence, but their positions on a host of religious and political issues had been absorbed by the

GOP. The "religious right" became an integral component of Republican Party strategy.

A development that was both opposite and parallel to the religious right took place among those Protestant Christians who still advocated the goals of the Social Gospel, although they rarely mentioned that heritage. Issue-oriented organizations like the anti–Vietnam War movement drew heavily on support among the churches, both Catholic and Protestant. Clergy like Rev. William Sloane Coffin and Father Dan Berrigan were among its most visible leaders. Black churches constituted the base for the civil rights movement, often led by ministers like Martin Luther King Jr. and Jesse Jackson, who had learned their political theology in seminary and from the progressive wing of the Black Church tradition. The American Roman Catholic bishops issued a blunt but eloquent statement against nuclear weapons in June 1998. In many ways, the impetus of the Social Gospel, and therefore of the spirit of the kingdom of God, albeit rarely identified as such, continued to influence religious and social life in America.

What was going on with "heaven" while the kingdom of God and the Social Gospel went through their ups and downs? The answer is that regarding the "next world" a kind of division of labor set in. Heaven became an even more individual or family-centered concept than ever. The kingdom of God became a communal vision, a quasi-utopian symbol of the fulfillment of history that required both divine and human effort. But why do we hear so little today about the kingdom of God, either in ordinary conversation or in explicitly religious gatherings, yet we still hear about heaven, and not just at funerals? After a succession of failed utopias in the past two centuries, both in America and internationally, some people have become suspicious of them as too grandiose or pretentious, and have retreated to more diminutive hopes for *my* family and *my*self.

But it was always a mistake to identify the coming of the kingdom of God with one or another social or political utopia, something liberal Christians were often prone to do. From a biblical perspective, God's kingdom is God's, a transformation initiated by him in which he invites human beings to participate, bearing in mind that human pride and self-deception will inevitably mar their efforts to some degree. Reinhold Niebuhr constantly reminded his readers, including a grateful Barack Obama, not to let the craving quest for perfection become the enemy of the good, and that it was urgent for Christians to involve themselves in the struggle for social justice even though their highest goals would probably not be achieved in their lifetimes. Indeed, Niebuhr adds, it is our confidence in the ultimate triumph of God's justice that empowers us to keep trying despite setbacks and failures.

So what is the relationship between "heaven" and "the kingdom of God"? As for heaven (and hell) I sense no diminution in ordinary conversation today. Switch on a car radio anywhere in America, not just on Sunday, and you will hear overwhelming evidence that talking about heaven and hell has in no way vanished from modern life. Nor is this language confined to radio preachers, as we will be reminded in the following pages of this book. A more accurate way of restating Loisy's statement that "Jesus preached the kingdom of God but what happened was the church" today would now be "but what happened was the hope individuals have of going to heaven." The main obstacle faced by anyone who tries to understand or write about concepts of heaven today is that the message of Jesus has been almost eclipsed by a massive tsunami of individualism fueled by a profit-driven consumerist economy, the cult of endless human potential, and religions centered on *my* happiness and *my* salvation.

This near displacement of the kingdom of God by heaven in

so much of Christianity today creates a problem. I have written that my home port for the circumnavigation recorded in this book would be the biblical tradition and the kingdom of God. Yet, what became clear to me in the course of this journey is that the kingdom of God, the heartbeat of the Old Testament and of Jesus's message, has been either disfigured into an ideology of empire or wrongly equated with a distant heaven or severely marginalized into a quaint relic on a back shelf that we may respect but which no longer guides us in Christian theology and practice. True, the energy of the kingdom of God still motivates many campaigns for justice, peace, and inclusiveness. But these often lack the sturdy link to the stirring history of the kingdom of God that would provide invaluable clues about how to steer clear of some of the deformation mentioned above. In short, what we need today is twofold.

First, we need to understand that heaven, in whichever of its multitudinous variations it appears, is not the kingdom of God. It is the symbolic expression of an elemental human hope, and as such we must take it with utter seriousness, but not literally. Some of the following chapters will document a few of the lavish depictions of the next life projected by different religions. As in the rest of this book, however, I do not want these to be dismissed as mere wishful thinking. They are more than that. They tell us something vital about how humans give shape to their deepest hopes and fears. We must be familiar with them to understand them in the light of the kingdom of God.

This second step is to reclaim and renew our understanding of this "reigning of God" in human history. In a culture in which "royalty" and "reigning," "king" and even "God" have become suspect for many people, we may need new terminology for eternal verities. This will require us first to become familiar with the way people talk and think today about what most concerns them, and, in light of this current worldview, to plumb what the Hebrew prophets and Jesus can still tell us about what they called the "reigning of God." We need to welcome the several guises, some of them not "religious," in which this reigning has appeared in the past, where it is happening now, and how we can nourish and promote it in the future: "Thy kingdom come on earth. . . ."

# 6

# *Jews, Heaven, and the Kingdom of God*

*The heavens declare the glory of God; and the firmament sheweth his handiwork. Day unto day uttereth speech, and night unto night sheweth knowledge. There is no speech nor language, where their voice is not heard.*

*Their line is gone out through all the earth, and their words to the end of the world.* (Psalm 19:1–4 KJV)

As they peruse this chapter, some readers may think it sounds like a digression, that it strays from the central focus of the book and wanders too far into the expanse of the wider Jewish tradition. But I do not see it as a digression. As I was starting to write the book, I dropped in on a colleague who is both an ordained rabbi and a scholar in Jewish history. I told him the book was about ideas of the afterlife, and asked if he could suggest some helpful reading on Jewish concepts on the subject, since I had not been able to find much.

"And I don't think you will," he replied. "We don't say much about it." I was a little surprised. "But why?" I asked. "It's an endlessly intriguing subject."

"Yes," he said, "that is just the problem. Endlessly intriguing, endlessly. But where does it get you? Maybe what you should look into is not what Jews think or write about heaven, but why we don't. Now that is worth spending your time on."

At first I thought this was a promising idea, although, at least for this chapter, it would require changing the focus. Instead of comparing views of heaven, it would mean exploring the meta-question of why some people say a lot on the subject and others very little. But as I wrote, it became clear to me that this was just the point. Views of the afterlife in any tradition are often a kind of key to the whole panoply of symbols and ideas by which a tradition is formulated. So, rather than backing away from this treasure house, I decided to explore it as best I could. Also, the more I delved into the Jewish tradition, I discovered that the rabbi had been only partially correct. Jews have written many thousands of pages, if not about heaven per se, then about death and the hereafter. Most of this is in the classical texts of Jewish mysticism such as the Kabbalah and the Zohar, and the commentaries on them. But so many of the ideas in these sources, like reincarnation, for example, have been strenuously rejected by scholars and rabbis that the problem is that it is virtually impossible to sort out what is authentically "Jewish" and what is not. And since Jews have no official creed, my solution to this problem was not to make myself a judge but to realize that engaging in this kind of sorting is not my responsibility. The Jewish tradition has been, and still is, so profusely rich and varied that I decided instead on something else: to discuss those aspects of it that enlarge and diversify the expansive celestial horizon constituted by the other perspectives in this book.

There is a story of an eager Jewish graduate student at a German university who paid a visit on a wise, aging rabbi to ask him a question. "Rabbi," he whispered, leaning close to the old man's ear, "some of my fellow students who are Gentiles tell me their courses in theology are fascinating. Rabbi, do we have Jewish theology that I could study?" "Ah," said the rabbi, *"Lassen die Goyim ihre Theologie machen. Wir haben Torah."* ("Let the Gentiles do their theology. We have Torah.")

This is only a story. But it is, in its way, a true story, and it has an important bearing on the theme of this book. It has been said that the Jews "do not have a theology." If "theology" means talk *about* God, then the claim has some truth. Starting in the earliest centuries of their long saga, the Hebrews were loath to talk about the Holy One. Above all, they never spoke his name but resorted to an assortment of nicknames and circumlocutions. They spoke *to* him in praise and prayer (and complaint). They sometimes *listened* for his voice. They tried, often without success, to obey his will. At times they even described his *actions* in creation, liberation, and redemption, and his promises. But, as for the essence of God, or his "nature," other than that he was merciful and wise, they said little or nothing. Not only was God, in their view, indescribable, but this indescribability was a primary element of his holiness.

When Moses responds to God's voice addressing him from the burning bush, telling him to "set my people free," he asks, "Who shall I say has sent me?" The voice answers with words that have been badly mistranslated into English as *"Tell them, 'I am who I am' has sent me."* But scholars of Hebrew reject this translation as far too static. They prefer, *"Tell them that 'I will do what I will do' has sent me."* In the centuries since then, faithful action in response to God's initiatives, not reflection on God's being, has constituted the axis of Jewish faith. Jews have continued to honor their mission: to obey God and to serve his purposes in the world, not to talk about him, which in any case would always risk slipping into idolatry.

Likewise, the ancient Jews were equally reluctant to talk about life after death. To "sleep among their fathers" or to rest in "the bosom of Abraham" was as much as they would say. Even when, at the height of the Hellenistic period, some Jews embraced ideas of a postmortem existence, they stopped short of saying what it would be like. It is noteworthy, especially for a book like the present one, concerned with ideas about the afterlife, that this Jewish reluctance to talk about either God or heaven has not changed. But, as we will see, it has never been airtight.

The reticence to speak of heaven springs from a long history. The ancient Jews lived among peoples who were not at all averse to chatting about their gods or envisioning the next life, often in explicit detail. Inevitably the Hebrews heard this talk, and because their own faith was still in process of formation, they picked some of it up, even sometimes, as we will see below, the concept of the immortal soul. And since they had no clearly defined convictions on a next world, they incorporated bits of their neighbors' religious idiom. But they were never comfortable with it. Jews were uneasy with body/soul dualism, and they noticed that in their neighbors' theologies, it was only the spirit, not the flesh, that had a future after death. This body/soul language would scarcely pass muster in the Hebrew antidualistic worldview. Still, despite this caveat, some fragments borrowed from these neighbors found their way into Jewish faith. Dualism, in a variety of guises, was always knocking on the door, and as we will see, sometimes it slipped in. It is still present, albeit not always explicit today.

Jewish mysticism has accompanied the mainstream for centuries like a persistent doppelgänger. Fiercely attacked and condemned by the rabbinical elite, it has nonetheless thrived in the interstices and continuously made itself felt as a permanent component of Jewish life. The main vehicle that incorporates this mystical stream is the kabbalah, which means "tradition." It consists of esoteric interpretations of biblical texts and Jewish rituals as well as other elements, adding up to what almost amounts to a theological system. About the year 1188 there appeared a book in southern France called the *Zohar* or *Sefer ha-Bahi*, a compendium of kabbalistic teachings on creation ethics and a series of descending worlds. It also seeks to explain the origin of evil, the role of human beings, and the levels of the soul.

Of special interest for a book on concepts of the hereafter is that the literature of kabbalah contains long discussions of reincarnation or the transmigration of souls, something few people today know was once so prominent in the Jewish tradition. It is also relevant here since, where the idea of reincarnation obtains, the idea of heaven is correspondingly diminished. If you are scheduled to be reincarnated, you do not "go to heaven" but into a different body.

How and when did the idea of reincarnation and the attempt to refute it find its way into Judaism? It was probably in the ninth century, when a similar process was under way in Islam and Christianity, originating among Eastern Gnostic Christians who brought along many of their Neoplatonic ideas into Christianity. In all three traditions, spokesmen for the established doctrine energetically rejected reincarnation. The Second Council of Constantinople declared it heretical in 553, but it lingered on in popular belief. Among Jews it was attacked and defended for years, but never disappeared. In the early tenth century the Jewish theologian Saadia Gaon contended that reincarnation was nothing but "madness and confusion." Thomas Aquinas, eventually recognized as the semi-official theologian of the Catholic Church, rejected reincarnation because it denies the unity of soul and body. The Protestant Reformers rejected it on the same grounds. Despite these condemnations, however, the idea of reincarnation persisted, albeit in a range of expressions. For many millions of Hindus and Buddhists it is not superfluous or optional but is integral to their traditions. Nor should we doubt that it is alive and well among some Christians. I have sometimes met people who seemed neither mad nor confused but who said they had the opportunity to travel though time to meet their ancestors.

Reincarnation seems to rise and recede periodically in Judaism. What was fascinating to me in reading about the ongoing controversy over reincarnation was that, for the Jews, it was often defended by an argument for justice: God allows some people who had suffered unfairly in life to have another chance, and some evildoers who managed to live a carefree life were made to return into reduced circumstances. Some Jewish and Christian advocates of reincarnation taught that there were people who would find themselves in the bodies of animals, and others said that a person might be reincarnated for up to a thousand times. Most agreed, however, that the process was not infinite, and that eventually souls would find eternal rest or, a few said, eternal torment. As I was reading these intriguing sources, it occurred to me that for some of its defenders, reincarnation served a purpose later assumed by purgatory, which was first coming into Catholic thinking in the twelfth century.

From the perspective of traditional Jewish and Christian theologies, however, the fatal flaw in ideas of reincarnation was, as we have seen, that they assumed a dualism of soul and body. But reincarnation is not the only view of life after death that violates the biblical doctrine of soul/body unity. Dualism rarely announces itself as such. From the soul vs. body of the ancients to the material vs. spiritual sphere of the medieval period to today's modern mind/body dichotomy, dualism keeps returning to bury its pallbearers. But it is almost always under attack. In our time, for example, the mind/body separation just mentioned is being questioned from many different sides, including notably, holistic medicine and neuroscience. It also remains a matter of contention in current thinking about death and the afterlife in the context of arguments about cremation vs. burial, and it therefore inevitably comes up in any discussion about heaven, as we will see throughout this book.

What does this debate mean for the belief, still held widely

today, in the "eternal soul" we may be in danger of losing, as
is spelled out in so many catechisms? The "eternal soul" is a
current version of dualism, premised on the assumption that
the body and the soul/spirit are separable. Early in their long
journey, the Jews had usually rejected this dichotomous notion.
They nourished the belief in a body-spirit unity. According to
Scripture, God had not created both a material and a spiritual
component in human beings. He had created Adam, breathing life (*ruach*, or spirit) into him in the act of creation. Thus, a
human was not a body *and* a spirit/soul but an embodied soul,
a spirit-infused body. Like the hydrogen and oxygen in water,
they were one substance. This conviction inclined the Jews to
be skeptical of theories of the immortality of the soul: God, and
only God, was immortal. But, being human beings as well as
Jewish, they could not help wondering. Death itself was not a
pleasant prospect. And from what little they heard about what
came afterward in Sheol, that was even more unpleasant. Yes,
they were aware of the promise of God's eventual restoration of
his people to their promised homeland. But in the meantime,
and even after they arrived, people would die. What about them?

For a long time Jews pondered this contradiction. As they
went on living under foreign rulers, the hope for Jewish nation-
hood in their own land became less plausible. They derived their
sense of identity from their families and their own life stories.
Now they hoped to somehow fuse their inherited teaching with
their new insights and concerns. The tradition held that God
would one day restore all Jews, both those who were now dead
and those still alive, to the Holy City, and might even permit
some worthy Gentiles to enter through the sacred gates as well.
It would be like those Gentiles who, according to the biblical
report, escaped from Egypt along with the Jews—like the miracle God had accomplished in the "Valley of the Dry Bones"
recorded in the biblical book of the prophet Ezekiel.

But this prophetic hope was something that God would bring to pass. It was not a hope based on some special quality, an "immortal soul," within human beings. Clearly, to invest such cosmic hope in some merely human quality, even if it was a gift from God, would be a blatant act of idolatry: attributing divine qualities to something other than God. Slowly it became clear to the chosen people that neither an Ezekiel-like resurrection nor an Isaiah-like restoration was the same as immortality, so most Jews rejected the concept, but not without a long internal struggle, one that had started in their earliest years.

In writing this book, as I talked with Jewish people about their thoughts on what lies ahead either for the individual or for the Jewish people, it became clear that nothing even close to a consensus exists. For most, neither the restoration nor the resurrection scenario seemed plausible. The older tension between the fate of individuals and of the nation had also lost its cogency. None were interested in some ultimate regathering of all Jews in their own land. As for the individual, most held to a respectful agnosticism. According to these prophecies, the whole people, the nation, would be restored. But some Jews began to ask two questions: What about *now*? What will be happening in the meantime? And if this restoration eventually includes everybody, does that mean that the righteous and the despicable, the virtuous and the evildoers, will all be swept up together? Would they all share the same heavenly plot? How could a just God allow that? And also, most importantly perhaps in the meantime, *what about me*?

This existential question of what happens to me after death has probably always been present, but it had been subsumed for centuries under the question of the ultimate fate of the people. But now, asking it as a concern separable from the nation's fate marked a decisive change. As the question became less national and more personal, Jewish scholars began to find precepts for individual salvation in the Bible that they had not noticed before. First, there were the accounts of how God lifted Enoch and Elijah into heaven, not after they died but while they were alive. Well, thought some Jews, if Yahweh can do that for those two, then in principle he could do it for anyone.

Then there were two psalms (43 and 73) in which the psalmists, who were temple singers, used the personal pronoun to describe when they would eventually meet God in heaven. These and other psalms were highly personal, with no mention of the nation. This clear reference to the individual, not just the nation, in God's ultimate plan marked a pointed shift with far-reaching implications for ideas both about heaven and about earthly governance. These ideas have lasted into our own times. They underlie the tension between the reigning of God that Jesus promulgated and the heaven that has largely replaced it in the common religious consciousness. It also reverberates in the never-ending dispute about the appropriate balance in any society between the individual and the collectivity. It is echoed in the sometimes heated conversation among Jews about whether they are a religion or a nation or a little of each.

This intra-Jewish debate is not just a theoretical one. It became noisier when the Jewish State of Israel became independent in 1948. Some Zionists declared that all Jews should now "return" to a land that was no longer only a distant promise. Most Jews, however, decided that Israel was a great asset for those who wanted to "make *aliyah*" (return from the diaspora) or needed to flee persecution, but that one could also be a "Zionist" and continue to live in Sacramento or Paris and support Israel politically and financially. In addition to these two parties, a third but smaller group had two wings. Some secular Jews were concerned that creating a national state defined by a religious identity of highly orthodox Jews posed the danger of creating a theocracy and might complicate their full participation in their own national communities. On the other hand, some highly orthodox Jews insisted that forming a national state was a gross violation of the long-held belief that only a messiah could do such a thing.

When I first visited Israel in 1979, I was surprised to discover that many of what are now called "ultra-orthodox" Jews there were still opposed to a Jewish national state, even though they lived in one. The rabbi of one such group regularly hoists a white flag upside-down on Israeli Independence Day to broadcast the group's disapproval. The situation is further complicated because, although the majority of Israelis are not "religious," only the Orthodox rabbis are recognized by the government. Reformed, Conservative, and Reconstructionist rabbis have no legal standing. This meant that when one of my wife's cousins, a citizen of Israel but a member of a tiny Reformed congregation in Haifa, wished to marry, she had to fly with her fiancé to Cyprus, where the rabbi of a Reformed congregation officiated under the wedding chuppah.

The outcome of this history is that both a distinct individualism and a deep-seated sense of corporate identity are alive and well in the Jewish community today, with both religious and political consequences. For example, it is at the heart of the riddle of what it means "to be a Jew," which has become a divisive issue in Israel. Since its founding, the policy of the Jewish state has been that any Jew is eligible for citizenship. But when some people think of themselves as part of an ethnic group, others, the inheritors of a tradition, and others members of a religion, what does that mean? When some years ago a Roman Catholic priest whose parents were both Jewish applied for entry into Israel, his application was denied. On the other hand, Gentiles who have converted to Judaism must have done so under the auspices not of a Reformed or Conservative but only of an Orthodox rabbi. There can be little doubt that the emergence of individualism within the tradition has contributed to the widely disparate opinions about the afterlife among Jews today. But why did this change take place, and why did it take place when it did?

The constant changes in where and how they lived forced Jews to cope with numerous challenges to their traditions. Among the different peoples they interacted with in their first centuries, some believed that a new life after death was natural. Both animals and human beings die, but every year at least the trees and grasses blossom again. And what appear to be the same wild animals are back. Several of the Jews' neighbors in the ancient Middle East associated this reappearance of life with the death and resurrection of a god or goddess of fertility, such as Isis and Osiris. However, some did not believe that this annual rebirth was an automatic, natural process. The god or gods who expired in the autumn had to be placated by rites and sacrifices to return. Otherwise, they might not come back to life at all, and this would spell doom not only for nature but for human beings as well. There would be no life on a barren, lifeless planet.

At first glance, this combination of terror and desperate hope might seem naïve. But as we learn more about how closely human beings and the world of flora and fauna, earth, sea, and sky are dependent on each other, this "primitive" outlook reveals a vital awareness, one that was nearly lost in the centuries of urbanization and industry. But it is an insight our current ecological crisis is forcing us to recognize anew. It turns out that as humans we are not as different from the fish and earthworms as we once thought. We are integrally linked to each other, in life and in death, something preliterate peoples recognized and respected, as is evident in their religious practices. They expressed it mythologically, not in scientific terms. But this interweaving is something we are now learning to appreciate and safeguard, though painfully. And we may have even more to learn from a sympathetic understanding of our preliterate ancestors and how they symbolized their environment. They knew something that they expressed in their own dialect that we need to translate into ours.

Sometimes theology and economics overlap. In any society's religion we can discern reflections of how its people sustain themselves. We can observe this, for example, in the distinctions between the religions of hunter-gatherers, nomadic herders, and those who plant, cultivate, and harvest. The changing spiritual practices in turn engender diverse conceptions of life, death, and the hereafter. But our question in this chapter is how did the ancient Israelites in particular, whose religion eventually became the progenitor of so many of our historic faiths, fit into this larger picture?

We know very little about the earliest history of the Israelites. By the time we catch our first glimpse of a people known as the "Habiru," they are nomadic herders, living in the highlands of what was later called Palestine. Their primary rituals appear to have been, first, the sacrifice of one of the animals from their herds to the God to whom they gave a succession of names but eventually called "Yahweh."

The second ritual pattern was that of shared ceremonial meals, from which the weekly Sabbath dinner and the Passover Seder grew. But we know little about their ideas of the afterlife. First, because they were Jews, and the reluctance we have just described was still strong. But also, because Jews avoided making images, we do not have the stash of sketches or illustrations others have left behind. Also, the reward God held out for faithfulness to his covenant was not, at least at this stage, eternal life. It was a land they could call their own where they could live out their years in tranquility. We can speculate, however, that when they did begin to envision a heaven (and no one is sure just when that was), it had to be a site where there was plenty to eat and an abundance of "green pastures" for the herds. The idea of an afterlife where the men would study Torah all day without worrying if supper was being prepared came in later.

The Jews have always been a people on the move. When we first see them, the Habiru/Hebrews were already migrating out of the hills and onto the fertile plains bordering the Mediterranean Sea, where they began new lives as farmers. And, along with this relocation, their religion soon started to echo their life change. As they settled in areas where the local Canaanite farmer-residents practiced seasonal fertility rites, some of the Jews were drawn to some of these rites, especially if the rituals were thought to be essential to success in agriculture. This is not hard to understand. As they migrated from tending sheep and camels to planting crops, they had to turn to their new neighbors, who had already mastered the agricultural skills. We can imagine these early Canaanite equivalents of county farm agents saying to the beginners, "First you dig this trench; then you drop in the seeds, like this; then you cover them like this; then you say this prayer. . . ."

I do not believe the newly arrived herdsmen, now junior farmers, thought they were blaspheming. Both for the instructors and for the Jews, who were eager to learn how to feed themselves, the technical and the spiritual components of agronomy were indistinguishable. Of course, the Jews recognized that the rites their new neighbors taught them looked and sounded different from the ones they were used to. But look, they were in Canaan now, and these locals knew how to coax the fields to blossom and the fruit to ripen. Would it not be prudent here in Canaan to "do as the Canaanites do"?

Still, they sometimes hesitated. Beginning shortly after the Israelite arrival in Canaan, Jewish prophets, such as Amos and Isaiah, began to insist that this was just the point. Wherever we are, they emphasized, we *do not do* what our neighbors do! We are a unique people, chosen by God for a special mission among the other nations; and God has explicitly commanded us not to worship foreign deities. Most of their hearers probably understood the prophets' condemnations. But much as they wanted to obey Yahweh, they also wanted bountiful harvests. Sometimes they tried to have it both ways. They attempted to combine these newly learned ceremonies with their own traditional rituals.

But this angered the prophets even more. They saw themselves as fierce guardians of the ethics and forms of worship Yahweh had bestowed on them at Sinai as integral to the covenant he had made with them. They strenuously objected to any mixing. They characterized such intermingling in the harshest language as "whoring and infidelity":

> *I am broken with their whorish heart, which hath departed from me, and with their eyes, which go a-whoring after their idols: and they shall loathe themselves for the evils which they have committed in all their abominations.* (Ezekiel 6:9)

The religious backbone of the prophets' tireless attacks was their confidence that God had created the whole world, including the plants and animals, the sun, moon, and stars, and seasonal change. All these were *creations* of God, *not* gods themselves. Unlike the idols of wood and stone, molded and pasted together by the Gentiles, Yahweh was both invisible and incomparably more powerful. He alone merited worship and service. He was a "jealous God," who made it clear that "Thou shalt have no other gods before me" was not optional. It was a divine commandment scorched into a stone tablet by the flaming finger of God himself (as those of us who grew up on Cecil B. DeMille's film *The Ten Commandments* can testify). As we have said, this did not mean that the ancient Jews were monotheists, as some

Christian and Jewish scholars have claimed. They were not.
They rarely questioned the existence of the gods other people
served. That was their business. But the Jews had been chosen
by the God of the Sinai Covenant and liberated by him from
their bondage in Egypt and commanded to serve him and him
alone. This is what religious historians call the "Yahweh alone"
theology, but it was not monotheism. Nonetheless, the reward
the Hebrews would receive for fidelity to Yahweh was that they
could look forward to long lives, big families, prosperity, and
the privilege of dwelling in the land God had promised. With
all this, who needs a heaven?

But, living together as closely as they did, eventually the Israelites absorbed some of the seasonal fertility festivals of their
neighbors into their own tradition. The annual Jewish holiday
of Pesach, now called "Passover," is a prime example. The roots
of Pesach reach back to just such a Canaanite spring fertility
ritual, which, when the Israelites migrated into Canaan in the
second millennium BCE, they gradually absorbed. For some
time, Pesach coexisted with a separate Jewish holiday called
"The Feast of Unleavened Bread." Little by little the two festivals
grew together, and eventually merged. But the holiday was still
not what it subsequently became, Passover, the most important
of Jewish festivals.

Only during the monarchy, after the revived and growing
impact of Moses and their miraculous escape from Egypt, did
Passover begin to signify this liberation. Now Moses became
the hero of the saga. And the reason for the unleavened bread
(*matza*) was explained in a new way: because in their haste to
leave the captives had not had time to allow their dough to rise.
The holiday was rechristened "Pass-over" because God's angel
of death had passed over the shelters the Jews had daubed with
the blood of a lamb, killing only the firstborn of the Egyptians.
In time, the Jewish elements of the holiday story predominated,

and the Canaanite roots faded. Passover, trumping all the others, became the principal holiday in the Jewish calendar. But what does it mean now? And what, if anything, does its centrality mean for Jewish ideas of a hereafter?

"Why is this night different from all other nights?" When this age-old question is asked by the youngest person present at thousands of Seder tables, piled with the special foods reserved for this occasion, the narrative response is the retelling of the Jewish story of enslavement, oppression, and liberation. And it is that account that has inspired so many emancipation revolts for so many years. It was, understandably, Martin Luther King's favorite biblical text.

It is not surprising that the Jews' exodus from Egypt has assumed a universal significance. We retell it again and again at our family's annual Seder, and it never fails to touch both our family members and our guests. I would not like to change that. But the meaning of Passover is not fixed or frozen. It has been adapted and reframed in many ways, but has an uncanny resiliency. For this reason, I sometimes wish that at the Seder table someone could also recount the longer history of "this night," how it originated as a "pagan" carnival, and how the Jews adopted it and merged it with a holiday of their own. In an increasingly religiously pluralistic country and world, we need symbolic reminders of the spiritual elements we share. This could be done, and should be done, without weakening the primary importance of freedom and liberation that Passover has come to mean for so many millions of religious and nonreligious people. This enlarged interpretation of Pesach/Passover would not be a dilution but an enrichment, and it would not be the last. Even today the reinterpreting goes on apace.

The epic of the Jewish people is one of defeats, expulsions, of captivity and liberation, of exile and return. And with each succeeding chapter, a new layer of meaning was grafted onto Pass-

over. It became not just the occasion to mark the deliverance
of the people from Pharaoh's Egypt, but then from captivity in
Babylon, followed by more losses and banishments, from all of
which at least a remnant of the people survived, albeit with the
constant realization that whatever "promised land" they were
now living in could be snatched away from them.

History had demonstrated to them that life had been, and
would probably always remain, uncertain. But, despite these
twists and turns, with some important exceptions (see my
discussion of the psalms) Jews usually did not compensate by
envisioning a "heaven" beyond death as a recompense for their
faithfulness. The closest they came was the idea of a divine Wisdom that, despite all the menaces, would eventually restore them
as a people to a renewed life in a land of their own. But whether
that "land" would be transcendent or earthly or something else
was never made clear. This ambiguity is especially evident in
the multiple meanings attached to "Jerusalem," which we will
discuss in a later chapter.

Still, throughout all these adversities, Jews recognized that
the threats to their worldly existence did not all come from
the outside. Century after century internal splits and divisions
threatened the fabric of the nation. When the Hebrew elites
who had been deported to Babylon began to return in 538 BCE
after seventy years, they found it difficult to settle in with their
kinsmen who had never left. The returnees had clung fiercely to
their ancestral faith as a means of retaining their identity when
they sang "the Lord's song in a strange land." But when they got
back home, they found that those who had remained had married and integrated more closely with their Canaanite neighbors, even adopting some of their customary religious practices.
The split was cultural, political, and religious. But it was also a
class divide since it was the ruling strata who had been taken to
Babylon while the lower orders had not, and those who returned

remembered that. Thus, the end of the Babylonian Captivity pitted some Jews against other Jews, and it was never fully healed. Echoes of this rift are evident throughout the Bible. When Jesus stopped and conversed with the Samaritan woman at the well, the rupture was still roiling. The woman reminds Jesus that his people prayed at the temple in Jerusalem, but her people prayed "here at this mountain" (Mount Gerizim). We will return to this issue later.

There is another essential Jewish category, perhaps the most basic one, that has become a point of conflict for centuries. It is the idea of a messiah. What is the relationship between heaven (the theme of this book) and the idea of a messiah? The answer begins with recognizing that in Jewish history, the hope for a messianic era, an epoch of peace and harmony, held sway long before the hope for "a" or "the" messiah as an individual person who would initiate the era did. The Jews believed the new era would unfold in stages. God would first free his people from captivity in Egypt; then establish them in their own land; and the temple would be rebuilt. Only after this would an "anointed one" come. But there were wide differences of opinion about what role the messiah would play. Some foresaw a kingly figure, a "Son of David," others a more spiritual figure, the "Son of Man." Some expected a huge but still earthly change; others something cosmic that might include the raising of the dead. Still, despite these different outlooks, it was the messianic *era*, not *the* messiah, that was central.

But then the central core of this expectant hope began to shift. The Jewish historian Zwi Werblowsky says, "Messianic expectations became increasingly focused on the figure of an individual savior. The Messiah no longer symbolized the coming of the new age, but he was somehow supposed to bring it about." The "Lord's Anointed" thus became the "savior and redeemer" and "the focus of more intense expectations and doctrines."

After giving it much thought, I have come to the conclusion that the transition from the hope for a messianic era to the hope for a messiah was not a good one. Without intending to, it has contributed to the "great man theory" of history in which too much hope and therefore too much power are invested in single leaders. Many other factors have contributed. And there are cultures in which the equivalents of these "leader cults," whether of emperors, khans, emirs, or czars, have taken their toll. Still, it is important to remember what more than one New Testament scholar has said: "Jesus did not preach himself or God; he preached the kingdom of God." The question is why and how, especially in Christianity, the message changed from the era to the person.

The word itself, "messiah," means "one who is anointed," but this does not tell us much. Anointing was not unique to the Jews. It was widely practiced in the Middle East. In everyday life, hosts customarily poured oil on the feet, hands, and heads of their guests, and anointing, usually with oil, is far from unusual in the Bible. Everyone's favorite psalm has the words "Thou anointest my head with oil, my cup runneth over" (Psalm 23). There was also a ceremonial use of anointing. Prophets were usually anointed by a priest, but kings always were. But few people realize that when God commissions a "great fish" (not necessarily a whale) to rescue Jonah by swallowing him, the word used is "anoints." People are anointing one another on page after page. In the New Testament it is sometimes the Holy Spirit who anoints, not with oil, but with the Spirit. I have attended enough Pentecostal worship services to have heard, "Wow, was he ever anointed!" after someone has testified in a particularly moving way. Anointing appears not to be a scarce resource, either in the Bible or in Spirit-filled worship today. So what makes the term "messiah" special?

One of the things I heard in Sunday school as a youngster was that the difference between Jews and Christians was that "while the Jews believe the messiah is yet to come, we (Christians) believe he has already come." But that is a cliché and helps very little in sorting out what the two traditions have in common and where they differ. I still remember my embarrassment when as a freshman in college, and the student in the dorm room next door told me one day that he was Jewish, I responded cheerfully, "Interesting. So you believe the messiah is yet to come, right?" He looked at me with a slightly puzzled face, then said, "Well, to tell you the truth, I don't believe he is coming at all." His answer confused me at first, but as I thought about it, I was glad that, at least for the moment, neither of us was expecting a messianic interruption of our enjoyment of college.

If I had known then what I have learned since about the different things "the messiah" has meant for both Christians and Jews, I might have pursued the conversation with my college friend into the labyrinths of Jewish history. Or I might have simply dropped it. Because of the Jewish hesitancy about speaking of "heaven," the answer is complicated. But, despite the many opinions about what a (or the) messiah should do, everyone agreed in principle that it depended on the nature of the messianic era. And because the idea of a messianic era is so closely related to Jesus's message of the kingdom, or reigning of God, which has so often been mistakenly equated with heaven by Christians, some sorting out is obviously needed.

The history of the term "messiah" shows that all anointings are not the same. It depends on *why* one is anointed, by whom, and for what purpose. Anointing was seen as conferring power as well as responsibility. When the prophet Samuel anointed David as king (in 1 Samuel 16), he did it secretly, presumably so as not to endanger the young man's life. So Samuel took the horn of oil and anointed him in the presence of his brothers, and from that day on the Spirit of the Lord came upon David in power. Many times someone is anointed as a symbol of their being selected for a special responsibility. This includes becoming the sovereign of the United Kingdom. But exactly what responsibility did the Jews think their expected messiah would undertake?

There was never complete agreement on the answer to this question. Just as various images of heaven so often reflect the fondest hope of a people in different stages of their history, so the hope for what God's Anointed One might accomplish varied. In their early years, surrounded by potential enemies, they needed a strong warrior messiah, just as they sometimes wanted a mighty, man-of-war king. When they were divided, they looked for a healer and uniter; at other times, a wise judge or a comforter who would bid them to lie down in green pastures. But there was one indispensable quality they always expected: that a messiah should liberate them from whatever their current bondage was. That done, he should then proceed to inaugurate a new age of peace and prosperity for the whole world.

The debate about what else a messiah, when one came, should do continued, and was still not settled when Jesus began preaching about the soon-arriving kingdom of God, which sounded very much like the messianic age. But when he did not liberate them from their captivity by the Romans, and died the death of a radical agitator, most of those who had followed him for a time gave up on him. Then, when his disciples announced that God had raised him from the dead, and that he was the Anointed One, and would return soon to establish his just kingdom on earth, a rupture opened among the Jews that still exists today. Something later called Judaism took shape, and the nuclei of what was later called Christianity emerged. Those who rejected the assertion that Jesus was messiah contended that, although they were not in full agreement about what the messiah should do to "prove his messiahship," there was one thing that was perfectly clear. The long-awaited one would *not* be arrested for treason, publicly humiliated, and tortured to death in a procedure reserved for those thought to be dangerous to the Roman imperium. Far from evidence of his being anointed by God, his scandalous fate amounted to proof that he was anything but God's messiah.

The schism between Jews and Christians about the significance of Jesus did not end the contentious quarrels among the Jews or among the Christians over who was or was not "anointed by God." In Christianity, shelves of books have been compiled about people who have claimed to be a "second coming" of Christ intent on establishing his kingdom. I will not attempt to recall the escapades here except to say that there is scarcely a mental hospital anywhere in the world that does not house at least one Christ figure.

In Judaism, the arguments were stoked by the repeated arrivals of "false messiahs," men who claimed to be the Long Awaited Anointed One, Messiah of God, who would liberate them from whatever tyranny was persecuting them at the time, and open the door to a messianic era, a kingdom of God. In historical retrospect it is easy to dismiss these self-appointed messiahs, like their Christian counterparts, as deluded or as charlatans. But in their own uncertain times, and with the idea of a coming messiah still alive, they were much more credible. Remember that in the twentieth century, Western civilization has had to cope with more than one leader making messianic claims, and clearly both Hitler and Mussolini grounded their claims on a mixture of religious and secular messianic conventions.

I once carried on a fascinating public dialogue about all this with a sympathetic rabbi in the course of which I asked him if he thought Jesus had been a "false messiah."

"Oh no," he replied, "not at all. I think he was a *failed* messiah." At that moment I understood more clearly than I had before the decisive role of what was *expected* of the messiah had played. Just what had Jesus failed at? He had not delivered on what at least many Jews, maybe most Jews at the time, expected of God's Anointed. But for Christians, Jesus had radically altered the job description of a messiah. He had both enlarged and transformed it. He announced a liberation not just from the Romans but from captivity to sin and death. And, searching the sacred texts to help them understand his disgraceful death, his disciples interpreted it as that of a messiah/suffering servant. It could be said that at the root of the disagreement between Jews and Christians is that Jesus either "threw away the script" or altered it in ways that rendered it unrecognizable to many of his own people.

In any case, after my conversation with the rabbi, I began to think that in some ways he had been right. In the way we usually use the term, Jesus was a "failure." After his death, even his own disciples apparently thought so and began to disband, and it took something like the event of Easter to cause them to change their minds. To his credit, my rabbi colleague had forced me to think about what we mean by "failure." How long do we wait before making that judgment? Was Dietrich Bonhoeffer, who was killed by the Nazis for his unsuccessful attempt to rid the world of Hitler, a failure? When we see that so much of the systematic racism he fought still infects us, was Martin Luther King a failure?

Just as I was finishing this chapter, I attended the funeral of a regal, elderly Jewish woman and witnessed once again the remarkable combination of stability and flexibility that has helped the Jewish tradition to continue to bear witness for so many centuries. The ceremony took place in a funeral home in New York's Upper West Side. As I entered I noticed an aged man with a long beard, dressed in black and wearing a yarmulke, seated near the coffin chanting. Someone whispered to me that he had been there all night and was intoning the psalms, a venerable Jewish custom. Then, I saw, only a few feet from the man who was chanting, a young woman kneeling just in front of the coffin, praying the rosary, and repeating the "Hail Mary" prayer, which I knew includes the words, "Pray for us sinners, now and at the hour of our death." As I sat down and listened, the two voices, one deep and masculine, one light and feminine, one in Hebrew, one in English, seemed to blend.

Then a third voice came in. At the request of the deceased, her daughter had just started to play a tape of the French chanteuse Edith Piaf singing "Je ne regrette rien." Once again, however, the result was not cacophony but an intricate melodic fusion. At that point the woman rabbi who was to lead the service walked in, sat down near the coffin, and smiled. After a few minutes, she stood and read two passages in English from the Bible, then recited some prayers in Hebrew and one in English; then invited those gathered to repeat together the Kaddish, which had been distributed at the door. When we had finished, she reminded everyone that this was not a lament or a prayer for the dead but a paean of praise to God for his goodness.

As I left, I again marveled at the balance of strength and generosity, tenacity and openness that has enabled the Jewish faith to sustain the human spirit of so many people and for so long. It was still flourishing now in a religiously pluralistic society without being any less Jewish. Whatever different thoughts about the hereafter were present in that gathering, they did not prevent us from remembering, mourning, and hoping together. "Hear, O Israel, the Lord our God is One."

# 7

# The Undiscovered Country

*Who would fardels bear,*
*To grunt and sweat under a weary life,*
*But that the dread of something after death,*
*The undiscovered country, from whose bourn*
*No traveler returns, puzzles the will,*
*And makes us rather bear those ills we have*
*Than fly to others that we know not of.*

Shakespeare, *Hamlet*

Despite the bard's warning that the "undiscovered country" is one "from whose bourn no traveler returns," history is replete with intrepid voyagers who claimed not only to have visited it but to have returned. Further, for good measure, these Elysian voyagers have "lived to tell the tale," or someone else has told it for them. Their ventures are documented, frequently in minute detail, and constitute a treasure trove of data on what our forebears, distant and recent, thought about heaven and hell.

But it is important to remember that these are *tales,* and we recognize them today as such. We do not value them, centuries after they were composed, as history, and that is one reason why it is vital to engage with them early in this book. They provide superb examples for us of what we intend to do in subsequent chapters. Our fundamental question will be twofold. First, what does any depiction tell us about the people and the era in which it took shape? Second, once it had been created, how did this image of the hereafter continue to shape their culture, laws, poetry, arts, social institutions, and religious worldview?

The first and one of the best known of these sojourners is Odysseus. According to Book 11 of the *Odyssey*, on his circuitous voyage back to his home in Ithaca from Troy, the prince of the Argives visits the island of Circe. The enchantress tells him he must visit the realm of the dead, Hades, so he can be told of his own fate by the prophet Tiresias. As I have said, we recognize that the *Odyssey* is a work of fiction, and Odysseus an imaginary character. But in this book the dichotomy we often like to draw between fact and fiction is not helpful. Whether we are talking about heavens or heavenly sojourners, we are looking for something else. We are listening to the sagas of galactic Marco Polos for what we can learn about the "lived world," which includes imagination, fantasy, dreams, and visions, and for this purpose, whether Homer's characters, for example, are historical or fictional is not significant. These villains and heroes have lived for two thousand years in the human imagination. They have enlivened our ways of seeing ourselves and one another for generations. And still do. Riveted by their exploits, can we truly think of Penelope, Athena, Dionysius, Odysseus, or Aeneas as dead? In one sense, they may never have actually "lived," but maybe we should not define "live" in such a narrow sense.

We will start with Odysseus and look over his shoulder as he visits the land of death and converses with the specters he meets with there. We will then visit Socrates in his prison, preparing to drink the hemlock while quietly conversing with his friends about what he expects in the next world. Then we will accompany another ancient traveler, Aeneas of Virgil's *Aeneid*, who also visits the next world but comes away with impressions quite different from those of Odysseus. Then comes St. Paul, who made a very short visit to heaven, and then Dante, who made a very long one. All the while, we will be asking what we can find out about what that "undiscovered country" was like for them.

First, Odysseus. During his visit to the chilling halls of Hades, he meets several people, including some of the brave Greek warriors who died in the disastrous Trojan War, the struggle that began when Helen's face "launched a thousand ships." Among these fallen heroes, Odysseus spots the greatest of them all, Achilles ("Favored of Zeus"), and plunges into a conversation with him. Some readers have thought that their exchange tells us all we need to know about how ancient Greeks envisioned the afterlife, namely, that it was gloomy and foreboding, not an inviting place to look forward to either after death or at any time. But, as we will see, this is not the whole story.

What does this conversation between Odysseus and Achilles really tell us? It gives us only one side of a chronicle that had many, often conflicting, threads. Maybe it would be better to say that it gives us Homer's idea of the afterlife. But Homer lived somewhere between six and ten centuries before Socrates and Plato, both of whom, as we will see below, held quite different views of death and its aftermath. First, let us listen to what Homer says through Odysseus and Achilles, then compare it to what Plato says through Socrates.

Odysseus says to Achilles,

> *"But you, Achilles,*
> *There is not a man in the world more blest than you.*
> *There never has been, never will be one.*
> *Time was, when you were alive, we Argives honored you as*
> *    a god, and now down here, I see*
> *You lord it over the dead in all your power.*
> *So, grieve no more at dying, great Achilles."*

Thus (says Odysseus), I reassured the ghost, but he (Achilles) broke out, protesting,

*No winning words about death to me, shining Odysseus! By god, I'd rather slave on earth for another man— / Some dirt-poor tenant farmer who scrapes to keep alive—than rule down here over all the breathless dead.*

Evidently, for Homer and his contemporaries, the "next life" was dark and dreary, not something to anticipate with serenity. There is nothing "heavenly" about it. Furthermore, no distinction is made in this Stygian sphere between those who have lived good lives and those who pursued evil.

Homer died in 701. Four hundred years later, Plato, who died in 348 BCE, voiced a very different view of the next world in the words of his literary persona, Socrates. In the *Phaedo*, Socrates, the sage of Athens, is pictured sitting in irons on his cot in prison, condemned for "corrupting the youth of Athens." He is calmly waiting to drink the poisoned cup that will send him to the precinct of the departed. He does not claim to have seen it, but he speaks as one who knows. He tries to assure the disciples who have gathered around him that they should not wail or grieve, because he is about to move on to a far better place. He realizes, he says, that not everyone will immediately go there after death, and in a prefiguration of the doctrine of purgatory, he says some will pass through a preliminary realm in which they will be purified. However only the most despicable transgressors will have to wait a very long time to move on. This may sound a little like hell, but there is a radical difference. Socrates does not say they will be there forever. He also assures his worried friends that those who have lived lives of philosophy, distancing themselves from bodily pleasures, as he himself has done, need not fret. A better existence awaits them beyond the veil. After these words, at last

the jailer enters carrying the cup. Socrates quietly drinks it
and dies.

Thus, Homer and Plato, two of the Greeks' greatest thinkers,
hold radically different views of "that undiscovered country."
But there is a further complication. The Romans inherited much
of their culture, including their gods, from the Greeks. But
in their understanding of the afterlife, the children of Romu-
lus and Remus introduce significant changes. About the year
20 BCE, the *Aeneid*, Virgil's Latin epic, appeared, with its own
version of the next world. Aeneas, Virgil's traveler, also visited
Hades, but before he arrives there, he meets a Sibyl, who tells
him that he will come to a place "where splits the road in twain."
In one direction lies the Elysium, but in the other Tartarus. The
first is a verdant landscape where the virtuous are welcomed:

> *The happy region and the pleasures of*
> *blessed woodlands, the abode of joy*
> *And ampler ether with perpetual light*
> *Clothes here the plain; another sun than ours*
> *And other stars they know.*
>
> *Aeneid*

This sounds like a lovely spot for an eternal picnic, but, alas,
it is not for everyone. The second path leads to a region filled
with darkness, lit only by fierce, flesh-scorching fires, where the
wicked must anguish for eternity. No picnic.

But the split in the road is something more. It marks an
epochal alteration in the meaning of heaven and hell, and a fundamental shift in values. Virgil's next world, with its division
into two realms, is markedly different from Homer's underworld in which both the upright and the evildoers all languish
in the same gloom, and the morality or immorality of one's
earthly life is of no consequence. What accounts for the dra-

matic distinction between these two perspectives on the meaning of life and death?

First, there are some similarities. Odysseus wants to meet his mother, but when he does and tries to embrace her, she fades into a wisp. Aeneas seeks his father, Anchises, with whom he has fled from Troy, but the result is the same. Apparently in both these postmortem worlds, reunions with departed loved ones, which for many people today is their idea of heaven, are not so easy to come by. Does this suggest that in both societies from which these classics emerged the same conflict between the claims of family and the polis or other loyalties so graphically dramatized in *Antigone* still obtained?

Some of the differences between the two epics are due to the reasons they were composed and how. Homer's works began as oral traditions spun out around campfires and were only later written down, thus allowing for endless variations depending on the venues. The *Aeneid* started as a written manuscript. The *Iliad* had no specific political purpose, but the *Aeneid* was intended to glorify the emperor Augustus and the greatness of Rome. Whenever any comparison is made, Virgil always favors Rome over Greece.

There are some important religious differences between the two descriptions of the underworld. Both see King Minos on a throne judging the recently arrived dead. But Odysseus is only told what happens to them, while Aeneas sees unborn babies being cared for, suicides being punished, loose women chastised, and groups of spirits being prepared for reincarnation. Odysseus sees none of this, or if he does, says nothing about it. On the other hand, Aeneas is only informed about the torments meted out to the serious sinners. He does not see them.

There is a reason for this omission. Unlike Odysseus, who is admonished to be courageous and honorable, Aeneas is commended for his piety and urged to continue to be "pious." To safeguard that piety, he is not permitted to visit Tantalus while in hell and, as just mentioned, is not allowed to witness the torments of the wicked. Perhaps sin, like some dreaded disease, is contagious, so the pious man should not come too close.

These are intriguing aspects of these two next worlds of Homer and Virgil, but the defining difference is of prodigious import. A moral component is now the *main* factor in determining where and how anyone will live in the next life. The stark contrast between Elysium and Tartarus foreshadows the conventional Christian ideas of heaven and hell. But even though Virgil's heaven and hell may be similar to Christian ideas, he has no parallel to the kingdom of God. In his famous *Fourth Eclogue*, Virgil predicts the coming of something akin to a messiah and a golden age, but these are not as basic to his thought as they are in the Bible.

These glaring shifts in images of the afterlife from Homer to Plato to Virgil took place over the span of a thousand years, and this makes any generalization impossible. It might be a little more conceivable to ask about the changes over a shorter period. For example, what happened in the four hundred years that separate Homer from Plato to make their pictures of the afterlife, epitomized by a discontented Achilles and a hopeful Socrates, so different?

The religion of the Greeks was not frozen. Gilbert Murray's brilliant *Five Stages of Greek Religion* clearly charts the changes. He also describes how influences from cultures outside Hellas sparked the evolution. He shows how upheavals in the terrestrial lives of the city states undermined inherited images of the next world, changes that were then projected onto the heavens, and—once projected—then shaped the rituals and beliefs of following generations.

Understanding these developments becomes even more difficult when differing cultures are involved. Plato was a Greek, writing in Greek at a time when the independent city states like Athens and Sparta were often at war with each other, and he yearned for a peaceful, united polity, ruled by men of virtue and wisdom. He sketched out such a realm in *The Republic*. But he never lived to see it. On the other hand, Virgil was an Italian living in Rome during the heyday of the lavish Augustan age. That emperor had ended a period of division and uncertainty. Now the solidity of the empire's laws and institutions was treasured, but fear of the recent period of disorder and lawlessness still haunted people's memories. Why should the assumptions of a Plato and a Virgil about the character of an ultimate human community not be affected by the worlds they lived in? For Homer, it was living this present life well that was man's foremost objective, not preparing for another life where, in any case, virtue and vice were not relevant. Virgil's afterlife, on the other hand, is one in which virtue, law, and order are fundamental; and given the tendency of the heavens to affect terrestrial ideals, it is interesting to recall that for centuries after the "fall" of the Roman Empire, the archetype of a world-inclusive (or at least Europe-inclusive) polity endured, and still does. It seems clear that, just as there is no single biblical view of heaven, neither is there a single classical view.

Before we leave the ancients, there is one more traveler who should not be overlooked, so we turn to St. Paul's short trip to (the third) heaven. In 2 Corinthians the Apostle writes,

> *I know a person in Christ who fourteen years ago was caught up to the third heaven—whether in the body or out of the body I do not know; God knows. And I know that such a person . . . heard things that are not to be told, that no mortal is permitted to repeat.*

Thus, seven centuries after Odysseus, and three after Socrates, St. Paul becomes yet another Greek-speaking wanderer, but this time one whose historical reality is not in dispute. Saul (later Paul) of Tarsus claimed to have completed a round trip to the other world, albeit a very brief one. In about 56 CE St. Paul wrote the words quoted above, addressing them to the small neonate Christian congregation in Corinth. He says that he "knew a man" who in body or in a vision was carried up to the "third heaven." That "man," Bible scholars agree, was of course the Apostle himself, speaking here in the third person. In any case, Paul does not tell us anything at all about what he ("a man") saw or heard during the brief visit. We can, however, garner something of interest from his few words.

First, historians have found that in Paul's time conflicting views about the geography of heaven jostled each other in the Mediterranean world, which makes it virtually impossible for current readers to settle on "*the* biblical" view of heaven. According to the New Testament scholar E. W. Bullinger, the Greek words in this text should be translated as "caught *away*," not "caught *up*," possibly reflecting Jewish beliefs that paradise was somewhere other than the uppermost heaven. Some held that there were seven heavens, stacked like a layer of pancakes. Today we still retain the expression "I was in seventh heaven," usually as a way of describing a supremely blissful state. Saint Paul, however, talks about the "third heaven." Whatever the number, historians agree that the idea of multiple "heavens" was common coinage in Paul's day.

What may be noteworthy for us today, however, is that even though St. Paul had a life-changing encounter with Christ on the road to Damascus and on a trip to heaven, neither of these changed his cosmology. He was, he often says, a "new person in Christ," but that new person still retained certain focal elements of the worldview he shared with his contemporaries before and after his Damascus-road vision.

This is a welcome insight. It means that faith in Christ does not entail or require any specific cosmology. Christian faith has coexisted with numerous changing cosmologies in the past, and whenever religious people try to identify any one of them as the only acceptable partner for faith, trouble always follows. Take, for example, the official theological consensus in Galileo's time, which dismissed his heliocentric view of the universe as incompatible with Christian doctrine, a dispute that pushed him into the maw of the Inquisition. Today there is no religiously established cosmology. There is not even a scientifically established one. New theories, each claiming the sanction of science, follow each other apace. We have watched Einstein's theories promulgated, accepted, debunked, then retrieved and discussed again. Is the universe bounded or unbounded? Is there only one universe, or are there many? What about string theory or gravitational-wave theory? And do the fascinating arguments that go on today among one or another of these competing cosmologies have anything to do with religious faith?

The history of religion suggests that the answer to the last question is no; they do not. But it is also crucial to see that St. Paul did not use his heavenly journey as a basis for his authority in the early Christian movement. On the contrary, he mentions it as an example of what he does not use. He rejects relying on any of what served as such bases for other early Christians. These included speaking in tongues ("of men or angels") or heroic sacrifice ("giving my body to be burned"). Paul rejects all these as the source of his authority and bases it solely on the assignment he has received from Christ.

Maybe Paul's example should be heeded by the current religious leaders who still flaunt their own "spiritual gifts" as a stamp of authority. Also, if St. Paul's visit to the "third heaven" does not provide us with any juicy information about "what it is like in heaven," at least it suggests that whichever of today's competing cosmologies appeals to us, it has little to do with the essence of faith. This should post a warning to those who lacerate each other over "creationism" or "intelligent design" or the spontaneous appearance of the universe. All these protagonists too often feel they need either to enlist religion or to deny it to strengthen their case. But shaping the argument this way goes nowhere. The Bible is not a scientific text, and modern science is not equipped to grapple with the questions of meaning and value with which religions have traditionally been concerned.

In his brilliant book *Rocks of Ages*, the late Stephen J. Gould, a renowned paleontologist, argues that science and religion have separate but mutually dependent responsibilities. The first describes and analyzes *what is*; the second deals with values and meaning. As Gould once said, "Science can tell you how to make a nuclear bomb, but it cannot tell you whether to make it or whether to use it." So long as science and religion work in their own spheres, no clash, let alone "warfare," is necessary. It is only when one impinges on the other, such as when a scientist announces that there is no God, or religion conscripts a biblical or doctrinal concept to oppose science, that conflicts arise. Of course, there will always be "border disputes," Gould says, but any civilization needs both.

Before Gould died a few years ago, we had been teaching a large lecture course together with Alan Dershowitz on "Science, Religion, and Law." Once I asked Gould if he ever felt a sense of awe when he uncovered a new stratum of fossils.

"Of course, I do," he answered. "It happens all the time."

"But can you incorporate that sense of awe into your science?" I asked.

"No," he said. "It's a wonderful feeling. But I have to set it aside when I do the science."

But I pressed on. "Steve, can you envision a *future* science that could incorporate awe and still be science, maybe even a better science?"

He smiled. "Well," he said, "let me think about that, and we can talk about it."

Steve Gould died a couple of weeks after this conversation. I hope he is still thinking about it. I know I am.

But back to St. Paul. Since his time, innumerable pilgrims have asserted that they have assayed the same celestial junket, have returned, and have written about it too many words to count. And with a boundless curiosity that persists from century to century, generations have wanted to hear about their impressions of that undiscovered country. These theological trekkies devour what the returnees spin out, whether in science-fiction stories and films, in religious and quasi-religious testimonies, or in reports of dreams and visions. It seems that so long as there are heavenly voyagers who are eager to share their travel logs, there will be stay-at-homes just as eager to savor them.

Throughout the centuries after the Apostle Paul, hermits, mystics, saints, charlatans, holy men, holy women, and heretics have tried to describe that undiscovered country, but with mixed success. Still, there is one such sojourner who so towers over the others that he can be taken to represent them: the great Florentine poet and political philosopher Dante Alighieri. He also paid a visit to that land and returned to tell the tale. More than just a tale, the *Divine Comedy* has become one of the most precious jewels in the Western literary canon. But what about its theology? Aye, there's the rub.

The Russian Orthodox theologian Nicholas Berdyaev may be the most blunt and uncompromising critic of Dante's theology, which Berdyaev claims is derived from St. Thomas Aquinas. Berdyaev complains that the underlying religious premise of the *Divine Comedy* is blatantly hedonistic and utilitarian, not Christian. It posits readers who are seeking ways to avoid punishment. Further, he says, Dante seems to want to frighten people into preferring heaven to the cruelly calculating tortures he details in the *Inferno*. Berdyaev views this as a kind of black-mail, of coercion, and a denial of human freedom. No genuine virtue, he insists, can result from such techniques. Real virtue must arise from unfettered human freedom. Berdyaev makes a convincing case. But it seems unimaginable to excise Dante from the Western literary legacy. What is to be done?

I suggest that the first thing we do is to recognize that the *Divine Comedy* is fiction, even superb fiction, and not theology. We can begin this by recalling what the book is about. In it Dante portrays himself in a kind of trance or dream, accompanied by the Roman poet Virgil, strolling through all three precincts of the world hereafter: purgatory, hell (the *Inferno*), and paradise. Of these three, however, readers have always found the *Inferno* the most absorbing. Here Dante passes through the portal bearing the soul-freezing words *Lasciate ogni speranza, voi ch' intrate* ("Abandon all hope, ye who enter here"). The message is unmistakable: Whatever terrors hell holds, the worst is the realization that, unlike purgatory, here you are never going to get out. As Jean-Paul Sartre puts it in his claustrophobic play about hell, there is "no exit."

Once inside, Dante catalogs in graphic detail the ingenious variety of tortures to which the damned are subjected, each in accordance with the nature of his transgression. To accomplish this perverse goal, hell is divided into nine circles. The eighth circle is devoted to those guilty of fraud, and is further divided into ten *Bolgia*, or trenches. In the first, the panderers and seducers are forced to march around in a circle single file while they are lashed by horned demons. In the second trench, the flatterers are immersed in an endless river of human excrement. In the third, those guilty of buying or selling church positions or services (Simoniacs) are suspended upside down in huge baptismal fonts while their feet are set on fire.

In a particularly apt twist, popes who are condemned to this level are pushed in on top of the popes who have arrived there earlier. They do not even have the privilege of their own place in hell. Astrologers, seers, and sorcerers who try to peer into the future, which only God knows, descend to the fourth trench, where their heads are twisted so that they can only look backward. Even the honored Greek prophet Tiresias is confined to this section. After this come places for extortionists and crooked businessmen (thrown into a vat of boiling pitch).

Next comes the trench for the hypocrites, forced to walk around in heavy, weighted robes that look like gold. Interestingly, on the side of this circles Caiaphas and the entire Sanhedrin must sit and watch the hypocrites for eternity.

In the seventh trench, thieves are bitten by snakes and reptiles. In a nasty twist, the bites of some of the serpents often cause spontaneous combustion, but the thieves quickly fly back together so they can continue to be bitten. Next comes the trench for those who have deceived others for personal gain. These are on fire with a blaze that never goes out. Dante places Ulysses and Diomedes in this quarter. In this (eighth) trench, the souls of deceivers who gave false or corrupted advice to others for personal benefit are punished. They are constantly ablaze, appearing as nothing so much as living, speaking tongues of flame. In the ninth trench Dante places those who promoted schism and discord—sinners who, in life, promoted scandals and divisions, particularly those who caused schism within the church or within politics. They are forced to walk around the circumference of the circle bearing horrible, disfiguring wounds inflicted on them by a great demon with a sword. The nature of the wound mirrors the sins of the soul; while some only have gashes, or fingers and toes cut off, others are decapitated, cut in half (as schismatics), or are completely disemboweled. It is noteworthy that this is the level to which Dante consigns the Prophet Muhammad. He is condemned not as a heretic but as a divider. He is split from the crown of his head to "where the wind is voided." With little regard for the reader's sensitivity or discretion, Dante adds that because of this gaping incision, various inner organs are spilling out for all to see. Naturally, many readers, and all Muslims, have found this passage cruel and offensive. A publishing house in Holland recently excised it from their edition of the *Divine Comedy*.

After this grotesque section, Dante keeps up the pace of his appropriate punishments. In the tenth trench we find the "falsifiers," those who attempted to alter things through lies or alchemy, and as counterfeiters of coins. After this appears the lower edge of hell, guarded by a ring of titans and earth giants, many of whom are chained in place as punishment for their rebellion against God. All in all, at every level, Dante's Inferno is not only a maliciously cruel place; it is also repulsive. Why then have I reminded the reader of its grisly features in a book about heaven?

First, we need to reply to Berdyaev's denunciation that Dante is anything but Christian. Berdyaev is surely right, and anyone who reads Dante as a kind of catechism will be well off the right track. But as a work of imaginative narrative that draws on the common beliefs and fears about the next life in his day, and elevates them into a masterpiece of narrative, the *Divine Comedy* will always hold a secure place on the "great books" shelf. Its overtones continue to appear in serious literature. The sermon on hell in James Joyce's *Portrait of the Artist as a Young Man* provides a stunning example of this longevity.

The main reason for my including Dante in this book, however, is to underline the *contrast*. So far in our visits to assorted heavens, it is noticeable that in nearly every heaven we have seen, we have also seen a reverse image. Is it imperative that every heaven must have a hell? This question somehow reminds me of those superlatively pious believers who used to say they were "willing to go to hell for the glory of God" (whatever that meant). Does every heaven require a hell? The answer to this question is beyond the scope of this book. But in my personal view, the only acceptable answer is no. Unlike, say Zoroastrianism, which is dualistic to its core, biblical faith envisions the ultimate triumph of a God of justice and mercy. In this connection it is useful to recall our title and the text from Revelation that tells of "a new heaven" but declares that the abyss (the sea) "is no more." The vision suggests that heaven will be restored and renewed, but hell (the abyss) will "pass away."

These are thorny quandaries. But there is a much earthier question: why do these grisly snapshots of the pains of hell continue to draw more devotees than those of the bliss of heaven? The question has prompted more than one observer to suggest that there may be a perverse streak in human beings that savors watching the writhing of others, so long as it is not us. Another theory is that not even the most inspired of writers can make the simple but immaculate joys of heaven as absorbing as the tortures of Sheol.

In the years since these veterans of the heavenly visitation genre, many others have followed, but most have had little lasting influence and have long since been forgotten. There is one, however, who did have significant impact on his era; and although he is little known today, he merits mention here, and as the reader will see, may be on the threshold of a rediscovery. He is the eighteenth-century Swedish scientist, philosopher, engineer, and mystical writer Emanuel Swedenborg (1688–1772). We will turn to him in the next chapter.

# 8

# *A Modern Visitor to Heaven*

*If we would know what heaven is before we come thither, let us retire into the depths of our own spirits, and we shall find it there among holy thoughts and feelings.* (Nathaniel Hawthorne)

In the latter part of the eighteenth and early-nineteenth centuries, Emanuel Swedenborg wrote hundreds of pages on heaven and hell, but he is almost forgotten today, which is surprising and disappointing. In the nineteenth century he attracted an enthusiastic band of intellectual followers as his thinking spread from Sweden to North America. Ralph Waldo Emerson, Louisa May Alcott, and Horace Greeley wrote of their admiration. So did Henry James Sr., the strong-minded father of William James, the psychologist, and Henry James Jr., the novelist. The latter wrote that Swedenborg's insights had helped their father pull out of a spiritual crisis. The father agreed. Swedenborg did so, he says, mainly by rescuing him from his individualism and by showing him how every human being is integrally related to every other human being, with all finding their ultimate unity in God. This decidedly communal vision is one that pushed believers in an individualistic salvation to reconsider. James Sr., however, always a harsh critic of "institutional religion," strongly disapproved of the Swedenborgian

"New Church," which sprang up among the Swedish mystic's American devotees.

Until I began to write this book, I had not thought much about Swedenborg, although where I live it is hard to escape him completely. On the corner of Prescott and Cambridge Streets near my home in Cambridge nestles a handsome little stone chapel in neo-Gothic style. It houses a miniscule congregation, one of some 140 others in the mostly unknown American denomination known as the Swedenborgians.

I have walked by the church hundreds of times and have grown rather fond of it. A small edifice, it is overshadowed on all sides by the buildings of Harvard University. Just beside it gleams the glass and steel School of Design, in which aspiring architects sketch and erase under immense skylights that admit floods of natural illumination. Across the street soars the twenty-story, ivory-colored William James Hall, the university's highest building. Next to it stands the complicated gray Adolphus Busch Hall, which houses a collection of Germanic culture and the Flentrop organ, made famous by the concerts E. Power Biggs once played on it. Facing the church, the massive Memorial Hall, built in the late nineteenth century in neo-Victorian Gothic style, honors graduates who died in the Civil War. It spreads over a triangle of stubby grass, its central tower casting a shadow over Harvard Yard. Tucked among these behemoths, the diminutive Swedenborg church modestly holds its ground like a plucky survivor of another era.

As one can imagine, the postage-stamp slice of turf on which the Swedenborgian church is located represents an almost priceless piece of real estate. It cannot help being an appetizing morsel for a university always hungry for more space for classrooms, laboratories, and offices. But although the congregation is tiny, it benefits from a copious endowment, bestowed by previous generations. Time and time again, the university has attempted to purchase it, with offers said to have been amply generous, but the church has always politely refused to sell. I am glad the congregation has not sold.

Every day numberless students, faculty, and tourists file by the church, the visitors sometimes stopping to admire its graceful lines, while the students scurry by to their classes. But hardly one of the thousands who walk by could, unless they spot the minute sign in front, identify it as a Swedenborgian church. Few, if any, would recognize the name, or have heard of the nineteenth-century theologian and mystic after whom the denomination to which this church congregation belongs is named, Emanuel Swedenborg.

There is little wonder why Swedenborg is so unknown today. Unlike other founders of new religious movements in the 1800s such as Joseph Smith or Mary Baker Eddy, the founders, respectively, of Mormonism and Christian Science, he is rarely mentioned in histories of American religion. But he was a fascinating man. In addition to founding the denomination, Swedenborg was also an accomplished scientist and inventor, and a respected theologian. But just as he is barely touched on in texts on religious history, he rarely appears on the syllabi or reading lists of courses in seminaries. He has faded into something of a nonperson; and in all my years as a divinity student and a PhD candidate, his name never came up, even though I spent some of those years at Harvard where Swedenborg remains today at most a minor figure in the long saga of Christian theology. But there are reasons to believe that this eclipse may be ending.

Most American religious thinkers ignored Swedenborg, but there was one striking exception, and it is a notable one, namely, Ralph Waldo Emerson. Emerson admired Swedenborg's mind and mentions him frequently in his own writings. In a long essay, "Swedenborg; or the Mystic," Emerson deemed the Swedish thinker worthy of comparison to Aristotle in his valiant attempt to bring everything into the big tent of his philosophy. This might seem to be an example of the hyperbole of a devotee, but it correctly expresses the high regard Emerson, who knew a fine mind when he saw one, held for Swedenborg. As I have learned about both the history of the chapel and about Swedenborg himself, I have become appreciative of both.

I value the chapel for its symbolic significance. Although Harvard College was founded in 1636 to train ministers for the Massachusetts Bay Colony, it has evolved into a recognized citadel of science and enlightened reason, a severe critic not only of superstition, but at times of religion of all sorts. But in recent decades scientists have begun to suggest that what we now know as "modern science," so remarkably adept at helping us understand our world, is not the only way of knowing reality. It is not equipped to address some of our most persistent dilemmas. Science is and always has been a work in progress. It changes and evolves, sometimes rather quickly. What we call "modern science" today is not the same as the "modern science" of fifty or one hundred years ago.

This growing recognition among scientists of both the strengths and limitations of their enterprise has nurtured a sense of humility, which has not always been there. In this situation, I see in this unpretentious little church, hemmed in by brick and glass landmarks of the sovereignty of the enlightenment worldview, a quiet visual reminder of the possibility of other ways of knowing. It should be said, however, that it is not the only reminder. When the plans for Emerson Hall, which was to house the "human sciences," were brought to then-president Charles William Eliot for his approval, as he picked up his pen, he noticed the words that were to be etched on the portal over the door: "Man Is the Measure of All Things," whereupon Eliot crossed out the proposed inscription and wrote in, "What Is Man That Thou Art Mindful of Him?" The president's action echoed a tension at the core of the university, sometimes creative, sometimes not, that has endured since its founding, and continues today.

I recognize that neither Emanuel Swedenborg nor the little church is the object of much attention today, but I regret it. In recent years, and somewhat to my own surprise, I have come to be thankful for Swedenborg as perhaps an idiosyncratic but significant, though overlooked, figure. And I believe that no one interested in the history of Christianity should allow him to fade from view. Like the Danish Søren Kierkegaard (1813–1855) in the nineteenth century, who was mostly unappreciated in his lifetime, only to be "discovered" one hundred years later, Swedenborg might soon become the overlooked treasure of another rediscovery. Especially now, when the relationship between religion and science has entered a promising new phase, with more openness in both camps to reconcile the two, we have something to learn from his life and his daring ideas.

Swedenborg began his career as a respected scientist. But, like some other notable scientists, including Albert Einstein, he also considered himself a person of faith. Swedenborg was not just a dilettante scientist. He published articles in scientific journals and is credited with several inventions. Raised in the Swedish Lutheran tradition, he insisted throughout his life that science and religion were not incompatible, and they could be partners in a common human enterprise. His opinion was very much like that of the late Harvard paleontologist Stephen J. Gould, whom I have mentioned above. As his thinking matured, Swedenborg developed a consuming interest in theology and published several books on a range of religious topics such as salvation and the Last Judgment. Of special interest for this book, one of his most widely read works is *Heaven and Hell* (1788). In this ambitious book, he gives each a creative and original reinterpretation. Perhaps at times a little too original, he was eventually declared a heretic by the Church of Sweden.

But was Swedenborg a heretic? Not in his own eyes. He called himself "a servant of our Lord and Savior, Jesus Christ." It is true that the ideas he presents in these volumes probably sounded beyond the pale in his own time and might sound far-fetched today as well. One reason for suspicion is that he often based his ideas on his dreams and visions. But another is that his views on heaven, hell, the final judgment, love, and the nature of the Christian life were, as we will see below, frequently at variance with the teachings of the Lutheran Church, which finally excommunicated him. Sadly, after he was shown the door, he became largely missing from Christian theological consideration, which is a loss. If everyone branded a heretic were erased from Christian history, it would be reduced to a very slim volume. Besides, many "heretics" were eventually exonerated, sometimes after centuries, and have been welcomed back into the fold from which they had been excluded. Church officials burned Joan of Arc at the stake in 1431 in Rouen, accusing her of witchcraft and of refusing to disavow her "voices," even when ordered to do so by priests and bishops. Her ashes were dumped into the Seine, but she was canonized in 1920, nearly five hundred years later, by Pope Benedict XV.

Might now be the time to reconsider the case of "Church of Sweden vs. Emanuel Swedenborg"? In being labeled a heretic by the established church of his day, Swedenborg is in the best company. Century after century some of the most honored figures in religion and philosophy have been branded as deviants or heretics in their day, only to be acclaimed later, sometimes much later, for the invaluable contribution they made. Remember that Socrates was forced to drink the fatal cup of hemlock because he was "misleading the youth of Athens." The brilliant Jewish philosopher Baruch Spinoza (1632–1677) was excommunicated in 1656 by his synagogue in Amsterdam. But now Jews, along with everyone else, laud his contribution to philosophy.

Yesterday's heretics and corrupters of the youth are honored, sometimes much later, for their wisdom and virtue.

But what about visions? Saint Teresa of Avila (1515–1582) is one of the most revered personalities in Christian history. A mixture of mystic and activist, a feminist *avant la lettre*, she scolded the pope, founded monasteries in Spain, and wrote meditations on prayer and mysticism, such as the *Interior Castle* (1588), which are still treasured today. But Teresa had to tip-toe carefully and keep moving to stay one step ahead of the Inquisition, which was always hot on her trail. Why? Because, like Swedenborg, she claimed to have visions, which church leadership frowned on severely. After all, visions can come to people without benefit of priests or a hierarchy.

There is little wonder that church officials had grown nervous about visions. In the sixteenth century Pope Leo X excommunicated an Augustinian monk named Martin Luther and declared him a heretic. But Luther is now one of the most respected theologians, studied by both Catholic and Protestant scholars. Luther, however, also had visions. One of his best known involved a spat with Satan, who bothered him when he was translating the Bible into German and Luther hurled an inkwell at him. Today, guides still show visitors the stain on the wall where the missile landed.

Nor, of course, are such extraordinary experiences restricted to Christians. For centuries Buddhists and Hindus have spoken about their visions. The Prophet Muhammad told his friends that one night he was carried off from his home in Mecca to the site of the temple in Jerusalem. There he was raised up to heaven, where he conferred with Moses and Jesus; and both assured him that his mission, to bring the worship of the one true God to the Arab nation, was a valid one. Muslims still mark a day every year to celebrate the Prophet's "night journey." And his experience on the Temple Mount often reminds Christians of Christ's transfiguration, in which Jesus, also on a mountain-top, was joined by Moses and Elijah, who validated his mission. These are only a small sample of the many who claim to have had visions or to have heard voices with messages from God. But if we delete them from the canon of saints and exemplary figures, we lose their invaluable influence. Also, since the patriarchs who appeared in the transfiguration and the night journey had already died, to recall their appearances strengthened those who hear about them in the conviction that the faithful dead are not confined to some distant realm but are still close and communicate with the living. Visions link this world with the next world, or the other world.

Where does Emanuel Swedenborg fit in this picture? Yes, he spoke and wrote at length about his visions; but if he is saying something worth hearing, this should not be grounds for removing him from our bookshelves. Still, do not the conversations Swedenborg says he carried on with angels cast some doubt on him?

We have already noted how frequently both angels and visions occur in the Bible and in Christian history. From Genesis to Revelation and ever since, visions are the rule, not the exception. It is also useful to remember that many great writers and thinkers have woven invented characters into their pages to serve their intellectual purposes. Plato was a student of Socrates, but few people think that the words of the "Socrates" who appears in Plato's dialogues are those of the sage of Athens. Undoubtedly some of his thought, maybe even a few of his words, appear in Plato's works, but "Socrates" has become the voice of his former disciple. For good measure, Plato also adds a couple other characters, as he does in the *Phaedo* with "Apollodorus" and "Simmias" to enliven the exchange with Socrates.

Inventing conversation partners is a common literary trope. The medieval Christian schoolmen invented critics with whom they held arguments (and always won). Søren Kierkegaard conjured a whole cast of characters—with names like "Victor Eremita," "Johannes Climacus," and "William of Afhan." These contrived characters allowed Kierkegaard to voice contrasting points of view. Likewise, Swedenborg introduces the voices of "angels" into his articles and books, and they serve the same purpose as the often lively, but fictional characters his intellectual forebears invited in to "advance the argument." Maybe our problem today is that we are so tightly wrapped in a literalistic culture that we often lose the capacity to appreciate the truths that are conveyed to us through poetry, metaphor, symbols, and imagined or invented characters.

This is precisely where Swedenborg's theology comes in. He was convinced that Christians have been tragically misled by reading the Scriptures *literally*. Like the medieval scholars before him, Swedenborg asserts that such a literal reading misses the point, that the *real* meaning is a *spiritual* meaning. He goes on to say that this spiritual meaning obtains not just in verses and passages but in every single word in the Bible. It was his mission, he said, to deliver these inner treasures from their literal imprisonment. Then with this formidable interpretive sword in hand, he sets out to confront nearly every historic doctrine to uncover its true "spiritual" meaning. The result of this bold project is too encyclopedic to summarize here. But for our purposes it is important to mention how he treats heaven and hell. Swedenborg does not leave us to guess.

I have already mentioned that Swedenborg's most widely read book is *Heaven and Hell*, first published in London in 1758. But in this fascinating work Swedenborg employs an approach that has confused and unsettled many readers. He claims that he learned what he describes in conversations with angels. But, given what I have just written in the preceding paragraphs, I do not believe his thinking should be ignored for that reason.

It is true that in *Heaven and Hell* he tells about conversations with angels, but in several places in his writings he says that these talks occurred during visions. One might still ask, however: What about the *content* of Swedenborg's visions? Are they intended to point to a reality or realities beyond themselves? If so, do we not have an obligation to ask *what* reality?

Interestingly, although, as we have seen, both the Old and New Testaments are reluctant to describe the characteristics of the next life, Swedenborg was not. His *Heaven and Hell* could hardly be more explicit. He leaves scarcely a corner of heaven or hell unexamined. The book has 493 packed pages, divided into numbered sections. What is his core message? It is the fundamental continuity between this life and the next. He is not interested in what has been called "the holy other." For Swedenborg, heaven is a "sanctified same" (my phrase, not his).

Throughout the present book I have suggested that descriptions of heaven are both aspirational projections of a culture and normative guidelines for conduct. They symbolize both what we *are* and what we *should* be. The axiom is that if this is the way it is in heaven, then this is the way it should be here. Even works ostensibly dedicated to discrediting ideas about heaven only succeed in creating new ones. This is the premise of Carl Becker's classic *The Heavenly City of the Eighteenth-Century Philosophers* (Yale University Press, 1932). Here Becker questions the idea that there was a deep rupture between the medieval and the modern era. He documents the often-unspoken continuity between the two. Both, he argues, postulate a more perfect possibility for human life, but one that is not wholly out of reach.

*Heaven and Hell* belongs in this category. Swedenborg's purpose is to displace current conceptions of the afterlife with a more just and credible one. His approach, however, is symbolic and metaphorical. To prepare the reader for his conversations with angels, he begins by declaring that all angels were once human beings whom God elevated to angelic status. But, some of these angels rebelled against God. Thus, Swedenborg's religious cosmology clearly implies two deductions. First, human beings possess "angelic" possibilities, and second, heaven and ordinary life are characterized by a radical continuity.

It is this continuity that is the continuing motif of Swedenborg's heaven: it is not that different from the life we already know. The difference is that it is a perfect version of what we now know only imperfectly. Here he reminds the reader of St. Paul's assertion that here we know only in part, but then "as we are known." Also, in heaven, he says, some of the things we are getting wrong will be corrected. Swedenborg then begins a systematic directory of a world of heavenly perfections and corrections. To illustrate how he does this I will mention a few here.

Swedenborg assures his readers that dying is nothing to be afraid of. In a paragraph that recalls Socrates's words to his followers, he writes that after death we are not radically different. We are, he says, "still human." He then immediately corrects something Christians were getting wrong. "All children," he says, enter heaven regardless of baptism or the church status of the family. Not only all children, but all people, including pagans and scoffers, will be in heaven.

Swedenborg then confronts the ageless "problem of evil" by postulating a device he often utilizes. He says that everyone has "spiritual eyes" as well as ordinary eyes, but that we have not learned to use them, something that will happen to us as we move into the spiritual state he identifies with heaven. As for evil, a good God allows it in the world to sharpen and perfect our moral sensibilities. It is hard for us to see this now, he says, but once our spiritual vision has been achieved, we will see it clearly, once again an echo of St. Paul.

When Swedenborg begins to describe heaven in specifics, he

leads the reader on a tour de force. His main emphasis is that heaven is not a collection of individuals. It consists of innumerable close-knit communities. The residents enjoy life in tasteful mansions located along clean, broad streets that are brightly lit. Inside the mansions one finds magnificent, tasteful furniture. But everything is so stunningly attractive, he adds, not because they are beautiful in themselves, but because the heavenly residents have such marvelously acute spiritual vision, which we can all enjoy.

Swedenborg knows full well that not everyone will believe what he says, so he writes something for these skeptics:

> *Many of those born within the church refuse to believe . . . saying in their hearts, "Who has come from that world and told us?" Lest, therefore, such a spirit of denial, which especially prevails with those who have much worldly wisdom, should also infect and corrupt the simple in heart and the simple in faith, it has been granted me to associate with angels and to talk with them as man with man, also to see what is in the heavens and what is in the hells, and this for thirteen years; so now from what I have seen and heard it has been granted me to describe these, in the hope that ignorance may thus be enlightened and unbelief dissipated. Such immediate revelation is granted at this day because this is what is meant by the coming of the Lord.*

One of Swedenborg's first corrective salvos is fired at what he sees as the current erroneous ideas held by what he calls the "Christian world" about angels. The mistaken belief, he says, is that in the beginning angels and devils were created in heaven, and that the devil was an angel of light, but having rebelled was cast down with his crew, and this is how hell was formed. Swedenborg emphatically disagrees. He states that, on the contrary, every angel or devil began life as a member of the human race. In other words, there are no angels or demons who were not people on Earth first.

Swedenborg was obviously quite fond of angels, who were, after all, his principal informants. But he was also fond of children, so he moves next to challenge the debased way the church regards them. Children who die, he says, whether or not they have been baptized, go directly to heaven, where they are raised by angel mothers to adulthood.

In his long portrayal of heaven and hell, the most fascinating point Swedenborg makes is how much they resemble the world we live in here and now. For example, when he meets and talks with angels, he assures us that they are not ephemeral specters. They live pretty much as we do. They eat and sleep; they breathe and talk and love; they play and worship. They inhabit a "spiritual body" rather than a fleshly one, but they enjoy the tasks they do in helping human beings and as God's messengers. In all this, however, angels possess no power of their own. The only power they have is God's, which works through them and is always benevolent. The angels, in other words, supply us with exemplary models of how we earthlings should be living on this mortal coil.

Swedenborg says little about government in heaven, but one thing is clear: like heaven itself, the government there must be suffused and guided by love. He says that there are many communities in heaven, each with its own "specialty," but he does not describe the specialties. They sound somewhat like the groupings by trades, vocations, and talents that combine to constitute a state, an idea under discussion at Swedenborg's time. In heaven these subcommunities are ruled benevolently by a governor, although we are told that the governors should be motivated by both love and wisdom. The love enables them to discern what is just, and the wisdom guides them in how to realize the good. But Swedenborg does not tell us how these governors are selected. All in all, his suggestions for government remind the reader of Plato's *Republic*. The key difference is that for Plato, the rulers/governors had to be philosophers, and therefore presumably both wise and impartial. Swedenborg also stipulates that the governors must be wise, but he adds another indispensable quality: they must also be motivated by love, a special kind of spiritual love that can only come "from the Lord."

It is here, however, that Swedenborg's concept of the unity between inner and outer, the spiritual and the physical, can become problematic to a reader who does not share his unitary psycho-physical premise. It leads him to mix psychological categories with metaphysical, philosophical, and theological ones. And this can sometimes be confusing. Swedenborg begins not by scanning the topography of the afterlife, but with a penetrating look *within* the soul. This is a method that is common in classical theological approaches, with overtones of St. Augustine's *Confessions* and St. Teresa's *Interior Castle*. Like them and like many mystics, Swedenborg sees a "greater life," beyond the individual, but one in which all people participate. This spiritual unity often manifests itself in visions.

Clearly, for Swedenborg, these exemplary angels do not just remain in heaven. Since they are spiritual beings, we do not see them except on the rare moments when God opens our eyes or ears to them. But nonetheless they live and move among us, protecting, inspiring, and comforting us, which—Swedenborg implies—is just what we should all be doing.

But Swedenborg's book is not just about heaven. It is about heaven *and* hell, so he sets out to explore the abyss with the same approach he used for heaven: he goes within. There, within every person we find a painful dichotomy. Within ourselves we are eventually touched by a consciousness of the spirit and, if we are patient and persistent, of the purpose for which we were created. But then we also find something else. We become aware of pain and suffering. This double insight, Swedenborg says, comes to us only at special times. It comes when we are experiencing stress or are outside our usual mental or physical location. And for Swedenborg, this awareness is a buried memory, the recollection of a previous time in our own lives or in that of our species. Here the similarity of his thought with that of Carl Jung is clear. The trouble is, says Swedenborg, in language that Jung might agree with, we reduce what come to us as powerful feelings into mere concepts. Then we manipulate and misuse them. This is the way the idea of hell has arisen in human history. It is man, Swedenborg asserts, not God, who has invented both heaven and hell. But since he has already reassured us about heaven, it is the deranged idea of hell that Swedenborg obviously finds odious. His analysis is similar to that of religious ethicists like Reinhold Niebuhr who, contrary to many previous moralists, argued that sin does not arise from the passions, but from the way we use them.

Building on this mystical conception, Swedenborg turns to examine current distorted ideas of heaven and hell. He finds them not only defective but destructive. Still, he rarely scolds; he reasons. Our misconceptions, he says, are a natural product of our inner awareness of what seems to be a fundamental dichotomy. This awareness is essential, he says, but it has "taken some extreme and some very distorted forms." For example, he says, heaven is often thought of as a reward for doing the right things in life, like believing in God and following his edicts. In this mistaken view, heaven is a "better life," but one that can be achieved only by fulfilling specific rules.

Swedenborg firmly rejects this idea of heaven, and in his rejection, we can hear overtones of the Lutheran condemnation of "works righteousness." Like Luther's, Swedenborg's heaven has no such requirements. It is a matter, for Luther, of grace, and for Swedenborg, of love. There are sinners there as well as saints, and (for Swedenborg if not for Luther) Muslims and Jews are there too. God's love is unconditional and universal.

Likewise, for Swedenborg, it is human beings, not God, who have created hell as a place of endless punishment, a terrible and ugly pit. Hell was invented, he argues, as a place of punishment for people who do not keep the rules. And Swedenborg is particularly vexed at the raw details of hellish punishments that have been devised in some religious traditions.

But, since we have faith in a God who is both all merciful and loving, none of this horror makes sense to Swedenborg. Besides, since God is omniscient, he must know that the world is a series of traps for the innocent and the unwary. God must know, he says, that we live in a reality "where error is so prevalent and the seductions of error are so great, there are very few people who could ever surmount them."

In addition to these theological arguments against what he held were serious distortions of the idea of heaven, Swedenborg had another argument: he had been to heaven, and it was nothing like its distorters picture it. Swedenborg even gets a bit sarcastic. "When you think about it," he says, to spend eternity

> *with no contrasts in life, with nothing really to do with this body that you still have in this imagined Heaven, Heaven becomes extremely dull and boring. You cannot sing, "Glory Hallelujah" forever without becoming weary of it. So, Heaven, though it seems a great reprieve from the difficulties of your current existence, seems to have no real relief on an ongoing basis.*

For Swedenborg, the silliness of most ideas of heaven is due to two related fallacies:

1. Identifying ourselves with our physical bodies when we are essentially spiritual beings, and

2. Thinking of heaven as a place when it actually is a spiritual condition.

The main reason why Swedenborg feels he needs to criticize and correct these infantile ideas is that they constitute an obstacle to genuine faith. "Of course," he writes, "some people look at all this and think it is madness and reject religion altogether, still holding on to the notion that they have some kind of connection to a greater life. . . ." He also regrets that the view of God behind this absurdity is terribly wrong because, "Here," he writes, "God becomes something you have to please, and when you have to please another, it breeds resentment and resistance."

The more I read Swedenborg, the more I was reminded of my own principal theological teacher, Paul Tillich. Tillich also held that the underlying obstacle to grasping religious language in our time is our entrenched literalism. During most of human history, Tillich believed, most people had the capacity, now largely lost, to absorb the intent of symbolic meanings directly, without channeling them through a cognitive grid. There were, of course, always a few people in any era who became cognizant of the binary structure of consciousness, but for the average person, it was—like breathing—something so ordinary that it did not require analysis or explication. As human beings they were at the same time both rational and symbolic creatures, although even this description might have sounded strange to them since the two faculties were so thoroughly fused.

But that was then, and this is now, and what they took for granted, we have almost completely lost, also without noticing it. For Tillich this is equally unfortunate. We live in an age in which the once-powerful language of traditional symbols barely touches us while we are inundated daily with a constant stream of invented pseudo-symbols, designed to manipulate our consciousness. And, like adults who were born blind or deaf, it is hard to imagine what sight or hearing is, cut off, as we are, from whole elements of the world without knowing it.

During the many years when our symbolic sensibilities were still alive, there were observers who understood the different levels of consciousness. In his own language, Plato often recurs to the distinction between the world of things and the world of ideas without denigrating either. The medieval schoolmen and Renaissance thinkers recognized a similar distinction. Theologians and students of Scripture contrasted the literal reading of texts, which they dismissed as superficial, with the metaphorical reading, which they sometimes called the "inner meaning," and which they held to be a vastly superior one.

But this often changed without our even noticing it. With the advent of the printing press, the Reformation, mass literacy, and the modern scientific mentality, we have gradually become symbolically tone deaf and less capable of appreciating anything but the literal. "Well, that is only symbol," we sometimes say, thereby demoting symbols to an inferior status, the opaque idiom of an archaic civilization or a bygone era. One of the most renowned theologians of the twentieth century was Rudolf Bultmann, who argued that the Bible was written in the age of the "three-decker universe," and was therefore cloaked in myth. For modern people to understand it, it must be "demythologized." This was a task Bultmann and his disciples set out to do, translating the New Testament out of myth and into contemporary existential categories. Their premise was that myth inevitably distorts and obscures. The ambitious project of liberating biblical ideas from their mythic wrappings was widely acclaimed for a time, and preachers tried their hand at "demythologizing" their Sunday texts, sometimes to the puzzlement of their congregations. But before very long this practice went out of fashion, and Bultmann has been largely forgotten.

Tillich, however, who was Bultmann's friend and contemporary, held an almost opposite view. He contended that symbol is not just the outer garb of religion but its essential language, and that what hampers our grasping its meaning today is our literalism. Thus, when we read the Bible (creeds and doctrines) literally, we miss their real significance. Therefore, Tillich insisted, the most important task of theology today is not to do away with myth, but to engage in what he called "deliteralization." In commenting on Tillich, a leading Catholic scholar said, "Yes, he is right, and that is why I say we should always *sing* the creeds. It helps to avoid taking them literally."

Tillich saw both liberal and conservative views of the Bible, for example, as snared in the same literalist web, the first trying to disprove it, the second clinging to its every page as free from any error. It is ironic that today's fundamentalists have seized upon the same literal view of Scripture, which was once looked down upon, as the defining doctrine of true Christianity.

Swedenborg was far ahead of his time. In one of his first books he set out to uncover the "inner meaning" of the Scripture, taking it verse by verse. He only got through Genesis and Exodus before he put this colossal project aside to work on other things, only briefly returning to the Book of Revelation later. But, a century before Tillich, he was deliteralizing.

Meanwhile, however, some modern philosophers have reopened the controversy about symbolism and literalism in a vigorous way. Ernst Cassirer in his *Philosophy of Symbolic Forms* and Suzanne Langer in *Philosophy in a New Key* have reinstated the symbolic as a critical dimension of human consciousness.

Still, there is little wonder why it remains difficult for many twenty-first-century readers to take seriously a thinker like Swedenborg who writes about his visits to heaven and his conversations with angels. Add to this some of the startling things he says he learned from these encounters. What can we make of this audacious thinker today?

To respond to this question, we need to recall two principles of interpretation I have already discussed but that are especially important in understanding Swedenborg.

The first, introduced in my opening pages, is that I have not been writing "about heaven or hell." I have been writing about what different people have thought about heaven and hell, and how they have made them a part of their lives.

The second is that in trying to appreciate what these elements of their "lived world" means and have meant, we must not be misled into literal readings. True, reports of visions and dreams may be articulated in a literal idiom, but their interpreters, like psychoanalysts, need to ask, what larger or deeper truth do they point to? True, Swedenborg recounted his visions in expressions that sound literal. But we know from his own writings that his intention was symbolic, and this is also borne out by his patient effort to work his way through the Bible to uncover its "inner meaning." It is both unfair and unproductive to read a writer who was a lifelong critic of literalism in a literal way.

Why do I believe Swedenborg should be invited back into both the theological fraternity and the larger public intellectual conversation today? There are three reasons.

First, we are now witnessing the revival of experiential and mystical spirituality. This is happening after many years of their being shunned, marginalized, and in some cases condemned by both church officials and theologians. Obviously, mysticism, as the direct, unmediated relation to God or the transcendent, has had a recognized place in the history of Christianity, but by the time I was a divinity student, it had fallen out of favor. For example, a book by the German theologian Emil Brunner, called *Mysticism and the Word*, had become one of the principal texts. In over three hundred pages Brunner left the reader little doubt which of these two he favored, and it was not mysticism, which he found to be vague, ephemeral, and untrustworthy.

Like his colleague Karl Barth, Brunner was a voice of what they called *Wort Gottes Theologie,* a theology based exclusively on the Word of God. Mysticism of any sort they discarded as just too subjective. But the antimystical fashion, like many others in theology, eventually passed. Today, both students and their teachers are reading Thomas Merton, Simone Weil, Dorothy Soelle, and others more friendly to a mystical approach.

Second, ever since the work of Freud and Jung, developments in the psychology of religion have opened the door to a more sympathetic view of both dreams and visions. The wind has now shifted on the interpretation of dreams and visions, which had earlier been dismissed as illusions and not to be taken with any degree of seriousness. Without taking them as predicting future events as people once did, both Freud and Jung saw them, in different ways, as keys to the human subconscious, and therefore as an essential factor in human behavior. As a psychologist who was one of my faculty friends once remarked while talking about the visions his patients sometimes reported to him, "I do not take them literally, but I do take them seriously." Interestingly, two hundred years earlier, Swedenborg had written about the value of dreams and visions, which, he said, using almost the same words, we should take "seriously, but not literally," and this is the standpoint from which he wrote about heaven and hell. It was the stylistic device he used to assert his description of himself as one of those rare travelers who have visited the "undiscovered country," and to describe what he saw, what he learned, and what he thinks we should know. How then should we take what Swedenborg tells us? In keeping with the writer's own self-description, I think there is only one possible answer: seriously, but not literally.

# 9

# *Heaven in the Desert*

*For now we see through a glass, darkly;*
*but then face to face:*
*now I know in part;*
*but then shall I know even as also I am known.*
(1 Corinthians 13:12 KJV)

This chapter recounts a brief visit I paid to an indigenous Indian community in the desert of northwestern Mexico. The reader who has perused the previous chapters may wonder why this one is included. What does it have to do with the afterlife? But I hope I can show why I think it is not only relevant but possibly even crucial. Throughout history, the mystics in every tradition have testified that they have been in some way, however fragmentary or fleeting, in touch with ultimate reality. Those nurtured in the Christian faith, like St. Teresa or St. John of the Cross, have often called it "heaven." The link between the two is the intimate connection of the visions of the mystics and the images of heaven found embedded in spiritual traditions. Virtually all the classical mystics have testified to a glimpse of the Great Mystery, real and powerful, but one they cannot describe in words. And it is precisely the frustrating quality of the mystical—the meeting with an undeniable reality, combined with the exasperating inability to describe it—that makes the present chapter so essential.

When I began to write this book, I knew there were topics I wanted to incorporate. Among these, I needed a comparative perspective to make it clear that our culture's ideas of heaven or the afterlife, however heterogeneous, are in no way universal. I had read a lot about alternative visions of the hereafter in a variety of traditions, but I wanted to experience some of them firsthand. It occurred to me that my experience in the desert many years ago was just such a firsthand experience and that it had something to contribute to this discussion.

My sojourn with the Huichole had not started as a quest for the numinous. I had different reasons. I knew the Huichole ingested peyote (mescaline) in their ceremonies, and I wanted to uncover more about the possible similarity between experiences of psychedelics and classical mystical states. I had also come to believe that the use of psychedelics in traditional ritual settings, as many tribal people do, was the safest and most beneficial way to use them. But this was a problematic subject to explore. The severe criminalization of these substances, beginning in the 1950s and 1960s, had made it almost impossible for researchers to do their work. Consequently, tall tales and horror stories thrived, and trustworthy data were hard to come by.

Then I received an invitation that eventually enabled me to pursue both of these interests. In 1975, I accepted an invitation to be a visiting professor for two semesters at the ecumenical seminary in Mexico City.

Protestants constitute a small minority in Mexico, so this school enrolled students from several different denominations: Baptists, Methodists, Lutherans, and Pentecostals. There were also a few Roman Catholics and some who claimed no denominational affiliation. I loved teaching them, even though my wobbly Spanish was sometimes a source of puzzlement.

After a couple of weeks, I ran into a visiting American scholar at a local restaurant. I had not known him before, but we chatted, and planned to have lunch. When we did, he told me he had come to work for a few weeks with a noted Mexican medical doctor who was doing research on the therapeutic possibilities of indigenous psychedelic plants, and did I want to meet him? I said I did.

The doctor's name was Soltano. He was a serious middle-aged man, wearing a rumpled blue suit and open collar. He said he was learning much from indigenous people about mescaline, peyote, and other lesser-known medicinal plants. He said that once a week he met with some of his advanced students to sample small portions of some of the substances he was studying. He asked me if I would like to attend one of these sessions, which he assured me with a smile were perfectly legal under Mexican law. Again, I said I would.

The following week I dropped in on one of the gatherings, and I found it so interesting that I attended several more, always as an observer. There were usually about ten people at each session, mainly young adults, both men and women. They sat on cushions scattered on a thick red rug. They always began by doing some yoga exercises for relaxation. Then Dr. Soltano talked briefly about what would happen and distributed the different substances being tested that evening. The lights were dimmed, and he played some music he had recorded in the villages on a hi-fi. The guests sat quietly or stretched out on the rug and remained that way for the five-hour session. Only once did I notice anyone who seemed to be agitated. A young man in a blue-and-white wool serape stood up, approached Dr. Soltano, and appeared to be talking to himself angrily. The doctor listened to him calmly, spoke to him in a quiet voice, then led him gently back to his place on the rug. I did not imbibe any of the substances. I was there, I told myself, to observe and learn, not to participate. But as the weeks passed my attitude changed.

I usually left before the session was over, but a couple times I stayed until two in the morning when the patients woke up, and Dr. Soltano led them in a group reflection on what they had experienced. To my surprise, they did not talk about the experience itself, or about the specific qualities of some particular substances. Instead, they talked about how, during the past hours, they had been able to see personal problems they were struggling with in a clearer light.

I was curious about whether this disappointed Dr. Soltano, who, after all, was mainly interested in the qualities of the preparations he was administering. He smiled and shook his head. He told me that, no, he was getting precisely the feedback he wanted. He said that if you listened carefully to what they said, you could determine the differences among the substances. I continued to drop into Dr. Soltano's clinic/lab, and one day he asked me to come into his private office. Every year, he said, he made a field trip into the desert of northern Mexico to spend a few days with the indigenous Huichole Indians, who, for generations, had used peyote, which grows at the root of the desert cactus, in their ceremonies. They camped in the desert to gather a supply of peyote, which they called the "little deer." They stayed for two weeks during this "deer hunt" before returning, and they had invited Dr. Soltano to join them. He accepted and asked if he could bring a few friends along. The Huichole agreed, as long as the doctor and his friends camped at a close but separate location. These "friends" were of course his patients/subjects/coworkers (any distinction was no longer clear to me), one or two staff members, and, if I wanted to, me. I accepted.

There are only about eighteen thousand Huichole left in

Mexico. They wear red, white, and black serapes and decorated sombreros with very wide brims. They construct picture paintings from colored thread, which they sell to support themselves. They are considered the last remaining people to have preserved their culture and way of life since the Spanish conquest. They have accomplished this by living in secluded villages in Nayarit and Jalisco states, and they do not welcome visitors. Dr. Soltano, however, had become their friend by intervening for them with the federal government, so he had been able to visit them before. He made the arrangements for our expedition, and the next week ten of us packed sleeping bags and water bottles and climbed aboard a train for the four-hour trip from Mexico City north to the desert. When we finally reached the modest rail station there, an open truck that Dr. Soltano had rented to take us into the desert was waiting.

After a bumpy ride over the dunes in blazing sun and billows of sand and dust, the truck stopped near where a Huichole man, who was to be our guide, stood signaling to us. We piled out and arranged our sleeping bags around a circle of stones indicating where our new guide told us we were to have our campfire. On a hill about a hundred yards away we could see the camp the Huichole had already set up and where they had been living for a few days while they scoured the desert for peyote plants, the "little deer."

After half an hour, four Huichole men in their colorful costumes walked over to our area. Since they do not speak Spanish, but their own Huichole language, Dr. Soltano translated. The men welcomed us briefly but warned us not to come close to their camp. They would be chanting to invoke their ancestral spirits, they said, and those antecedents did not like to come in touch with outsiders. Surely, they said, we must have our own ancestral spirits, everyone does, and we should get in touch with them while we were here, not with theirs.

His remark made a couple people in our group smile. Like
me, they probably wondered why anyone would ever want to
be in touch with our bygone forebears. But it also reminded me
of how different our current ideas about our ancestors are from
those of most people in most of history, among whom the links
are far more significant.

We accepted the suggestion, and the warning, and then one
of the Huicholes lent each of us a small, sharp knife. The way to
hunt the little deer, he said, was to kneel next to a cactus to find
it just where the cactus came up from the ground. Then, he said,
we should say a short prayer to the little deer explaining why
we were cutting it, apologizing, but assuring it that we were not
cutting its roots, so it could grow back. The prayer, he said, had
of course to be repeated in Huichole, and he would teach it to us.
He was ready to start right away.

There were seven of us who wanted to learn the prayer so we
could join the "deer hunt." We sat in a circle while our Huichole
instructor began to voice the words phrase by phrase, asking us
to repeat them after him. It was, however, not a short prayer. We
tried, and we tried again. But Huichole is not an easy language,
and the prayer lasted about five minutes. Try as we would, our
efforts to mimic our teacher soon trailed off into incoherent
muttering. Our tutor, however, saw both that we really had been
trying, but that we would probably never master this prayer. He
looked disappointed, but not angry. Eventually he indicated that
we should sit still while he walked over to his own camp. We felt
discouraged. Had we ventured so far into this wasteland only
to concede that the deer hunt would have to go on without us?

In a few minutes however, our teacher came back with Dr.
Soltano and another Huichole, a somewhat older man who
smiled at us and nodded. Translated by the doctor, he said he
understood that we were having trouble learning the prayer.
But, he said, he had a suggestion. He would now teach us a

very short prayer, also in Huichole, which would suffice. It was indeed short, and within a few minutes we had memorized it.

What, I asked Dr. Soltano, did the prayer actually say? He thought for a moment, then gave us his own Spanish translation. "Oh, little deer," he said, "I am sorry that I cannot speak to you in your own tongue. But if you will listen to our brothers on that hill who are praying to you, you will understand why I am cutting you . . . and leaving your roots." Within half an hour we had all learned to say this prayer, or a reasonable facsimile, and we set out with our sharp knives to seek the little deer.

By evening we had each gathered a little bundle of pieces of the peyote root. We roasted corn and turnips over the fire and ate dinner. Then, instructed by Dr. Soltano, we sat in a circle around the flames and swallowed one bite of peyote, waited, then swallowed another. It had the consistency of a raw sweet potato, and it was tasteless. But it did not take long for the state of what some people called "expanded consciousness" to set in. For me it was a pleasant, calming sensation. But when I looked at the stars that were just beginning to appear, they seemed enormously larger and brighter than anything I had seen before. Friends later told me that in the desert, due in part to the absence of the obscuring pollutants of the city, the stars always appear brighter. That may be true. But for me the scrubby, dark jade bushes, the orange flames of the fire, the people seated around me or stuffed into their sleeping bags, had also become many times more vivid. It was as though I had been seeing the world through a foggy screen, or maybe, as St. Paul says, "through a glass darkly." I could understand why people preferred to call peyote and similar substances not hallucinogens but psychedelics, which means "mind expanding." I did not hallucinate that evening, not even once. But I did see what was around me and, later, my inner thoughts with a crystalline clarity. A powerful awareness came over me that these stars and I need not be strangers, but that somehow we belonged together.

Nothing I saw or felt was frightening to me, and when I noticed we still had some chunks of peyote in the bowl, I ate another piece. Then I stood up and began walking around our group and took a few steps out into the desert. I looked up again at the thousands of stars, then the words of our Huichole guide, that we should invoke our own spirits, came back. And then I also suddenly remembered a song I had learned in church as a child:

*Bright morning stars are shining,*
*Bright morning stars are shining,*
*And day is breaking in my soul.*

I did not think of it at the time, but later it occurred to me that the words suggest a kind of mysterious link between the universe and myself, and in another song, Jesus is called the "bright morning star." I also remembered that the Judeo-Christian religion had originated among a desert people, and that according to the gospels, Jesus had had one of his most telling experiences in the desert. Had this curious bit of desert sweet potato somehow enabled me to get back in touch with the origins of my faith?

I think it was about three in the morning when I crawled into my sleeping bag and fell asleep. The sun woke me up at about six, and as I glanced around, I saw that my companions were stirring too. One of the women was sipping coffee and applying lipstick, with the lower half of her body still wrapped in the canvas sack. Then, I also noticed a Huichole man seated on a brown-and-white horse just outside our circle. He was smiling and nodding. It was almost a morning benediction.

We cooked oatmeal and boiled water for coffee and tea over the coals of last night's fire. Some of us were still wrapped in the bags. Others were stretching and walking around. Then Dr. Soltano asked us to gather around the fireplace so we could compare notes on the previous evening. I knew the doctor usually did this, and I was looking forward to the conversation. But I was disappointed. As we went around the circle, everyone spoke of the previous night in positive tones: positive, but vague, even flat. When my turn came, I could see why the words the people used sounded so hollow, because mine did too. How could I describe the luminescent stars, the kinship I felt with the universe? It was not the "oneness" with it that many mystics have spoken about. I had not been absorbed into the cosmos. Rather, I had felt what I could only characterize as a profound friendship, something close to love. But in our modern world both words, "love" and "friendship," had lost much of their edge. And the universe, the "starry skies above" that Kant had called the sources of the natural law (the other was "the moral law within"), has become something we scrutinize through a powerful telescope. At times we may even feel a sense of awe toward it. But we rarely embrace it as a lover or a friend.

After a somewhat unsatisfactory hour of desultory chatter around the waning campfire, some of the campers began to drift away from the circle, and Dr. Soltano ended it by suggesting that we start cleaning up our site and packing to return. As we did so I realized that although the sharing session had been frustrating, we had all had a hint of the classical mystic's dilemma: the stubborn ineffability of the experience. I could see more plainly why mystics had turned to the language of metaphor and symbol, why, when they spoke of visions and dreams, and maybe of journeys to heaven, it often sounded incoherent. And I could also see why, in our age of radical empiricism, when so much of our capacity for the symbolic has been lost, anything that appears to be beyond the range of objective observation can be dismissed as illusory, insignificant, or perverse.

True, we have all learned a lot and gained much from this objective, "scientific" way of relating to the world. But if this way becomes the only acceptable way, is there a danger that we are missing something vital? I am glad that there are still people like the Huichole, and other people like them who have nourished an alternative way, but I do not think we need to abandon our "objective" way in order to incorporate the "other" way. A few decades ago, the philosophers who predicted a "meeting of East and West," such as F. S. C. Northrup and Alfred North White-head, thought that these two "ways" might one day be woven together on a global basis. That has not happened. The "East" has in many respects caught up with the "West" in hard objective science. But the "other way" has not disappeared. There are still mystics and visionaries on every continent. Some of them are disguised as filmmakers, some as poets, some as writers. Some do not possess these gifts, but are still, in their own lives, showing us "the other way."

As I was coming to the end of writing this book, I was still wondering just what the Huichole heaven is like, and I still do not know. I had not asked that question in that way when I was with them, and besides, I did not speak their language. Without a doubt, however, the Huichole, like so many of the other people I mention in this book, think of heaven in two closely related ways. First, it is where their ancestors dwell; and when they become ancestors, they will join them. But at the same time, this domain of the ancestors is very close. The ancestors are still members of the community, and one can communicate with them on some occasions, such as when one partakes of the little deer. They demonstrate once again that the paradoxes of near and far, or of coming and already here, as Jesus expressed it, seem to be universal elements of the "ultimate," which we share with a vast multitude.

I have never partaken of the little deer since that visit with the Huichole. The visit did not convert me into a nature mystic, although I sensed the temptation. It is worth noting that the biblical writers were fully aware of this temptation:

> *And beware lest you raise your eyes to heaven, and when you see the sun and the moon and the stars, all the host of heaven, you be drawn away and bow down to them and serve them, things that the Lord your God has allotted to all the peoples under the whole heaven.* (Deuteronomy 4:19 ESV)

But the visit did persuade me that some of those who criticize Christianity for emphasizing the God who acts in history to the detriment of the God who is also present in nature have a point. This one-sidedness distorts our idea of God, and it deprives us of full access to the maker of *both* heaven and earth. Once, while I was visiting rural Baptist churches in West Virginia some years ago I became sharply aware of this imbalance—and the efforts ordinary people sometimes make to compensate for it. As I worshiped in small wooden churches, I noticed that the members had all painted lush scenes of trees, grass, and flowing creeks on the wall behind their baptismal pools. At some level of their minds, they wanted to bring nature back into Christian worship. Also, nearly every painting I have ever seen that seeks to picture heaven incorporates trees and hills. A heaven without nature, it seems, would not be heaven.

# 10

# *The Death of Purgatory*

*All who die in God's grace and friendship, but still imper-*
*fectly purified, are indeed assured of their eternal salvation;*
*but after death they undergo purification, so as to achieve*
*the holiness necessary to enter the joy of heaven.* (The Catholic Catechism)

*We should exclaim with all our might, that purgatory is*
*a pernicious fiction of Satan, that it makes void the cross*
*of Christ, that it intolerably insults the Divine Mercy, and*
*weakens and overturns our faith. For what is their purga-*
*tory, but a satisfaction for sins paid after death by the souls*
*of the deceased? . . . [but] the blood of Christ is the only sat-*
*isfaction, expiation, and purgation for the sins of the faith-*
*ful. What, then, is the necessary conclusion but that pur-*
*gation is nothing but a horrible blasphemy against Christ?*
(John Calvin, *Institutes of the Christian Religion,* Book 3)

When my grandmother Maud, a pillar of our Baptist
church, died at eighty-seven, two well-meaning Catholic
neighbors dropped by to offer condolences to my grandfather,
a deacon in the same congregation. In their conversation, the
guests assured the old man that they were praying every day to
get his late wife out of purgatory. But their assurances did not
have the desired effect. My grandfather, a man who never cried,

momentarily removed the ever-present cigar from his mouth and broke down into spasms of sobs, and his comforters left puzzled. When he told his son, my father, about the exchange a few hours later, he was still weeping. "Well," my father said, "don't worry, Papa, that is what *they* believe. But we do *not* believe in purgatory."

My father was no historian of doctrine, but he was right about that. And why not? If there is one idea that people in the pews of Protestant churches pick up from sermons that touch on the difference between Catholics and Protestants (usually on Reformation Sunday), this is it. Ever since the Reformation, Protestants have rejected the idea of purgatory as a denial of the all-sufficient grace of God both to forgive sinners and to make them ready for the divine presence. They have also rejected the idea of praying for the dead at all. The Westminster Confession of the Reformed churches states this quite explicitly: *"Prayer is to be made . . . for things lawful, and for all sorts of men living, or that shall live hereafter; but not for the dead."*

Today, Protestants still do not believe in purgatory, or—more likely—do not think about it at all, or have the vague impression that it is an unpleasant place, is not heaven, and anyway *we* do not believe in it. But what about Catholics? Do they "believe" in purgatory, and, if so, what meaning does it have for them nowadays?

In official Catholic teaching, purgatory is "a condition or state of suffering in which those who have died as friends of God pay the debt of temporal punishment and are purified of all possible venial sins and evil habits." The teaching supposes that before death the sinner has been justified by faith in Christ. His eternal destiny is assured. But before entering the full presence of God there remains the need to expiate the temporal sins he has committed. This purification is the purpose of purgatory. This expiation is derived from the grace of Christ, but according to the teaching, it can be helped by the prayers and good works of those who are still living.

The idea of purgatory has a long history, going back to similar ideas that predate Christianity. As we have seen, Plato wrote about an intermediate stage that human beings enter after death where they remain until they either ascend to a celestial paradise or are reincarnated to return to this world. Other ancient thinkers held similar ideas. But they also argued in a way that seems entertaining to modern readers about just where this interim way station was located. Some thought it hovered between the sun and the moon, others that it was farther up and out, maybe in the Milky Way. These ideas were still circulating when Christianity was born, and since the early Christians had no theories of their own on the subject, some adopted the pagan notions, adapting them in various ways. The theological basis for these teachings was twofold, both illustrating the conviction that prayer precedes doctrine ("as we pray, so we believe"). The first was that since we pray for the dead, they must need our prayers, so they have obviously not reached the ultimate state of bliss. The second basis was that since nearly everyone falls into sin after baptism (which was said to wash away original sin), and may not have received the sacrament of penance regularly, further expiation was needed, and it can continue after death.

As different versions of the interim status of the dead (not yet called purgatory) emerged, differences appeared between the Latin church in the West and the Eastern churches. The former taught that suffering had to be an essential component of the purification, but the latter rejected this notion. Centuries later, at the time of the Great Schism in 1054, this dispute had still not been resolved. One feature of the argument among the Western theologians sounds odd, even abhorrent to most people today. It centered on the nature of the flames. Augustine distinguished between the purifying and the punishing blazes, reflecting the notion that purgatory had two purposes: expiation and purification.

A crisis of the doctrine of purgatory broke out in the sixteenth century. By then the Catholic Church had determined that living people could procure indulgences, issued in the pope's name, that signified pardon from certain sins for those in purgatory, presumably shortening the time they needed to stay there. The system seemed almost designed to create misuse, and it did. Soon, one could purchase indulgences for a price, and Rome created a kind of franchise system, farming out the sale of indulgences to people who would market them energetically and were allowed to retain a portion of the profit for themselves. Some of these salesmen contrived assertive pitches to market their spiritual product. Their sermons/sales pitches beset their potential customers with the plea that if they listened closely, they would hear the wretched moans and screams of their suffering loved ones, and would also hear their pleas to their living relatives not to harden their hearts but to obtain an indulgence that would shorten their misery. Among these hard-sales indulgence pushers, one stands out. His name was Johannes Tetzel (d. 1519). Tetzel merits a special place in the long saga of religious charlatans. Centuries before "Things Go Better with Coke," he used a rhyming limerick to hawk his spiritual wares:

*As soon as the coin into the bucket pings,*
*The soul out of purgatory springs.*

The sale of indulgences aroused widespread criticism among Catholic priests and lay people. A key aspect of the practice was that it involved two elements. First, it assumed the reality of something called purgatory, where the dead were suffering. Second, it also assumed that the pope, as Christ's earthly representative and the keeper of "the keys of the kingdom," had the authority to cancel or shorten people's terms in the flames.

One of the Catholic critics who decried the practice was a young German Augustinian monk named Martin Luther. But there were many others. We have cited the view of purgatory of another theologian, John Calvin, at the head of this chapter. By the time the Reformation reached full swing, all three moving parts of the practice—indulgences, purgatory, and the power of the pope—were thrown into question. And by the time it ended, a large segment of Europe had not only rejected indulgences and purgatory but the authority of the papacy as well. Much of the money that had flowed into Rome from the sale of indulgences was used to build St. Peter's Basilica, but it came at a steep price. A friend once told me that when he visited St. Peter's, his group visit was being conducted by a young seminarian. As they gazed at the splendor of the basilica one of the other guests asked their guide, "How much did this all cost?" The guide paused and smiled wryly. "Well," he answered, "it cost us northern Europe." Was it worth it? What is happening with purgatory in the Catholic Church today?

When I asked my Catholic theological colleagues about this, I got mixed answers. None of them wanted to go into my question very deeply. Most said that little is made of purgatory in recent Catholic theology, and that it is now rarely mentioned in Sunday sermons or at funerals. But when I sent an email to my friend Fr. Gerald Whelan, a Jesuit who teaches at the Pontifical Gregorian University in Rome, his response sounded somewhat equivocal: "I am afraid that purgatory is still alive and well in Catholic theology." I believe that, short of the pope himself, there is no more authoritative source on Catholic theology than "The Greg." But how was I to understand his message? In what way was purgatory still alive and well? And why the "I am afraid"? Do I detect some ambivalence here?

In any church, the opinions of theologians are not the same as that of the laity, the people Catholics call "the faithful." How does the teaching about purgatory stand today among them? I have noticed that, apart from the unfortunate conversation my grandfather had with his neighbors, mentioned above, I never hear my Catholic friends or students even mention the word "purgatory." What is going on? The question felt like an important one to me. If the doctrine of purgatory did not still claim the importance it once did, what were the implications for relations between the two traditions or for their ideas about life after death?

In assessing the status of purgatory in everyday Catholic life today, there is one small piece of evidence that might shed some light on the larger picture. In what is thought of as the Italian American "North End" of Boston there stands a picturesque little Catholic church which, until quite recently, displayed inside its front door a graphic three-dimensional model of "Souls in Purgatory." It depicted a dozen naked men and women writhing amid curling red and cobalt blazes. Next to it stood a box with a sign requesting visitors to pray for these unfortunates and to make a cash contribution that could speed their release. (The sign did not specify the destination of the gift or just how it would accomplish its salvific purpose.)

The model remained in the church for years even after the Second Vatican Council, and I often took visitors there to see a living example of "that old-time religion." After a brief visit we would then drop in for lunch at a small Italian restaurant down the street called Alfredo's, where I always ordered the lasagna and a glass or two of Chianti, followed by soft ice cream and a cup of cappuccino. I also usually bought a copy of *La Republica*, the Roman daily paper, from the kiosk on the corner, where elderly Italian men in a day's growth of beard and wearing suits with open shirts watched passersby. I did not read Italian well, but I liked sipping my coffee while perusing the headlines, and wondering why anyone would spend hundreds of dollars on a flight to Milan or Rome when the best of what Italy offers is a twenty-five-minute bus ride from Harvard Square.

But what about purgatory? The last time I visited the church a few years ago, I was sorry to see that "Souls in Purgatory" was gone. It had been replaced by a gently smiling Lady of Guadalupe, with no flames in sight. I say I was sorry not because I harbor a belief in purgatory, which I do not. But I always regret seeing the symbols of a devotion people once found inspiring brushed aside to make room for those expressing a newer style of devotion. The Catholic churches I most appreciate are the ones that preserve the material reminders of the devotions of previous generations. Seeing them helps us maintain a sense of continuity with our spiritual forebears, even when we do not pray as they did. As I began to write this book, however, it occurred to me that the disappearance of the "Souls in Purgatory" from the church might have a significance beyond the changing ethnic composition of the North End.

I also have nothing against Our Lady of Guadalupe. Quite the contrary. Ever since I first "met" her during the fiestas and pilgrimages I took part in when I lived in Mexico, where I first learned what she means for the poor and excluded people of the continent, my fondness for her has deepened. As a Protestant, I did not grow up with the idea of having a patron saint. But if I could, Our Lady of Guadalupe would be my choice. Still, I was regretful that she had not only *re*placed but *dis*placed the "Souls in Purgatory." Couldn't that church in the North End have found perhaps a less prominent location for the souls struggling amid the blazes? But this left me with a more basic question: How could a doctrine that once loomed so important that it contributed to an agonizing schism in Christianity become so inconsequential? Were there cultural, political, or other factors that hastened its demotion? Then, an even more baffling question becomes unavoidable: As Catholics or Protestants, do we have doctrines or practices that seem utterly foundational today but might seem less prominent in the future? Might any of these have to do with death and the afterlife?

The shrill dispute over purgatory became the most controversial issue during the sixteenth-century Reformation. Catholics fought bitterly with Protestants over whether it existed, but they argued even more furiously over whether the pope had the authority as the heir of St. Peter and the custodian of the "keys to the kingdom" to release souls from its flames. This dispute has long since virtually disappeared. Since the Second Vatican Council (1962–65) Catholics and Protestants have left behind many of their inherited disagreements. But it might be asked, "Whatever happened to purgatory?" And where do the two traditions stand today on the deeper question, the status of the dead, which the idea of purgatory was intended to address?

Some of my musings about the changes in the little church in the North End had a less spiritual, more sociological tone. I knew that during recent years the Italian Americans who had for a couple generations constituted the majority had been moving to the suburbs, and that Latino/a immigrants had been moving in. It occurred to me that there might be a link between the change in the ethnic composition of the neighborhood and the transition from purgatory to Guadalupe. This might present an intriguing question for an aspiring researcher to investigate. Clearly Latino/as have more affection for Guadalupe. But had the earlier Italians been that concerned about purgatory? This question points to a larger one. Do popular devotions originate at the grass roots and percolate up to official church approval? Or are they the product of hierarchical teaching that spreads among the flock? Or is it a combination? The same question could be asked about, for example, devotion to the Sacred Heart, which flourished widely a century ago, or to the more recent devotion to the Immaculate Heart of Mary. For this book, the same query could be posed about changing ideas of heaven. And what about current views of purgatory? How accurate is it to say, "*They* believe, but *we* do not believe in purgatory"?

There is no doubt that whatever its current official status, purgatory has receded as a prominent Catholic teaching. There may be many reasons for this, but one is a decided change in the Catholic theology of grace. For years it was claimed, not quite correctly, that while Protestants held that salvation is entirely a gift of God (*sola gratia*), Catholics taught that it requires both faith and works. But hardly any Catholic theologian would support that contrast today. The late Hans Küng, who along with Bernard Lonergan and Karl Rahner was the most prominent Catholic thinker of the twentieth century, insisted emphatically that salvation is a gratuitous gift of God. "Good works" should be the "fruits" of this gift, not something by which one earns God's favor. But even if Catholic theologians decided that the church would be better off without purgatory, what would happen then, if anything? Could the pope decide to eliminate or demote it?

This idea fascinated me. Then, in April 2007 Pope Benedict XVI signed a theological report that implied that he could. It had to do with "limbo," which the Catholic Church had taught was the destination of babies who died unbaptized. The pope said that limbo would now be replaced with "the prayerful hope" that these infants might reach heaven. The *New York Times* reported, "Many in the church felt the idea (of limbo), never formally a part of church doctrine, was outdated and caused undue worry for parents."

The more I learned about purgatory, the more I realized that I could not be satisfied with a merely descriptive treatment of it in this book. So far, I had tried to retain a measured distance from the disputes I described. But on the issue of purgatory I began to think that I had to close this chapter with a clear suggestion that it is time to allow purgatory, which has been a contentious and harmful doctrine, to fade into memory. But I also realized I had to make sure that this was not just my Protestant bias intruding. I finally decided, however, that although this prejudice might have entered in, there were other reasons to suggest the shelving of purgatory. Surveys of Catholic lay people indicate that, among all the teachings of their church, they are most uncomfortable with purgatory. An essential component of Catholic theology has been that the "consent of the faithful" (*consensus fidelium*) should be taken into serious consideration in the formulation and clarification of doctrine. I do not believe that such a consensus among the faithful exists today for purgatory.

Eventually, I decided to think about purgatory with the same approach I have employed with other religious configurations. It is the "answering theology" method I learned from Paul Tillich, and it is similar to the theological style of Pope Francis. One starts by asking, what is the existential question to which this doctrine is supposed to respond? Then one asks how that question expresses itself today, what Tillich called a "hermeneutic of culture." Finally, one tries to reformulate both the question and the answer in the idiom of current life. Pope Francis advocates what he calls a "theology of the people," suggesting that even beneath the crudest of spiritual practices there lies a genuine religious concern that must be addressed. But how can this approach be applied to purgatory? There are two existential concerns to which the idea of purgatory, its antecedents, and its parallels in other faiths seek to respond.

The first concern is what might be called the "threshold syndrome." There is a universal human need or desire for a transitional area between the outside and the inside, which is most clearly evident in architecture. There are few structures that one enters directly from outside without passing through a foyer, hallway, porch, or even a "mud room." Even a simple igloo made of snow and ice has a short tunnel one crawls through before standing up within. There is a custom in Russia that one does not shake hands with a guest in the threshold, but only after he or she has come inside. People speak of their desire to "get to know" someone before becoming more intimate. Institutions have training periods and sports include times for warm-ups. Human beings seem to need time and space, however short, to make transitions. They require what psychologists call a "liminal" phase. Perhaps the gap between this world and the next or the other world is wide enough that, for millennia, people have thought that an interim level was needed. That need is still alive today in our so-called secular age. When Paul Tillich was on his deathbed in a Chicago hospital, his wife told me later that he was reading *The Tibetan Book of the Dead,* which is seen by many Buddhists as a kind of guide book for souls passing from this life either to another life or to nirvana. A few years ago, a novel entitled *Lincoln in the Bardo* by George Saunders won a large readership in America. In Tibetan Buddhism, the bardo is the state of existence immediately after death but before an individual is reincarnated. In Catholic Christianity, purgatory has often been thought of as just such an in-between stage. It is neither heaven nor earth but a way station between the two realms.

The main problem with the traditional idea of purgatory is that it was seen not just as an interim stop but as a place or condition of suffering, symbolized by flames that both purify and cause pain. I am sure my grandfather knew little or nothing about either expiation or purification; but the impression he had was that purgatory was an awful place, and he shrank at the thought of his wife being there no matter how fervently his Catholic neighbors were praying to get her out. But the underlying question is whether subjecting the dead to such torment is necessary to prepare them for their entrance into the divine presence. Both Catholic and Protestant theologies teach that Christ is the "suffering servant" who takes our pain upon himself and "bears our sorrows and iniquities." Life on earth, even for the most fortunate, is suffused with sickness, loss, and grief, full of suffering, a "vale of sorrows." Why would a gracious and merciful God find it necessary to load on more after death?

What about "expiation," the deeply held feeling that we need to repay or make up for the harm and hurt we have done to other people? The Twelve Steps of Alcoholics Anonymous recognizes this necessity. It is called "making amends." The point is that we make amends with someone not just to restore a damaged relationship with them but to heal ourselves. This process never ends because we never cease to hurt other people in large and small ways, often inadvertently, and this goes on for as long as we live. But what happens if we die before we have finished making amends? The result is that the damaged relationship is still not repaired, and a part of me is still not healed. Purgatory, according to some theories, provides us with the opportunity to complete the process, to mend the relationship and complete the healing.

In theory this sounds sensible, but the concept has grave flaws. The main defect is that making amends for pain we have caused to other people requires that we do it with those other people. But as we are "in purgatory," those other people are probably not there with us. For anyone with a sensitive conscience, this is not easy to accept. There have been people in my life to whom I wish I could have made amends but who died before I did. Films and novels are replete with accounts of deathbed attempts at reconciliation. And when someone we know dies we often regret that we did not see them more often before it was too late. These are feelings we all have at one time or another. But does purgatory respond effectively to them?

Again, in its traditional form, I think it does not. We suffer its torments alone, not in company. Maybe a better remedy for the nagging sense of incompleteness we feel when we have not rectified a relationship in time is to learn from it not to postpone the opportunities we still have with other people. While that person is still alive, it is never too late. A few years ago, a person I had almost forgotten wrote me a letter to "make amends" for something he had done that he thought had hurt me, even though I had by then no memory of it.

All this suggests to me that, in the notion of purgatory, we have projected onto another level what we should be doing here and now. In a famous saying, Jesus told his disciples that if they were on the way to the temple to make a sacrifice but remembered someone they had offended, they should first reconcile with that person, only then proceed to the temple to make the sacrifice.

It need not be officially abolished the way Pope Benedict dealt with limbo. Maybe it could be placed in a back room, like the suggestion I made for the "Souls in Purgatory" in the North End. There are commanding reasons for such a move. As we have seen, there is considerable evidence that the idea may not figure in Catholic practice with anything near the prominence it once did.

Purgatory, as we have said, has a long and conflictual history. Does it have a future? In this chapter I have been highly critical of the way the doctrine has been formulated and applied in Christianity. But simply to eliminate it, even if that were possible, would still leave the existential question it seeks to answer unaddressed. But how can that be done? I am aware from my study of the history of religions that doctrines and rituals cannot be simply invented. They begin gradually in the life of a people, develop, and are then formulated and routinized. Prayer and practice precede theology. What we need is what Tillich called a "hermeneutic of culture," a search for what is already present in our lives, albeit often unrecognized as "religious," but that responds to the same questions.

The next step is based on the core thesis of this book: that Jesus continuously urged his listeners to stop searching for God above and beyond and to look and listen to what was going on among them. The displacement of Jesus's message of the here-and-coming reigning of God by the endeavor to "get to heaven" is a fundamental distortion that has affected nearly every dimension of Christianity. This distortion is particularly evident in the idea of purgatory. But when we think of the questions that gave rise to purgatory in the light of Jesus's message, a viable reformulation comes into view. Regarding the present status of the dead, as we have seen, Jesus does not respond to questions motivated by curiosity. Rather, he talks about a new creation, the redemption of the whole cosmos and all of history, a transformation that includes the fate of individuals but is vastly more encompassing. By contrast, both going-to-heaven and purgatory amount to a radical diminution of the immense scope of the biblical promise.

What about purgatory as preparation for life in the full presence of God? Here it should be remembered that the call to "prepare" is integral to Jesus's proclamation. "Prepare ye the way of the Lord." His preparation had two facets that can be encapsulated as "repent and follow me." His point, however, was not to admonish his hearers to prepare for a journey they were going to make, but to prepare for the new era that was dawning in their midst. In his parables he constantly warns those who have not made preparation: they have not brought enough oil for their lamps or they have thoughtlessly built their house on sand, or they have just not paid attention to the signs of the times. In other words, this life and this world, not another one, are the arena in which we are told to "get ready." It is here that God's reigning is happening and will one day appear in its fullness "in your midst."

The other part of preparation that purgatory was thought to speak to is cleansing, or purification. This might once have been an issue on which Catholics and Protestants saw things so differently that no reconciliation, and therefore no rethinking of purgatory, seemed possible. But in recent years the gap has been reduced as Catholic theologians have increasingly embraced what was once a perspective identified as Protestant. The emerging ecumenical consensus is: (1) That the redemption of human beings is not something we earn, but it is an expression of God's grace and mercy. When, after Vatican II, Catholics and Lutherans met in a series of conferences, they finally adjourned and issued a document stating that on the idea of grace, they had found no disagreement. (2) That Christ's sacrifice is an act both of forgiveness and of purification. Countless prayers and hymns speak of the blood of Christ both as making payment for sins but also as cleansing ("washing away") sin. One hymnbook I consulted listed thirty-one titles that referred to the blood of Christ. These references are often linked to its "all-sufficiency," which means that nothing else is needed, an implicit critique of purgatory.

In addition to a growing consensus about grace, Catholic and Protestant theologies have also moved closer in their understanding of sin, and this could have considerable significance for the doctrine of purgatory. For centuries both traditions have conceived of sin both as original sin and as sins (plural), discrete thoughts or deeds enacted by a person partly but not entirely as the result of original sin. There was in both communities something close to a numerical view of sin(s). They could be added up, and after the action of grace, they could be subtracted, or weighed in a balance against one's good deeds. The image of an angel holding a scale just outside the gates of heaven became a familiar one.

In more recent theologies, but with roots in both Reformation and Thomist thought, theologies shifted their focus away from good and bad deeds to a reinterpreted understanding of a deformation of the self that stems from a separation from God and from one's fellow human beings. This is often referred to as "alienation," and it was conceptually closer to the older idea of original sin than the concept of sin as distinct actions or thoughts. Among Protestants, Reinhold Niebuhr in America and Karl Barth in Europe advocated this interpretation. But again, Catholic theologians like Bernard Lonergan began thinking along the same lines.

A convergence of these different theologies of sin and grace is slowly appearing, and I welcome it. In effect it renders the long-standing and misplaced argument about grace through faith versus grace plus works moot, an archaic leftover of previous debates. But what does this theological détente mean for the "purgation" for cleansing and forgiveness that were said to be the purpose of purgatory? As far as I know, no official Catholic statement has been issued on this question.

Where does that leave us? In her *Treatise on Purgatory*, St. Catherine of Genoa (1447–1510) writes that in purgatory all the cleansing and purification is still entirely the work of God's grace. She even says that the reason the souls in purgatory can bear up in the midst of the suffering they experience is that they realize it is an expression of divine grace. But frankly, I do not find this suggestion persuasive. The classical understanding of Christ's atoning death on the cross is that it includes both forgiveness and cleansing. Here I think that Calvin, in the excerpt quoted above, was right. To suggest that after death people must endure even more painful expiation is to belittle the fullness ("sufficiency") of Christ's sacrifice. I do not think, however, that this need be a "Protestant" point of view. A favorite hymn when I was younger was "Rock of Ages," written by an Irishman named Augustus Montague Toplady (1740–1778), a disciple of John Wesley, the founder of Methodism. But twice now when I have attended Catholic churches the congregations have sung it:

*Rock of ages, cleft for me*
*Let me hide myself in Thee.*
*Let the water and the blood.*
*That from thy wounded side did flow*
*Be of sin the double cure*
*Saved from wrath*
*And make me pure.*

But does the fact that Catholics and Protestants now sing some of the same hymn lyrics make any difference? I think it does. I am convinced that people learn more theology from hymns than they do from sermons. Also, hymns often assume the form of prayers, as does "Rock of Ages," so this is a further example of "as we pray, so we believe."

I do not intend to conclude this chapter with the suggestion of a doctrinal replacement of purgatory. That would be both pretentious and useless. I wish only to observe that the idea of purgatory, as formulated and as presently practiced, may once have served its purpose (although it never did for me or for my grandfather). But it has been unnecessarily divisive, and now seems not to command widespread support even among "the faithful," and none among other Christians. It may be reaching the end of its run. But if conjuring an alternative is neither possible nor desirable, what can we do? We can wait for the Spirit, for the new to appear, and in the meantime try to understand and be patient with those who still believe in purgatory, those who pray for the souls that suffer in it, those who quietly disbelieve it, and those who rail against it. Like all of us, these all now see only through a glass darkly. In the final canto of Dante's *Purgatorio*, the poet and his companion, Beatrice, are ready to leave it behind. But before they do, Beatrice says to Dante, *"Brother, it is my wish that you from now on free yourself from fear and shame, and cease to speak like someone in a dream."*

# 11

# *Angels in Heaven and Elsewhere*

*Therefore with Angels, and Archangels, and with all the company of heaven, we laud and magnify thy glorious Name; evermore praising thee, and saying: Holy, holy, holy, Lord God of hosts, heaven and earth are full of thy glory: Glory be to thee, O Lord most High. Amen.* (Eucharistic Prayer, *Book of Common Prayer*)

*And he shall send his angels with a great sound of a trumpet, and they shall gather together his elect from the four winds, from one end of heaven to the other.* (Matthew 24:31 KJV)

*Innocence, once lost, can never be regained; Darkness, once gazed upon, can never be lost.* (John Milton, *Paradise Lost*)

What would heaven be without angels? From before the Bible up to the cartoons in the latest *New Yorker*, angels continue to be recognized by everyone. In cartoons we recognize them because they are perched on clouds, clothed in white robes, wear haloes, and often play on small harps. But angels, or at least replicas of them, are not confined to paradise. Just look. They can be seen everywhere. One of America's biggest cities is named for "Mary, Queen of the Angels" but is better known by its shortened appellation, "Los Angeles." All around the country there are churches named "St. Michael and All Angels." The angel Moroni (not Gabriel), a long trumpet pressed to his lips, stands atop almost all Mormon temples. A Catholic website announces that "All the Angels Are at Your Service." But, other than sing and strum, what do angels do?

They are most often messengers from God or agents accomplishing his purposes. They populate the whole Bible. In the first book, Genesis, an angel with a flaming sword guards the gate of Eden, barring the return of our first parents following their exile. In the last book, Revelation, myriads of angels, along with the "living creatures" and elders, are too many to count. As the text says, *"Then I looked, and I heard the voice of many angels surrounding the throne and the living creatures and the elders; they numbered myriads of myriads and thousands of thousands"* (Revelation 5:11).

In between these two biblical bookends, angels make regular appearances. Among many other instances, an angel speaks to Hagar in the desert. An angel appears to Abraham and to Moses. Later an angel speaks to the unwilling prophet Balaam, and to Manoah and Gideon, among others. In the Book of Zechariah (1:12) an angel pleads to God to have mercy on Jerusalem and the other cities of Judah.

In the New Testament angels show up eighteen times, first to Zechariah (Luke 1:11–29), the father of John the Baptist. Then they reappear to reassure Joseph (Matthew 1 and 2) after his discovery that Mary, his betrothed, is "with child"; then to Jesus's mother, Mary (Luke 1:26), and later to the shepherds in the fields (Luke 2). Jesus encounters angels twice (Matthew 2 and Luke 22). An angel speaks to the women at the tomb (Mary Magdalene, the other Mary, Salome, and other women; Matthew 28:1–7; Mark 16:1–7; Luke 24:1–7, 23; John 20:11–13). Angels materialize in person or in dreams or visions. They serve as God's messengers. But they do not discriminate. They appear to good people, like Peter and Mary, and to bad people, like Herod, with good news and bad news. It is hard to imagine the Bible without angels.

After the period in which the Bible was being written and edited, a series of sometimes acrimonious debates broke out among Christians about angels. A special division of theology appeared called "angelology." The most rancorous of these disputes began in the fourth century, soon after the Nicene Creed had been formulated (331). The creed included words that state only that "we believe in the Holy Spirit" but does not offer any description of that Spirit. Soon there were theologians who taught that the Holy Spirit was more like an angel than like God or Christ. Maybe the Holy Spirit was the head of the angelic host, but—like the angels—a created being, not an uncreated one. Like the angels, the Holy Spirit "participated" in the divine, but was not itself (or herself or himself) divine.

This formulation, however, was totally unacceptable to those Christians who held to the idea of a trinitarian God. The theologian who jumped in to combat what he (and others) saw as a serious error was Athanasius (293–373). He summoned references from the Bible and from earlier Christian writers to make a case that since the angels were created entities, and all such entities are in danger of "falling," the Holy Spirit was not either one of the angels or even the chief. The Spirit was, he insisted, fully divine, and should be worshiped along with the Father and the Son. It was not until 451, however, that the Council of Chalcedon spelled out the true nature of the Holy Spirit as one of the co-equal members of the Trinity. Athanasius had won the debate, but his solution created more problems for the angels. This centered on the role of the angels in human governance.

For several centuries, based on biblical accounts, Christians believed that angels, along with "powers and principalities," played a decisive role in the ruling of nations and empires.

(See, among others, Colossians 1:16: "*For by him all things were created, both in the heavens and on earth, visible and invisible, whether thrones or dominions or rulers or authorities—all things have been created through him and for him.*")

The Bible also reported that the angels are organized into hosts, hierarchies of angels, archangels, cherubim, and seraphim. But the anxiety of the theologians was whether these hierarchies were "stable." Scripture stated that some of the angels had once "fallen" and were now serving Satan. Could the same thing happen again? This possibility was vexing because any shakiness in the angelic hierarchies could have damaging repercussions for political life in this world. Can we understand today what they were worried about?

I think we can. The powers, authorities, and principalities (and angels) were the nonempirical entities on which political institutions were based. Over the centuries, these bases, which once had a quasi-personal (angelic) profile, evolved into the equally nonempirical but also equally foundational concepts on which modern societies arose. Two closely related examples of these nonempirical concepts are the "creator," or "nature's God," to whom the authors of the American Declaration of Independence attributed "certain inalienable rights," which they believed that governments were supposed to defend. The other is the "natural law," from which human laws were derived. Historians generally agree that the idea of the natural law is derived from that of divine providence, which in turn is based on what Aquinas called the "eternal law," or—in more explicit theological language—"the will of God." It is held in this theory that the natural law is implanted by God in all rational beings, giving them the capacity to distinguish between good and evil. It is true that in more recent years some political thinkers have argued that such metaphysical categories are no longer necessary, and that, when they are wrongly applied, they can undergird tyranny. The defenders of these categories, on the other hand, declare that without them societies could descend into anarchy.

The argument is still going on, but it is worth mentioning that over the huge doors of Langdon Hall, the library of the Harvard Law School, stand carved the following words: *Non sub Homine sed sub Deo et Lege* ("not under man but under God and the law"). The fact that this discussion still goes on, albeit using some different terms, enables us to grasp the significance of the ancient concepts we have been reviewing here, and why they were so important to those who debated them. Angels *were* important. People may or may not "believe in angels" today, but the question of whether we can survive without what angels once did is still unresolved. And this was the core of the dilemma about the "stability" of the angelic hosts.

It was a contentious question. Evagrius of Pontus (345–390) argued that since angels were not divine, and since some had "fallen" before, they could fall again, with the dire consequences that entailed. But Augustine of Hippo took the other position. Angels were not divine, he agreed, but they "participated" in the divine life of God. Consequently, their hierarchies were solid, and the earthly systems they ruled over were secure. Some scholars have suggested that since Augustine, the bishop of Hippo, depended on the stability of the Roman Empire, he might not have been entirely neutral in the matter. But in any case, he seems to have won the argument.

In the medieval period, Thomas Aquinas (1224–1274), the leading theologian of the era, picked up the discussion about angels, but he did little more than systemize the received tradition. For example, he laboriously follows the precedent of Augustine and Gregory that angels neither have nor assume bodies in the ordinary sense, but they do have spiritual bodies. As Thomas puts it: *"Further, angels do not assume bodies from the earth or water, or they could not suddenly disappear; nor again from fire, otherwise they would burn whatever things they touched; nor again from air, because air is without shape or color. Therefore the angels do not assume bodies" (Summa theologica I).*

But Thomas would later write of angels that their spiritual bodies enable them to move about effortlessly, something the souls of the blessed in heaven would also be able to do. He further surmised that since animals do not have souls, there were neither plants nor beasts in heaven, which was reserved for the angels and the souls of the (human) blessed. This dictum must be disappointing news for those who hope to be reunited to their pet cats or collies in the hereafter. (But, not to worry, Thomas did not have the last word on this question.)

After Aquinas, the history of angelology becomes more interesting both for angels and for animals. There are times in religious history when artists and poets run ahead of formal theology in the case of "angelology" and depictions of heaven. This is what happened as the medieval age faded and the Renaissance began. After Thomas had penned his volumes, visual artists went to work elaborating a different and much richer vision, and it was an evolving visualization. The most promising place to look for these visualizations is in depictions of the Last Judgment. My favorite is Fra Angelico's version, painted two hundred years after Aquinas, in 1451. It stands out for several reasons. First, the artist is not content with showing only the usual scene of the throne and the torments of hell. He devotes half of the painting to illustrating the pleasures of the blessed in paradise, where we see angels warmly welcoming newcomers like skilled hosts and hostesses to what appears to be a party in full tilt. The new arrivals are invited into a dance, and they all accept.

Most interestingly, however, we watch a dancing couple in the lower part of the frivolity. It consists of an angel, clearly a female, dancing with a monk. This constitutes a radical break with the received orthodox tradition. It violates the doctrine that angels have no gender. But it also allows a monk, who in life has been forbidden contact with the opposite sex, not only to enjoy that physical touch but to move and prance in a most unmonk-like manner. A life of voluntary sensual deprivation is compensated for: *Que la fête commence!*

Also, before Fra Angelico, artists generally adhered to the idea of heaven as a city, the New Jerusalem. But on this canvass, Fra Angelica lays out a sumptuous garden full of flowering bushes. But he has not forgotten the urban tradition. Just above the garden stands a walled city with its gates open. The angels and human souls are disporting themselves on a broad lawn, and they seem not at all concerned that they are not inside the city. The urban and the rural have been reconciled. Further, in Fra Angelico's paradise, there appears to be no privilege. There are no hierarchies. People of all types mix freely and converse with those who have preceded them. It is an open and democratic place. "Y'all come." One recent scholar even called it "communistic." As I have written before, heaven here performs a normative function. Look, it says, this is heaven, and this is what cities *ought* to be like.

After Fra Angelico, artists widened the tendency to transfer the joys of earth to heaven. The faces of the saints and angels smiled more, and the artists added animals (previously excluded by Aquinas), beginning with the rabbits, to the celestial greenery. This humanistic trend spread from artists to poets and mystics, some of whom envisioned the lively presence of romantic physical intimacy in the next life. In any case, the angels seemed safe and not worried about their "stability," at least for a time. But what standing do they have today in either the ordinary world or even in the religious sphere?

At first glance they appear to be quite secure. Angels don't just sing at Christmastime. For most Americans, they're a year-round presence. Recently an Associated Press poll showed that 77 percent of American adults say they believe angels are real.

Belief is primarily tied to religion, with 88 percent of Christians in general, 95 percent of Evangelical Christians, and 94 percent of those who attend weekly religious services of any sort saying they believe in angels. But belief in angels is surprisingly widespread even among the less religious. A majority of non-Christians think angels exist, as do more than four in ten of those who never attend religious services. Have at least some angels slipped out of the confines of the religious sphere? Previous polling has found the public a bit more likely to believe in God, but far less likely to believe in other other-worldly beings. Ninety-two percent of adults told Gallup pollsters they believed in God, but just 34 percent in an AP-Ipsos poll in 2007 said they believed in ghosts or UFOs. But what do these opinion surveys tell us?

Not very much. The real question is not about "belief," which is a cognitive, transient, and often individualistic category. Someone can tell an interviewer that, yes, they think angels are real, then not think of the subject again. Meanwhile, discussions about angels have almost completely disappeared from serious theological discourse. In July 2017, a theologian from Eden Seminary named Adam Ployd published an article in the *Harvard Theological Review* (vol. 110, no. 3) lamenting the paucity of attention now given to angels. Ployd pointed out correctly, and we have seen in this chapter, that in the early centuries of Christian thought, extending into the medieval period, the study of angels ("angelology") was a significant section in the theological discipline. This interest was not restricted to Christian writers. Jewish thinkers addressed themselves to the topic as well. Unlike them, however, the Christians had to wrestle with a particular problem. For them, since they wanted to avoid any threat to monotheism, their main concern was to clarify the nature of these angelic beings who were not mortal but not divine, who had some human qualities but were not human either. They also needed to make sure that the Holy Spirit, which they considered one of the three persons of the Trinity, was not an angel. After endless debates, church officials finally decreed that the angels were, like humans, created beings. Thus, any whiff of polytheism was avoided, or so they hoped. After the medieval period the study of angels virtually disappeared from the theological agenda. In my many years in seminary and graduate school, I do not remember any mention of angels.

In previous parts of this book I have tried to suggest what might be the functional equivalents today of the doctrines and practices of previous ages. In the previous pages of this chapter I have suggested the historical and religious link between the angels and principalities on the one hand and, on the other, more recent ideas about the transcendent grounding of terrestrial political systems. But what about the role of angels as messengers? The focal question is: do there exist today parallels to the go-betweens linking everyday reality to some other dimension, including the domain of the dead? But it might be asked, does anyone believe in any such "other dimension," because without it, there would be nothing for the go-betweens to do?

The answer to this is yes; many people do believe in another dimension. Casey Cep reports that roughly two-thirds of Americans say that they have communicated with someone who is dead, and they spend more than two billion dollars a year on psychic services (Casey Cep, "Kindred Spirits," *New Yorker*, May 31, 2021). And evidence suggests that these purchasers are not just the uneducated. Seances also attract the well-to-do and those with advanced degrees. I live in a city, Cambridge, Massachusetts, which is said to have one of the most educated populations of any municipality in America. But just two blocks from my home, located between a post office and an upscale Thai restaurant, stands a shop that offers psychic readings. Also, there are in America one hundred "Spiritualist" churches that hold to the possibility of communicating with the dead. (There are three hundred in the United Kingdom.) Cep writes that there is currently a boom in Spiritualism, and the number of those who practice it is surging. Where, if anywhere, are the angels?

We have noted above that the Greek word for angel means "messenger." Angels are envoys to human beings from God, and occasionally to God from human beings. They link our world to another one. As the Olympian pantheon faded and the Christian era began, the angels took over the responsibility once held by Hermes, who is often pictured with wings on his feet. Now angels also had wings, but mounted on their backs, near their shoulder blades.

But as charming and picturesque as it is to see angels on these occasions, when it comes to the real thing, angels as couriers between heaven and earth? Well no, that was then, and this is now; and since there is no such "other dimension" and the present visible, tangible world is all there is, we have no need for Hermes or for angels. Not only have the angels themselves vanished, but the jobs they once did, like those of blacksmiths, have vanished as well. No such messengers need apply.

This sounds at first like a straightforward and sensible point of view, and many thoughtful people hold it as the only outlook that coheres with modern science. But when we look at what is going on in our culture today, a world totally devoid of any non-empirical qualities leaves a lot of our experience out. Why do so many people consult the horoscope columns that appear every day in respectable newspapers? Why do a significant majority tell pollsters that they do pray, if not regularly, then "sometimes"? Why do public officials, including the president of the United States, take their oath of office in a ceremony that almost always includes a prayer? Why do so many who are not regular churchgoers want to have a religious ceremony of some kind when they marry? Why did Albert Einstein, perhaps the most admired scientist of the twentieth century, write, in response to the question of a prominent rabbi, that he considered himself to be "a religious person"? And why did Robert Oppenheimer, the other most respected scientist of that century, quote a verse from the *Bhagavad Gita* when he witnessed the first atomic explosion at Alamogordo on July 16, 1945? That moment shook him. It was soon after this that he wrote, "the physicists have now known sin." He became such a vociferous opponent of nuclear weapons that he tried to dissuade young physicists from working on them and was deprived of his security clearance, which pushed him into a deep depression. Are some of the things that happen to us so powerful that they open a crack in our otherwise snugly empirical composure?

The psychologist Abraham Maslow asserted that to reach full human maturation, we need to have certain moments that, however transient, carry us beyond our normal lives, enabling us to touch on aspects of life that we normally do not notice. He called these "peak experiences," and he came to believe that they were a key to understanding religion. In his research, he interviewed hundreds of people who spoke of having had such experiences, some in religious settings, some not.

I do not believe that this theory explains all "religious experiences," some of which, as Dorothy Day often wrote, occur to us in our ordinary, sometimes boring daily routine. But I do think Maslow was on to something. It can be during such peak experiences that we catch a passing glimpse of a realm of our inner or outer world we had not noticed before. Various individuals describe what they have glimpsed in different ways, but all agree that it is real.

The question of other dimensions of reality and communicating with them is one that will not go away. And sometimes it becomes controversial. A few years ago, a dispute erupted at Harvard about a colleague and close friend named John Mack. At the time John was an esteemed member of the Medical School faculty and chairman of its psychiatry department. John had once served as a medic in the Air Force and spent a few years in Japan, which sparked his interest in the comparative study of religious cultures. He and I had been friends before the controversy blew up. His specialty was adolescent psychology, and he had considerable success in helping young people plagued by drug problems or who were suicide prone. He was also fascinated by the psychology of religion but never taught it. Since my concentration was in contemporary Christian theology and world religions, when I asked him why he did not teach it, he told me that he found the current methods used by scientific psychology such blunt instruments that they were totally inadequate for understanding religion, and I agreed with him.

Throughout his career John's persistent fascination was with how a person's worldview influences their attitudes toward other people and themselves. It was about then that John published a biography of "Lawrence of Arabia," which he titled *The Prince of Our Darkness*, for which he won a Pulitzer Prize. Not only a masterful recounting of the life of a complex man, the book also revealed John's focus on the connection between worldview and life attitude. In the late 1990s John began to take an interest in the people who came to public attention when they reported having had contact with aliens from another planet or another realm of reality. There were numerous press reports. Some told interviewers they had been kidnapped by these galactic visitors, and traveled with them to extraterrestrial destinations before being brought back home.

To many people, these accounts sounded like hallucinatory babbling or bare-faced publicity seeking and were mostly dismissed as not worthy of further attention. But John looked at them in a different light. Having helped scores of young people whose symptoms often included hallucinations, John approached these abductees in the same way. He started by listening to them carefully and respectfully, as he had the young people he had treated so successfully. It was his way of uncovering what was going on underneath. Many of them recovered, and they all spoke with appreciation of John as the one person they had met during their illness who treated them with dignity and not "like crazy people." Now, with the space travelers, John wanted to use the same approach.

During the next years, John interviewed some two hundred men and women who told him their stories of meetings with aliens or of sometimes being whisked away, always temporarily, in a spacecraft. Their accounts differed in many respects, but all carried on a similar theme: the aliens were unfailingly friendly. They had said that we were ruining our planet by destroying trees, polluting the water, and filling the air with carbon waste. They warned that we urgently needed to change our ways or face extinction, and these messages arrived long before our current concern for planetary survival.

Contrary to most popular media images of aliens as destructive invaders, the people John worked with told him they had never been harmed or threatened by their hosts. When John asked them what they had learned from such extraordinary experiences, what was their takeaway, they again recurred to a common theme (even though they had not known each other before). In one way or another they all said that their adventures had made them "more spiritual" and more interested in expanding (not abolishing) the modern scientific worldview so that it would be more "eco-friendly" and would make room for "visionary episodes" instead of simply dismissing them as abnormal.

As a theologian I found John's summaries of what these

"abductees" said not crazy at all but welcome and urgent, although I harbored my doubts about the sources of the messages. Among other things, I could not help noticing how much of what they said mirrored John's own outlook.

As his interviews and treatment (the two were never completely separated) of the returnees continued, I sensed a change in the way John talked about them. Others of his friends did, too. True, he had done his best to "get inside their heads" and become familiar with the worldviews of his patient-interviewees. Most of us agreed that this was a promising approach, one that had seemed to work well for him in the past. But, was there a difference in how he was interpreting their alien narratives now? Some of his colleagues and friends thought he had slipped over the line between taking them seriously and taking them literally. As one friend put it, had John gotten caught in the psychiatric equivalent of "going native," as anthropologists are said to do?

I also found that I was becoming uncertain about what John was saying, but when I talked with him about it, he was always reassuring. He said, not to worry. He knew perfectly well the difference between "seriously" and "literally." He then sometimes changed the subject and asked me, as a student of world religions, about civilizations, past and present, where "visionary experiences" were welcomed and encouraged and not summarily shelved as symptoms of a mental disorder. I told him that of course there were. I mentioned a Native American society in which, when someone reports a vision to one of the elders, they go to great lengths to "stage" what the person had seen in order to discover its meaning, and to make it a part of the whole group's experience. Still, John often raised the same question with me, and asked for more examples.

Our conversations often took place over coffee or a beer. As they did, although I was sometimes puzzled and skeptical, I never doubted John's integrity as a scholar. But not everyone at the university felt as I did. Eventually complaints about him poured in from other professors, alumni, and the public, some demanding he be removed from his position. These sentiments reached the dean of the Medical School, Daniel Tostesen, who delayed acting but appointed a committee of Medical School faculty, his "peers" as the dean phrased it, and began what was to become a fourteen-month-long investigation. It was during that time that John invited me for lunch at a restaurant in the Porter Square area, near my home.

I remember the luncheon well. We met during the winter holiday season, and the restaurant's sound system was playing Christmas carols. As we ate our grilled-cheese sandwiches and sipped beers, John asked me if I would be willing to testify before the faculty committee on his behalf. I told him I would be happy to do so, but I added that, although I could certify his integrity and general intellectual acuity, I could say nothing about psychiatry since I knew nothing about the field. If he approved, I added, I might also say something about his groundbreaking thinking on the expansion of science.

John nodded and thanked me but seemed a little disappointed. Just then one of my favorite Christmas carols started to play, "Angels from the Realms of Glory." Perhaps to lighten the tone of what had been a quite serious conversation, I smiled and said, "See, John, in my field we also have visitors from another realm of reality, and they sometimes bring us important messages."

John was not pleased. In a tone of voice that I had not previously heard from him, he said, "Harvey, the work I am doing has nothing to do with religion. This is science!" I was somewhat taken aback. I thought of the many times he had voiced an interest in religion, or at least "spirituality," and his complaints about the narrowness of our current science, but I decided this was not the moment to pursue that topic. Shortly thereafter, John, despite my protestation, picked up the check; we put our coats back on, and stepped out into the snow.

John never did ask me to testify. I wondered why at first, but then it came to me that my offhand quip about angels had worried him about what I might say to the tough-minded faculty committee that could incline to be more suspicious of him. In any case, after the long investigation, the dean issued a report stating that, since Dr. Mack had committed no professional offense, he was now again a faculty member in good standing. John had been completely exonerated. But what a price he had paid!

I often saw John after that, but our relationship was not as close as it once had been, and I was sorry. Years before, I had written my PhD dissertation at Harvard on the interaction between religion and technology. Although I thought I had left that subject behind, after my chats with John I had been musing about it again. I continued to be attracted by the idea of "expanding" science. Now and then I hoped I could pick up the threads of my conversations with John. But then, in September 2004, John flew to London to give a lecture at a gathering of people interested in T. E. Lawrence. After one of the sessions, John, who as an American was used to traffic driving on the right, stepped out into a busy street, was struck by a speeding truck, and died instantly.

John's memorial service took place in Harvard Memorial Church in Harvard Yard. Several colleagues and friends offered eloquent tributes, but the one I remember best came from a young woman, an "abductee," who had been one of John's patients/subjects. In a voice that fell on a quiet and attentive congregation, she spoke of how John had "given me back my life." She said that John had seen her neither as a subject to investigate nor as a patient to be cured, but he had listened and identified with her. "Thank you, John," she said in conclusion, and holding back tears, she left the pulpit.

As I walked out and down the broad steps of the church suddenly some words from *Hamlet* jumped into my mind:

*Now cracks a noble heart. Goodnight, sweet prince;*
*And flights of angels sing thee to thy rest.*

I did not think John, given his suspicion of talking about angels, would want this read at his funeral, but, knowing him, I also knew that he would not disapprove of my recalling them. Then I remembered that these were the words of Hamlet's friend, Horatio, who utters them with Hamlet's dead body lying on the stage along with the bodies of other characters who plotted against him. Hamlet had been vindicated, but too late for him to enjoy it. I realized how much I would miss John, and I felt angry that his vindication had not come sooner. There was so much more that we still needed to talk about.

# 12

# *American Heavens*

*Lord, while for all mankind we pray,*
*Of every clime and coast,*
*O hear us for our native land—*
*The land we love the most.*
*O guard our shore from every foe,*
*While peace our borders bless,*
*With prosperous times our cities crown,*
*Our fields with plenteousness.* (John Reynell Wreford,
    *The Church Hymn Book* [1876])

*Can you imagine anything more idiotic than the Christian*
*idea of heaven? What kind of deity is it that would be capa-*
*ble of creating angels and men to sing his praises day and*
*night to all eternity?* (Alfred North Whitehead)

Alfred North Whitehead is usually recognized as America's greatest philosopher. But Americans do not seem to have paid much attention to his cryptic dismissal of heaven. According to a recent Pew Research poll, 72 percent of Americans say they believe in heaven, while 58 percent believe in hell. Notwithstanding Whitehead's remark, and those of many other commentators, Americans persist in talking and thinking about heaven, with or without choirs of angels. They have re-interpreted it, argued about it, discarded it, composed songs about it, and many have continued to "believe in it," though in a thousand different ways and usually not in the images Whitehead refers to.

To present a complete catalog of this universe of celestial visualizations would be well beyond the scope of this chapter. It would have to begin with the views of the afterlife nourished by dozens of indigenous nations before the arrival of Europeans, but also reflect on the spiritual rebellion called the "Ghost Dance," which began in 1869, sparked by a vision of an elder of the Paiute people, and was soon enlarged by several other native nations. Space will not allow us to describe the Ghost Dance here, but it should be noted that it reveals something important about Native peoples: their dead ancestors were not far away or inaccessible. They could and did return and join the living to fight back against the takeover of their lands.

To be comprehensive, the chapter would have to encompass a hodgepodge of short-lived sects and older movements, some of which, however, left permanent marks. To be balanced, the chapter should also introduce ideas that run counter to those presented elsewhere in this book. But there are so many, I will be able to select only a few.

One of these other voices is that of a group many Americans have met when its representatives rang their doorbells. The Jehovah's Witnesses stand out in part because, unlike many other Christians, they do not look forward to "going to heaven." They hold that since Jehovah-God and Jesus already established their kingdom in 1914, and although it has not yet become visible on earth, it soon will. Meanwhile, a limited number of Witnesses, which they call the "little flock," 144,000 to be exact (a figure extrapolated from biblical texts), will ascend to heaven or are already there. The rest of us will remain on an earth that will be restored to its original paradisiacal condition, a pristine new Garden of Eden where the lion will lie down with the lamb and wars will cease. Therefore, what Witnesses anticipate is not leaving this world but continuing to live here in God's presence eternally. There is therefore little place for a conventional "heaven" in Witness theology. Although this might seem to disqualify this group from a book like this one, when we become familiar with the other "in-your-midst" heavens that have come and gone in Christian history, we can understand the Witnesses as one of them, a somewhat radical variety of a wider genre.

Nevertheless, I hesitated before devoting any attention to the Witnesses partly because when I mentioned them to friends who asked me about how my book was going, they usually grimaced. Their experience of the group was based on being annoyed by the doorbell ringers with their smiling faces and free copies of *The Watchtower.* I could understand their uneasiness, but I also had another, more favorable memory that stuck in my mind. When I was in fifth grade, a "new girl" joined our class in the Malvern Public School. The teacher introduced her as "Doris." She was attractive and plainly dressed. At the beginning of that first day with us, the whole class stood up, as we did every day, placed our right hands over our hearts, faced the American flag, and repeated in unison the Pledge of Allegiance. But Doris did not stand. She remained sitting with her head slightly bowed.

After a few minutes, our teacher approached and quietly said, "Doris, you should stand up now and join us as we pledge allegiance to our flag."

"I am sorry," Doris said in a soft tone, "but I can't do that. I am a Witness of Jehovah God. We do not pledge allegiance to the kingdoms of this world." The teacher nodded and walked away. Doris never joined in the pledge recital. I learned later that the teacher had asked the principal what to do, and he had advised her not to push the issue. A few years later the case of another Witness reached the United States Supreme Court, which found that students should not be compelled to violate their religious principles.

When I first read about this decision, I remembered Doris in fifth grade. But I also remembered the ringing words of Handel's "Hallelujah Chorus": "the kingdom of this world is become the kingdom of our Lord and of his Christ"; and when I hear these words sung I cannot help thinking about Doris, who moved away after fifth grade, and feeling grateful. The courage and persistence of her "little flock" had widened the scope of freedom for everyone. In the Germany of the 1930s, Witnesses were among the most unwavering, albeit nonviolent, opponents of Nazi rule, publicly refusing to give the required "Heil Hitler" greeting. They also refused military service, and their stubbornness infuriated the Gestapo. There were more Witnesses per capita in concentration camps than any other (non-Jewish) religious group.

In America, year by year, other court decisions upheld the right of religious minorities, and later of nonreligious people, to object to military service. For me, the moral of the history of this "little flock," as the Witnesses call themselves, is that we should be careful not to assess religious groups by their explicit theologies, which I admit in the case of the Witnesses, I find implausible. We must appreciate them for their actual accomplishment in extending the reigning of God. "By their fruits shall you know them."

In a subsequent chapter I will treat perhaps the most influential religious minority in America, the Black churches. But there are other religious minorities that have made their own contributions to the dawning reigning of God's "beloved community." Among these I would count the Mennonites and the Amish people, among whom I grew up in southeastern Pennsylvania, who also conscientiously refused to take up arms but served as medics. I would also like to have included the Ameri-

canized versions of Asian-born traditions, like the practitio-
ners of Krishna Consciousness (the "Hare Krishnas"), whose
creative adaptations of their imported faith show us what they
think needs to be kept and what modified to make a spiritual
practice more "American" without losing its soul.

To add to the challenge of examining American heavens, it
would be hard to draw a clear line between "religious" movements and those that made no "religious claim" but shaped public thinking on questions of life and death. This would include
Masonic Lodges, whose funeral services differ from the ordinary Christian ones, sometimes giving rise to controversies
with pastors who oppose their being held in churches. Is there
a Masonic view of death and the afterlife? Since their doctrines
and rites are not made public, it is hard to say.

Given the impossibility of doing justice to everything that
might be covered in a chapter, I have chosen only some of the
most popular views Americans have held on the subject. I will
begin with a man who was, perhaps, the best-known religious
personality in late-twentieth- and early-twenty-first-century
America, Billy Graham.

When William Franklin Graham Jr. died on February 21,
2018, at his home in Montreat, North Carolina, the obituar-
ies rightly identified him as one of the best known and most
admired figures in America. What did Billy think about heaven?
The leading evangelist of his epoch, Billy spent much more time
advising people on how to get to heaven than on what they
might find when they got there. But sometimes he responded
to people's questions about the next life. Once, for example, he
quipped that he was sure that there would be a golf course in
heaven. But he was usually careful not to engage in speculation,
though some of the questions he answered pushed him close
to the border. Among the most difficult questions he handled
were those concerning visions of heaven, especially those that

came to people, as they often do, on the threshold of death. In one of many challenging queries, a woman wrote to him that on her deathbed, her aunt, a "very spiritual person" who "read the Bible every day," had actually seen heaven and Jesus waiting to welcome her. Did he think this might have been a hallucination?

In his answer, Billy was careful not to dismiss the claim. He said that God does sometimes grant us a "glimpse of heaven" just before we die. Characteristically, Graham based his response on the Bible. He recalled the account of the martyrdom of Stephen. As the stones thrown by his enemies rained down upon him, Billy wrote, Stephen *"looked up to heaven and saw the glory of God, and Jesus standing at the right hand of God"* (Acts 7:55). About this aunt's experience, Graham wrote, "I am convinced it was not a hallucination." It was instead a "God-given glimpse into eternity." But why does God send the "glimpse"?

God does so, according to Graham, because "he is reminding us that . . . eternity is real, and Christ is waiting to welcome us into heaven." Having first anchored his answer in the Bible, Graham went on to link the "glimpse" to the message of Evangelical Christianity, for which he was such a dedicated spokesman. Through such glimpses of Christ welcoming us to heaven, God reminds us that "he alone is our hope, because by his death on the cross he paid the price for our sins, and by his resurrection from the dead he conquered death and hell and Satan."

Another questioner asked Billy if she and her mother would recognize each other in heaven. She was worried because her mother had died when she was a small child, and they never got to know each other, and she had heard that the Bible says that "the former things will not be remembered" (Isaiah 65:17).

Once more, in his response, Graham is reassuring, again quoting Scripture. He recalls that when King David's infant son died, David declared, "I will go to him" (2 Samuel 12:23). However, in this answer he goes on to add something that inadvertently reveals the problematic relationship between his concept of heaven and the kingdom of God. "But this verse" (Isaiah 65:17), Billy writes, "has nothing to do with whether or not we will be reunited with our loved ones in heaven if we know Christ. Instead, it gives us a great promise: someday all the sins and pains and failures of this world will be over, and we will be with Christ forever." True to his core message, Graham sees the message of the prophets in the light of the sacrificial death of Christ. "I am not an Old Testament prophet," Billy once said in an interview, "I am a New Testament evangelist." But this subsuming of the prophets raises two questions.

First, Jesus understood himself to be *continuing* the prophetic tradition in Judaism as he makes clear in his first sermon, reported in Luke 4:14–20:

> *Then Jesus, filled with the power of the Spirit, returned to Galilee, and a report about him spread through all the surrounding country. He began to teach in their synagogues and was praised by everyone. When he came to Nazareth, where he had been brought up, he went to the synagogue on the sabbath day, as was his custom. He stood up to read, and the scroll of the prophet Isaiah was given to him. He unrolled the scroll and found the place where it was written:*
>
> > *"The Spirit of the Lord is upon me,*
> > *because he has anointed me*
> > *to bring good news to the poor.*
> > *He has sent me to proclaim release to the captives*
> > *and recovery of sight to the blind,*
> > *to let the oppressed go free,*
> > *to proclaim the year of the Lord's favor."*

Billy's statement dilutes a key aspect of Jesus's mission. His reading borders on an idea that was advanced by a leader in the early church, Marcion of Sinope (c. 85–c. 160 CE), who said that Christians did not need the Old Testament. But Marcion's position was rejected, and the Christian Bible now includes both Old and New Testaments. Also, since Jesus derived his emphasis on the reigning of God from the Old Testament, Billy also runs the danger of diluting this fundamental motif of the Gospel. It blurs the importance of the fact that the biblical message is a continuous narrative.

But, despite his rhetorical emphasis on heaven, in his actions Billy often revealed that the kingdom of God as a promise of social justice and world peace was not absent from his life or his message. A Southerner, he nevertheless insisted that the seating at his rallies not be segregated, often to the displeasure of the local sponsors of these gatherings. When he was invited to preach in Russia during the height of the Cold War, State Department officials strongly urged him not to go. But he did, and thus, without using the language, became a symbol of a possible conciliation. When he spoke to an overflow crowd of students and faculty at the Harvard Kennedy School of Government on September 27, 1999 (a meeting I attended), his topic was "Is God Relevant for the Twenty-First Century?" There were many things he might have said under that heading, but to his credit, he devoted his talk to warning against nuclear war, and advocated a freeze on the production of such weapons, a highly controversial question at the time. The "New Testament evangelist," it seems, had not forgotten the "Old Testament" prophets' message of beating swords into plowshares. Billy's conservative followers were often displeased with his political positions, and many of them found his growing appreciation for the wider Christian community a betrayal. The accusations increased when he arranged that the people who were converted ("saved") at his rallies should be encouraged to affiliate with a local church, causing some to grumble that these churches might not be "theologically correct." But Billy's theological horizon continued to widen.

The first time I met him personally was in India at an assembly of the World Council of Churches, which religious conservatives had condemned for years for what they considered its "liberal" theology. I was a little surprised to see him there (he was not one of the speakers), but there he was, smiling and shaking hands. When I asked him how he liked it his answer was enthusiastically positive. "Wonderful," he said, "all these people from so many parts of the world, all praising Jesus Christ together!" Clearly, the theology of the hidebound Southern fundamentalist revivalist had evolved and matured, and he had become something of an ecumenical statesman.

Buildings associated with any religious movement or person can, in their shape and profile, say something noteworthy about what they represent. Thus, a basilica, a Zen temple, a cathedral, a mosque can express the ethos of a faith. When faced with the challenge of designing a building for the Billy Graham Library in Charlotte, North Carolina, what did the planners and the architects, Jenkins, Hancock & Sides, decide on? They chose a barn, a palpable icon of the simple, hard-working, God-fearing ordinary folks whose faith he personified and carried to the ends of the earth. No palace, marble mausoleum, or cathedral, and no soaring tower would be right for the Billy Graham Library, which squats squarely on its earthy plot.

This is no ordinary barn. It is a five-star edifice, unassumingly pretentious. Or pretentiously unassuming. It may look like a barn, but it occupies a space, not in a field of corn or wheat, but on a middle-class suburban street. It contains forty thousand square feet of exhibition space and cost twenty-seven million dollars. Like the American people, and the country preacher whose name it bears, the library, and the scrupulously manicured grounds, the monument tells the story of someone who both *was* good and *made* good. It assures visitors that you can be a born-again Christian, perfectly assured that you will go to heaven, but also be secure and comfortable here on earth.

The entrance to the barn-library is an opening in the shape of a giant cross, clearly suggesting that one can enter the heaven Billy preached about only by way of the sacrificial death of Christ—not all that different from the blood-red doors of cathedrals and other churches. But at the first step inside the library it is evident that there is something different here. Once inside, one is immediately greeted by an exhibit showing a straw-filled cattle stall. Standing in it is the life-sized model of a cow from which a deep recorded "moo" greets the visitor. "Well, this is mainly for the kids," a guide said. "After all, Billy was brought up on a farm with animals." Unspoken, the similarity to the birth of Jesus, surrounded by the friendly beasts, can hardly be missed. All that is missing are a few shepherds and wise men.

For some, however, the mechanical cow projects another meaning. This is no commonplace cow. It is a technologically enhanced cow. It does not represent nature, but nature upgraded by human (here American) technical know-how. Nothing could be more American. The other galleries were designed by Itec Entertainment, which was one of the principal planners of Disney World, where even the cobwebs are artificial. The galleries retell the life story of Billy. They start with a replica of the tent in which Billy staged his first "crusade" in 1949 in Los Angeles. That revival went on for eight weeks, was attended by 350,000 people, and made headlines all over the country and around the world. Billy became an internationally known celebrity and continued to have that status for the rest of his life. He is said to have preached to 210 million people on six continents. He was sought out by eleven consecutive American presidents. At the national memorial service after the 9/11

attack, it was of course Billy Graham who delivered the sermon. He had become "America's pastor," and he had a key role
in bringing Evangelical Christianity into American political
life. Yet, despite all the fame, Billy retained a modest, sometimes self-effacing persona. The first time he visited the library
built to honor him, he complained that "it was too much Billy
Graham." He told friends that he was disappointed because he
had wanted the library "to please the Lord and to honor Jesus,
not to see me or to think of me."

As one wanders through the Billy Graham Library, another
clue to the exquisitely American element becomes evident. It is
the need for a history that makes the present more intelligible.
This was never an easy assignment for the founding generation.
They wanted both to insist on the clean break they had made
with tyrants and old regimes but also to root their claims for
their new republic in the heritage of the ages. What resulted was
a selective genealogy. George Washington could be compared
with the orators and benevolent rulers of ancient Greece, where
it was held that democracy had been born. But the Father of His
Country could not be identified with the Roman emperors, so a
heroic statue of him in a Roman toga was displayed briefly but
now gathers dust in a back room of the National Museum.

Those who designed the Billy Graham Library wanted their
man to be the present incarnation of an American religious
ancestry. Therefore, the library features displays of earlier
evangelists such as Jonathan Edwards and Charles Grandison
Finney, the founder of Oberlin College and a staunch abolitionist. But after Finney, this social justice dimension of American
Evangelicalism went into decline, and the individualistic aspect
became predominant. The "getting to heaven" perspective overshadowed the kingdom of God perspective. Revivalists often
fulminated against any kind of Social Gospel. Billy Graham
came from this ultrapersonalistic tradition. He never escaped

it entirely, but he was not a complete captive of it either. He was not "so fixed on heaven that he was no earthly good."

Not long after Billy's death, some American Evangelicals initiated a movement that, had he lived, I like to think Billy would have supported. Self-identified Evangelicals like Soong-Chan Rah of North Park University, Alexia Salvatierra of Fuller Theological Seminary, and Jim Wallis, the founder of *Sojourners* magazine, have made an effort to reclaim the social dimension of earlier Evangelicalism, especially on issues like racism, gender equality, and economic justice. Political and social opinions of young Evangelicals are becoming more liberal, with special concern for peace, racial justice, and the environment. Whatever the view of heaven and the reigning of God this vigorous new generation develops, it will certainly not replicate revivalist Billy Sunday's statement that his job was just trying to get as many souls into the lifeboat as possible. It will not be a lifeboat heaven or what I have called the "extricationism" promoted by many of their Evangelical predecessors.

If Billy Graham was the quintessential personification of a dominant strain of American religion in the twentieth century, then the Church of Jesus Christ of Latter-Day Saints is the most impressive American-born religious movement of the nineteenth, continuing into the twenty-first century. Historians have rightly named it the "most American" of the denominations that were born and have flourished here. It originated in upstate New York, when a young man named Joseph Smith, who was struggling with doubt and uncertainty about faith, was led to discover some lost sections of the Bible. They were in a language that he did not understand but which God helped him to translate into English, *The Book of Mormon*. Smith (what name could be more American?) soon attracted followers, and the small assembly he initiated became, within a few decades, one of the fastest growing churches in America, then rapidly spread around the globe. Mormons do not believe in counting their adherents, but estimates put the number at about seventeen million.

The Mormon idea of heaven is in some measure a product of their stormy history. They lived through a difficult early existence in America. Despised and persecuted by their neighbors in New York State in part because of their practice of "plural marriage," they set out on a long trek across America to find a place where they could live their faith in peace. But the journey was a painful one. They were assailed and sometimes driven out of communities. In Missouri their leader Joseph Smith fell victim to a lynch mob. But undaunted, they went on singing the hymn for which they have become famous, "All Is Well, All Is Well."

After Smith's martyrdom, they were led farther west by Smith's successor, Brigham Young, until they eventually crossed a ridge and looked down on a fertile valley in Utah. Young then said, "This is the place!" These words are still dear to the hearts of Mormons, and when I visited Utah in 1959 with a delegation of peace advocates, whose main purpose was to plead with the Mormon leadership to prevent plans to install intercontinental missiles in the state, we were ushered in to see the president of the church. He told us that he had not yet made up his mind on the question. Then, just as we were leaving his office, I suddenly remembered the words of Brigham Young. "Mr. President," I said, "we hope that you will decide that as for nuclear missiles, this is NOT the place." Soon after that, the church took a public stand against the missiles.

As for polygamy, in Utah, the Mormons mainly just wanted to be left alone. But the United States was expanding, and on July 4, 1896, Utah was admitted to the union. It soon became clear that legal polygamy would no longer be tolerated, and the church officially discontinued the practice. But some Mormons disagreed with the decision and continued to enter plural marriages, often not making the additional marriages public to avoid legal harassment. Then, in 2020, the state passed an ordinance legalizing "domestic partnerships" with more than two people, and some commentators predicted that the idea was sure to spread to other states. If it does, will the Mormons be credited or blamed?

Meanwhile, there is another feature to Mormon marriages that is probably more unique than polygamy, and which has greater significance for life in heaven. Mormons do not exchange vows with the words "as long as we both shall live," or "until death do us part." Mormons marry for eternity. Marriage and family bonds are indissoluble, even by death, and Mormons do not believe this violates Jesus's statement that there is no marriage in heaven. People do not *get married* in heaven, but married people stay married to each other. This doctrine may bring comfort to those who have enjoyed a happy marriage on earth and look forward to more of the same. But it may not appeal to those who, regardless of whatever degree of satisfaction their partnership has produced in this life, are not eager to have it continue forever and ever.

In addition to the marriage forever, is there any other connection between Mormon marriage practices and what they believe about the afterlife? In short, the Mormons teach that there are three heavens. In Mormon theology, the three heavens are arranged in concentric circles. The central circle is for true believers, those who have been "sealed" in a temple. The next is for those whose beliefs and practices are close to those of the Latter-Day Saints but who have not been "sealed" or become members. The third circle is for "good people" who do not otherwise qualify. The Mormons do not have an understanding of a hell, maybe because they hold to a conviction that eventually all people, including the non-Mormons, whom they call "Gentiles," will come to see the truth and be appropriately welcomed into one of the circles. This rather generous, even universalistic doctrine has not, however, lessened the saints' zeal for enlisting converts, as anyone who has answered their knock on a front door can certify.

However, perhaps the most fascinating of Mormon beliefs about life after death is the church's practice of baptizing the dead. Undoubtedly, this custom springs from the Mormon hope, mentioned above, that eventually everyone will become a beneficiary of God's ultimate and inclusive community. Therefore, they have been baptizing the dead by proxy since their earliest days. But a few years ago a minor fracas erupted in America when some people who had not known before discovered that the Mormons were "baptizing," by means of surrogates, not only their own dead forebears but growing numbers of other people as well. Originally this baptism included only those parents and other ancestors who had died before the revelations to Joseph Smith. But gradually other deceased people were also baptized. Then, in theory at least, the Mormons came to believe that no one should be excluded. The church developed one of the most extensive programs of genealogical research and expanded its baptismal activity to anyone whose name they could discover. It was not long after this that complaints from outside the church began. Why did the Mormons suppose they had the right to baptize my deceased Methodist (or Catholic or Jewish) grandmother without her or her family's permission?

Mormons insisted that their freedom of religion allowed them to extend their mission to others if they chose to. Further, they explained that this baptism did not make its recipients into Mormons. It meant only that if, in life after death, they wanted to join the church, they would have the advantage of already having been baptized, and thus, according to Mormon belief, a better place in heaven. The argument that took place had a bizarre irony. If the critics did not believe that Mormon baptism had any validity, then why did it annoy them? The dispute has never been settled, but it suggests that, despite the influence of secularization, some people still think about the well-being of their dead.

The dispute ignited by Mormon practice also found its way into formal theological discussions and drew in scholars of the Bible and of early Christianity. It was soon evident that baptizing the dead is hardly a new issue. As we discussed in an earlier chapter, St. Paul addressed this question in his first letter to the tiny Christian congregation in Corinth, where some members of the congregation were being baptized on behalf of deceased relatives and friends. Paul might have been expected to condemn this practice, but instead he cited it in support of a long argument against skeptics who doubted whether the resurrection was real. "If the dead are not raised at all, then why are people baptized on their behalf?" Paul asked (1 Corinthians 15:29).

I think St. Paul handled the question correctly. Concern for the welfare of the dead, especially of those close to us, is a deep and troubling human instinct. It finds expression in an array of ways in virtually every religion. Tibetan Buddhists chant passages from the famous *Book of the Dead*, believing it helps their deceased relatives negotiate the perilous journey to the realm of light. The Catholic practice of praying for the "souls in purgatory" to speed their voyage to heaven provoked fierce debate during the Reformation, and still continues today. And Protestants pray that the dead may "rest in peace." Jews recite prayers at the "Yahrzeit," the annual anniversary of the death of a loved one. Every year on the "Day of the Dead," Mexican Catholics eat and drink at the graves of their departed loved ones. Africans, both Christian and non-Christian, bring gifts to the places where they have buried their dead. When Mormons today baptize the dead by proxy, it should be remembered that they are merely doing—in their way—what religious people have been doing, in numberless diverse ways, for centuries.

Psychologists say that from the first appearance of human beings, dead bodies have evoked deeply ambivalent feelings in the living, both horror and dread on the one hand, and awe and fascination on the other. Nonetheless, remembering and honoring the dead is one of the marks of what it means to be human. Even the most intelligent animals, though they use primitive tools and language, do not appear to express reverence for their dead. Reports that elephants pause at the places where other elephants have died have been discounted by zoologists. Anthropologists suggest that the surest evidence of when Homo sapiens emerged from his humanoid predecessors is burial mounds and grave markings. To discover one's own mortality in that of another person is to raise questions about the meaning of life, and to recognize that past, present, and future generations constitute parts of the same bundle. "Ask not for whom the bell tolls. . . ."

At its heart, concern for the dead reflects the hope that no one, not even the dead, are ultimately lost from the all-encompassing human family. The old Appalachian hymn, "Will the Circle Be Unbroken?" voices the desperate hope that somehow the broken "circle" might one day be mended, with everyone included. Even the somewhat diluted affirmation heard so often at modern memorial services, that he or she "will live on in our hearts," suggests that both the secular skeptics who have left sacred rituals behind and the religious people who still observe them have something in common. They both share a longing that the dead can still be with us in one way or another, and their practice of baptizing the dead is an expression of this munificent attitude.

It could be argued that the deep-seated human longing for a comprehensive community is at the heart of nearly all utopian aspirations and of all conceptions of heaven.

This yearning has also spawned significant organized and unorganized religious movements in America and elsewhere. One of these is often given the loose label of "Spiritualism." In 1860 there appeared in America a book by Robert Dale Owen (1801–1877) entitled *Footfalls on the Boundary of Another World*. Rarely read or cited today, it was enormously popular in its time. And it is thought by historians to epitomize Spiritualism, one of the most enduring and influential movements in American religious history.

Spiritualism is a wobbly term. It covers a plethora of varied sects, philosophies, popular medical nostrums, and theological currents, many of which would resist being grouped with the others. With roots in mesmerism, animal magnetism, hypnotism, and occult sects as well as in the thinking of philosophers from Paracelsus to William James, Spiritualism never became a denomination, but in the mid-nineteenth century it claimed thirty million adherents.

The reasons for the popularity of Spiritualism speak directly to the concerns of this book about the significance of the afterlife, and echoes themes I have already touched on. Many Spiritualists were fascinated, if not obsessed, with detailed descriptions of heaven. But we must notice that Owen's book refers to "*another*" world, not "*the next*" world. The import of this is critical. Owen was not talking about a dawning kingdom, or reigning of God. He was writing about a spiritual world that closely coexists with the everyday world.

In his classic *A Religious History of the American People*, Sidney Ahlstrom suggests that American Spiritualism emerged from a dizzying cast of what can seem like incompatible sources. First there were the renowned Fox sisters (Leah, Kate, and Maggie) of upstate New York, the "burned-over district," who heard "rappings" around their house and convinced themselves, then many others, that the noises were communications from the dead. The fame of the sisters grew and eventually two unlikely personalities embraced their message. One was Horace Greeley of the *New York Tribune*, one of the most respected journalists of the era. The other personage was P. T. Barnum, of circus fame, who initially celebrated their gifts. But in a book *Humbugs of the World* that he wrote in 1865, Barnum, who once uttered the timeless truism, "There is a sucker born every minute," condemned the sisters as frauds. There is little wonder that Spiritualism exploded into a congeries of entertainments, healing techniques, religious sects, philosophical gambits, and countless seances that purported to communicate with the dead.

The Spiritualist impulse has never disappeared. The impact it once made, and, I would add, continues to make, is due to a combination of factors. First, there will always be the bereaved who wonder and worry about those they have loved who are now deceased, and any practice that responds to their concern will inevitably attract attention. Second, Spiritualists have usually been suspicious if not disdainful of established creeds and rituals. There will always be people who long for a more direct access to the "other world" that Spiritualism promises to provide. Finally, in an age shaped so much by science, several streams of Spiritualism have asserted that their insights are not based on blind faith but are the result of careful empirical investigation.

It should not be surprising that the most widely known present representative of Spiritualism today is called "Christian Science." It has common roots with other efforts to combine science with Spiritualism but has probably exerted more influence on religion in America than the others, although that influence has not always been recognized. For example, its founder, Mary Baker Eddy, was one of the first to teach that God should be thought of as "Father and Mother." When her movement first appeared, most Protestant denominations, fearful of being con-

fused with self-promoting "faith healers," rarely prayed for healing. They were content to leave that to Pentecostals, Christian
Scientists, and the Catholics who visited Lourdes. But in recent
decades this attitude has changed dramatically. Using both masculine and feminine language in prayers is now more common
in many churches, and there is only a rare congregation that
does not incorporate prayers for healing into its services.

Christian Scientists are often characterized as teaching that
such "negative concepts" as sickness and death are not "real" in
the ordinary sense but states of mind which a pure and right
kind of thinking can replace. They often put this conviction
into practice by refusing ordinary medical treatment in favor
of prayers and readings from Mary Baker Eddy's *Science and
Health with Key to the Scriptures* (1875). As for death, the official
position is as follows:

> *It can be said heaven is awareness of our unity with God,
> while hell is feeling separated from Him. Jesus described
> "the kingdom of God" as "within" us (Luke 17:21). That
> introduces heaven as essentially mental and always avail-
> able.* (*Christian Science Monitor*, August 19, 1999)

Today there are legions of people who like to describe themselves as "spiritual but not religious." When one of my classes
did interviews with some fifty individuals who labeled themselves this way, they found that "spiritual but not religious"
meant different things to different people. But the common
thread is a rejection of what they see as the rigidity (which they
call "dogmatism") and narrowness of the existing religious
options. Many had undergone unpleasant or even painful experiences in conventional religious institutions in early life. But
among the subjects of this survey there was not one who wanted
to be thought of as "atheist," which they rejected as just another
close-minded dogmatism. They described themselves as skepti-

cal when asked about life after death, but they did not reject the possibility completely.

When my students reported these findings in class, they elicited a variety of responses. Some of the students said that they found they shared many of the criticisms those interviewed had described. Others were less sympathetic. Some said the people they spoke to just wanted to "eat the cake and lick the icing of religion but never wash the dishes." Others felt that their interviewees were mistaken to think that a genuine spiritual life was possible without a supportive faith community of some sort.

As I thought about what this informal survey of a small sample revealed, it seemed to indicate that the boundary between "religious" and "spiritual" may not be either fixed or clear. My guess is that a considerable number of the parishioners in any congregation might have expressed similar views, including uncertainty about death and what follows. Surveys show that people attend or belong to (or absent themselves from) religious observances for numerous reasons. These include family tradition, local custom, and personal habit. They choose this congregation rather than that one because it has a more commodious parking lot or better childcare. To the chagrin of clergy, theology does not weigh heavily in the choices most people make in this area.

But, as I listened to the findings of the "spiritual but not religious" survey, I also thought of something else. When the German pastor and theologian Dietrich Bonhoeffer sat in a Gestapo prison, accused of taking part in the attempts to assassinate Hitler, he smuggled out some letters to his friend Eberhard Bethge. In one of the last of these, dated April 30, 1944, he wrote,

> *I believe we are proceeding towards a time of no religion at all . . . how do we speak of God without religion . . . how do we speak in a secular fashion of God?* (*Letters and Papers from Prison*, 1955)

Bonhoeffer never had the chance to respond to his own questions. He was killed by the Gestapo in April 1945, just hours before the Allies liberated the concentration camp where he was being held. Since then more than one theologian has tried to answer them, but with little success. Some have even suggested that Bonhoeffer was wrong in his prophecy of a "time of no religion at all." Since his death, they ask, have we not witnessed an unexpected *resurgence* of religion, for bane and for blessing, all around the world? But I think Bonhoeffer's forecast still holds. Neither the traditional religions nor the new ones speak to people as religion once did. As we have seen in this book, the images of heaven that we have inherited no longer seem plausible, but we have not found anything to replace them. We are all in some ways like T. S. Eliot's "children at the gate," who "cannot pray but will not go away." We are searching, but not sure what we are looking for. In their own clumsy way, the people who say they are "spiritual but not religious" are part of this search.

America is religiously fecund. Its unprecedented admixture of so many traditions and of piety and secularity has prodded the loam from which denominations, sects, cults, saints, and charlatans have sprouted. Some have flourished; others have quickly died out. But I have little doubt that this fruitfulness will persist. As Pastor Robinson told the passengers on the *Mayflower*, "I am persuaded that the Lord hath more truth yet to break forth out of His Holy Word."

# 13

# *Black and Brown Heavens*

*And I heard a loud voice from the throne saying, "Behold, the dwelling place of God is with man. He will dwell with them, and they will be his people, and God himself will be with them as their God. (Revelation 21:3 ESV)*

*And afterward, I will pour out My Spirit on all people . . .*
   *Your sons and daughters will prophesy, your old men will dream dreams, your young men will see visions. (Joel 2:28 KJV)*

*. . . lashes in the drip black heaven.*
*I see the things I always see.*
*I taste the sweet of swarming bees.*
*Warm and droning summer lost you.*
*Whitewashed Hawaiian houses. (Laura Sidhwa,*
   "Black Heaven")

I have visited heaven, four or five times. I met God and dined with him and some of the angels. Then I met God in his office on the second floor of heaven. All this happened when I was a student at the University of Pennsylvania in the 1950s. The heaven was located at 40th and Chestnut St., a few blocks from my dormitory room. It was one of about one hundred heavens founded by one of the most remarkable religious personalities of the twentieth century, Rev. Major Jealous Divine, better known as "Father Divine," who his followers believed was God incarnate. Theologians have a term, "realized eschatology," the conviction that the kingdom of God that Jesus announced has already come, albeit not visible to everyone. Father Divine's movement, the Peace Unity Mission, represented realized eschatology at its most realized. For example, since God and heaven were already here, then in a Communion service we should no longer partake of the mere symbols of something yet to come. Rather, we sit down now to a multicourse banquet and God/Father Divine, sits with us. And, rather than waiting for an afterlife to hear angels sing, residents in his heavens, decked out in appropriate costume, serenade us while we eat.

I realize that for other Black religious leaders of the time Father Divine's views were deeply suspect, and that some dismissed him as a charlatan. But nonetheless I think his Peace Unity is highly pertinent to a book on heaven and to this chapter. His network of heavens embodies his convictions about the Social Gospel, though he did not use the term. The hungry were fed, the homeless were sheltered, and the outcasts were brought inside. And he called his theological philosophy "Americanism." No advocate of Black separatism, as were some other Black religious spokesmen of the time, Father Divine advocated thoroughgoing racial integration. At his weekly Communion feasts he interspersed Black and white guests around a huge circular table that accommodated eighty people. Each dish among the twenty or thirty that were carried from the kitchen by "angels" in starched white shirts and crimson jackets was first set before Father Divine himself. He blessed every bowl by vigorously plunging in a spoon or fork. The dishes would then be passed all around the table with each guest placing a portion on his or her plate. A choir of the angels in robes sang throughout the meal. I still remember one of their lively anthems:

*This is God's administration,*
*And we're on the winning side.*
*This is God's administration,*
*And we're on the winning side.*

The reader who has heard of Father Divine and of the severe economic depression going on when his movement was thriving must now be perplexed. Didn't Father Divine claim to be God? Did that not make him an obvious charlatan? How could I take part in the "Communion feast" of such a blatantly non-Christian or even blasphemous ceremony? I will return to Father Divine's eccentric theology below. Here I will only say that as a college student from a small town, I was fascinated by the dizzying array of religions on display in the City of Brotherly Love. Also, as a sometime penurious student, I was always ready for a good meal, and I always felt welcome at the heaven, even when I appeared with two or three skeptical classmates. I suspect that in his effort to intermix the colors of his guests, the host was sometimes a little short of white people. It was during my third visit that one of the angels tapped me on the shoulder while I was lacing into fluffy mashed potatoes and gravy, and whispered that "Father" had noticed I had attended more than one Communion and would like to see me in his office after the Communion dinner. I gladly accepted the invitation, and when I walked into his carpeted study with two fellow students I had, with the permission of his secretary, brought along, Father Divine himself was seated behind a glistening mahogany desk. A short, plump, dark-skinned man, wearing a neat blue suit, he rose to greet us and offer us seats. As we sat down, I noticed two women stenographers standing attentively behind him, each with a notebook, writing down every word he said.

Father Divine welcomed us and asked if we had any questions. I did, but I avoided asking the most obvious one ("Do you really think you are God?"), at least at first, and asked him to tell me how he organized his heavens in such a way that everyone seemed so satisfied. This gave him a chance to lay out some of the basics of his theological perspectives. Why should people not be satisfied? he asked. His angels had everything anyone could ever want. They lived in clean, warm rooms and ate good meals. He said that Jesus had never intended for us to wait until we die and go to heaven to enjoy the fruits of creation. Had he not said that he had come to bring us all life abundant? Also, he said, the angels enjoyed working together and, within the heaven, were not exposed to the wiles and temptations that might corrupt them on the streets. I had heard that Father Divine also promised those who entered his heavens that if they stayed, they would become immortal, and never die. But he did not mention this, and I did not bring it up.

However, my effort not to bring up what might be embarrassing questions was not shared by the students I had with me. A young woman, a sophomore, finally said, "Father, do you really believe you are God?" Father Divine was not embarrassed or offended. I am sure he had been asked that question before. "Well," he answered, "that is what my people say." But the sophomore was persistent. "But what do you think?" she asked. "Well," he said, smiling, "I just do not think about such things." I took that as as much of an answer as we were likely to get, and signaled my student to drop it, which she did. It was only later that I discovered that our host had, in fact, thought about that question a lot.

A reporter from a local newspaper who had spent time with him told me that Father Divine had once been struck by Jesus's statement in John 14:12, "In that day you shall know that I am in My Father, and you in Me, and I in you." As a young preacher he took these words about "oneness" with God and with Jesus literally. At first, in his sermons as a young preacher, he emphasized the presence of God in everyone. Later, it seems, he tended to focus more on the "in me" part more than the "in everyone." Then there is the established custom in Black preaching to "enact" the persons and voices in a Bible passage, sometimes in the form of a spirited dialogue between God and Adam or God and Noah or Moses and the pharaoh, or between Jesus and someone he confronts. Talented Black preachers learn how to use different voices. Some observers of Father Divine think he slid from this enactment into addressing his congregations using the personal pronoun in the voice of God. One way or another, Father Divine's relationship to God, whatever it was or how he understood it, inspired him to found what is reported to have been a hundred residential heavens with angels, banquet-sized Communion meals, a chain of small businesses, and other indications that the kingdom of God is now actually "in the midst of you."

The idea of unity with God is not strange to the Christian tradition. Saint Paul wrote, "I have been crucified with Christ; and it is no longer I who live, but Christ lives in me; and the life which I now live in the flesh I live by faith in the Son of God" (Galatians 2:20). Eastern Orthodox theology recognizes what they call "apotheosis" (usually translated as "divinization"), by which certain human beings are enabled to share the divine life of God. Athanasius (ca. 296–298 to 373), the Coptic Orthodox bishop of Alexandria, was one of the first theologians. In discussing the incarnation of Christ, he once wrote, "He became what we are that we might become what he is," which suggests that everyone could experience apotheosis. For centuries, Christian mystics have testified to feeling "at one with God," albeit in a variety of ways. Saint Teresa of Avila claimed she heard the voice of God within her. Saint Francis identified himself so closely with Christ that it is believed that the stigmata, the marks of the crucifixion nails, appeared on his hands and feet. In the nineteenth century, "Spiritualists" taught that life after death is a long process of growing ever closer to perfection, and since God is Perfection, eventually becoming one with him. The Mormon (LDS) Church teaches that God was once a human being, and that we as human beings can become gods: "what we are, God once was; what God is, we shall be." Father Divine's purported oneness with God may sound brazen, but it is not unprecedented.

I am aware that Father Divine's understanding of heaven and the kingdom was not wholly in keeping with the ideas of other Black and white religious leaders at the time, and still is not. The explanations I have listed do not, in my view, justify his encouraging his followers to call him "God." And his exaltation does make it questionable to regard his movement as representative. But I do not think we should allow Father Divine's alleged apotheosis to prevent us from appreciating the extraordinary achievements of his movement. My interest in his Peace Unity Mission has to do with those accomplishments, not with the man.

The Black religious tradition, even though it has been marginated by American culture and often treated dismissively by white religious leaders, has nevertheless had an enormous and continuing influence on America. It is hard to imagine what our music, literature, politics, entertainment, and especially our religion would be without it. But it has always been contentious. Racism has accurately been called the "original sin" of this country. It has tainted our national life and split local communities. But the struggle to eliminate racism has also been a constant theme. The conflicts between the two forces have drummed a pulsing background, and often a shrill foreground, in virtually every aspect of our history. And throughout this saga, the faith of Black people has resonated. It is often recognized that the only institution in America that people of African extraction controlled were the Black churches. They provided the rallying point, the protection, the inspiration, and the spiritual confirmation without which it would have been virtually impossible for the community to survive. But these congregations, some small, some large, from the slave revolts to the voter registration drives, also sparked the principal opposition to racism. It is understandable that the enemies of equality have directed so much energy to burning down Black churches.

Little by little these indispensable contributions are being recognized by the wider community. What is not often recognized is the rich insights these churches have contributed, albeit also mostly unappreciated, to Christian theology. The reason I say this goes back to my earlier assertion that in America, the dominant white theology has been distorted because "heaven" has displaced the reigning of God as the axial Christian category. The Black churches, however, with some exceptions, have avoided this crippling bifurcation. Through a tortuous history of enslavement, segregation, and exclusions, Black Christians have learned how to combine the personal with the social, piety with politics.

I was always impressed when I attended Black churches during the civil rights movement by how the congregation could sing a punchy freedom song and then a quietly devout hymn, and then file out of the church to face billy clubs and tear gas. What made this feat possible is that Black Christians could see symbols of heaven and the reigning of God as both transcendental and earthly. But this affirmation is not peripheral to Christianity. It is the meaning. But when it is applied to the relationship between the heavenly and the earthly, it remains a theological insight whose full implications most white churches and theologians have rarely fully grasped. The division between the "spiritual/pietistic" wing and the "social action / peace and justice" wing continues. There are, however, some hints that the

breach is not unbridgeable. Theologically conservative Evangelicals have become much more active in efforts to eradicate racism, and young Evangelicals have thrown their energy into the
climate crisis, some calling themselves "creation keepers." This
emerging overlapping makes it even more important that the
Black churches, with their long experience in combining these
elements of the gospel, be integral to the conversation.

The life of Martin Luther King Jr. provides an example of how
personal devotion and social engagement coalesce in one person. He said that at a time when the Ku Klux Klan had threatened his life and his family, he had almost decided to withdraw
from the battle. Confused and discouraged, he sat at home in
his kitchen, thinking and praying. As he sat there, he said, the
voice of God spoke to him softly, "I will never leave you or for-
sake you. . . ." With this reassurance he decided not to give up,
but to press on with his nonviolent struggle. When I read these
words, I recognized them, as most people could not have, as the
text of a hymn called "The Promise," by an unknown composer,
that both King and I had sung many times in church:

> *I will never no never forsake thee.*
> *Never no never forsake thee.*
> *I will save and guide and protect thee*
> *For my own and mercy's sake.*

King's faith was not just one aspect of his persona; it was its
core. I have often been annoyed that in the abundance of tributes paid to King on the holiday that bears his name, his role
as a "civil rights (King never liked this term) leader" is understandably featured. But the role that was always most important
to him, a preacher of the gospel, is often slighted. A few years
ago, a TV camera focused on the Abyssinian Baptist Church
in Harlem where a memorial service was in progress. The nar-
rator murmured, "It is so appropriate that the service is being

held here since Dr. King's own father was a Baptist minister." I almost threw a cushion at the TV. "His father!" Had they forgotten that King himself was a Baptist minister, and that he always considered the work he did as an expression of his ministry? His life epitomized the fusion of personal and Social Gospel that the Black church has accomplished, a gift to American Christianity that has not yet been fully embraced.

As he always insisted, King was not an exception. Starting in 1619 when the first kidnapped Africans were unloaded into slavery in the Virginia colony, the spirit of Black people has played a dominant role in American religious, political, and social history. Slaveholders utilized their better-by-and-by distortion of Christianity, and justified slavery as a means of civilizing and Christianizing the allegedly benighted people they abducted. And from those first years, the slaves called on the Bible to justify their demands for freedom. And these demands have not been merely rhetorical. Historians have listed forty-three slave rebellions, and they were all in some measure religiously inspired. In the first one, in 1739, twenty South Carolina slaves began a march down the Kings Highway toward St. Augustine, Florida, where, because it was then a Spanish colony, they would be free. As they marched, they sang a word, "Liberty!"— *lukango* in their native Kikongo, a word that expresses both the English ideals embodied in "liberty" and "salvation." This revolt failed, and its leaders were executed. But its fusion of the religious and the political continued in the African American community in revolts and uprisings, culminating in its most eloquent practitioner, Martin Luther King Jr.

King built on a history of faith-based American Black refusal to accept subordination, and Blacks demonstrated this refusal in defiant agitation, frequently led by religious figures. One of the most noteworthy, and a clear example of what had come before and would follow, was Nat Turner (1800–1831), who led a slave revolt in southeastern Virginia in 1831. Turner was an Evangelical Christian, a Baptist minister who drew directly on Scripture and on the Baptist distrust of worldly authority over "soul freedom" as the basis for the rebellion. Like other spiritual revolutionaries, however, Turner also relied on visions and messages from heaven. This is how he describes one of them:

> *I heard a loud noise in Heaven, and the Spirit spoke to me and said, the Serpent was loosened, and Christ had laid down the yoke he had borne for the sins of men, and that I should take it on and fight against the Serpent, for the time was fast approaching when the first should be last and the last should be first.*

There are two notable elements in this message from the Spirit that we will return to later,

First, the biblical symbol of the serpent, which is first mentioned in the creation story in Genesis, has reappeared, identified here with slavery. It will reappear more than once in the rest of the Bible until its denouement, crushed by "the woman," in Revelation.

Second, the "great reversal," when "the first shall be last and the last shall be first," which Jesus and the prophets reiterated, and which is a strong continuing trope in Black preaching, is also vividly present in Revelation.

When I first read Turner's testimony, it reminded me of Joan of Arc. At first, this might sound unlikely, but there are striking likenesses. Both the maid of Lorraine and the Virginia slave heard "voices." Both claimed to have been called by God, not to a quiet life of prayer but to violent action against subjugation. For Joan, it was the English domination of her homeland. For Turner, it was the oppression of his people by the slave holders. The innocent shepherdess who heard "voices" and persuaded the king to allow her to lead a discouraged army into battle suffered betrayal and death by fire. Likewise, the incensed slave heard voices from heaven, led people into battle, was defeated and slaughtered. The parallels are obvious. Yes, it has been reported that Nat Turner told his followers to "kill all the white people," but no one knows if he really said that or if it was attributed to him by his enemies. But is Joan so innocent of bloodshed? Her "voices" told her to liberate France from the English and install a questionable pretender, but obviously that would require the spilling of a lot of English (and French) blood. Both Joan and Nat Turner lost and paid for their actions with their lives. Five hundred years after her agonizing death on the pyre, decreed by a cabal of church and state officials, she was declared a saint by Pope Benedict XV in 1920. But there is no movement today, even as we celebrate how "Black lives matter," to recognize Nat Turner as a pioneer of Black liberation.

It is also significant that both Joan and Nat are summoned to their deeds not by visions but by voices. This is clearly within the biblical tradition. In the Bible, God seldom "appears" to people. Rather, he or his Spirit "speak." Yahweh speaks to Moses from the burning bush. He "calls" Amos, Isaiah, and Jeremiah to their prophetic missions. At the baptism of Jesus, the Spirit does appear "in the form of a dove," but it is a "voice from heaven" that says, "This is my beloved Son, in whom I am well pleased." On the road to Damascus, Paul is blinded and can see nothing, but Jesus commissions him verbally for his mission to the Gentiles.

It is worth noting here that Turner's account follows a classical paradigm of prophetic calls. It is voiced, not shown. As we have noticed before, the invisibility of the God of the Hebrews is a prominent dimension of his holiness: "No man shall see God and live." And this is also focal for understanding why, except for the Book of Revelation with its vividly symbolic streets of gold and gates of pearl, there are so few visual portrayals of heaven in the Bible.

Like the South Carolina revolt a century earlier, Turner's took the form of a *march* across the state. It is worth noting how many Black liberation movements have relied on marches, including the now famous march for voting rights from Selma, Alabama, to the state capital at Montgomery. That was the non-violent march that was brutally attacked on the Edmund Pettus Bridge by mounted police and deputized civilians. But when Martin Luther King invited people to travel to Selma to complete the march, he attracted hundreds of sympathizers to the city, which became a turning point in the civil rights movement. I was one of the hundreds who responded to King's invitation. Even now, years later, I recall joining the crowd streaming out of Brown's Chapel toward the bridge; and as we moved through the streets, everyone was singing. One of the songs was the old hymn "Marching to Zion."

The ongoing attempt to unshackle Black Americans took on a different shape under Marcus Garvey (1887–1940), the leader of the American "Back-to-Africa" movement. Garvey was also, in his own way, a religious leader and innovator. He is known for founding the Universal Negro Improvement Association, but for years he nourished a dream of organizing a church, especially if not exclusively for African Americans. Eventually he joined forces with an Anglican priest, and together they established the African Orthodox Church of St. Augustine in 1921 on the corner of Cedar Street and Hawthorne Street in the Highland Park section of Boston (in what is now called "Roxbury"). Its constitution states, its "faith . . . as declared, is orthodox, in conformity with the Orthodox Churches of the East from which its Episcopate is derived. The A.O.C. admits to membership and other privileges persons of all races. It seeks particularly to reach out and enfold the millions of African descent." The document then goes on to say, the church "declares itself to be and is perpetually autonomous and controlled by Negroes.

Hence the name, African Orthodox." Garvey wanted both a country (later Liberia) and a church where white people would not be excluded, but "Negroes" would be firmly in charge. And if this inversion of the social hierarchy of America suggested the "last shall be first" pattern he foresaw for heaven, it also meant that Garvey's prescription for society had radical political consequences. Blacks were and would remain a minority in a land with a white majority that would never accept such a transposition. It would necessitate Black Americans to create a new country and then their massive immigration.

As might have been expected, many white racists who would have liked to see the Black people "sent back" supported Garvey's "back to Africa" movement, as did the American Colonization Society, which Abraham Lincoln supported for a time. The latter urged Black Americans to join a settlement on the West Coast of Africa, which declared its independence in 1847. Still, the United States did not recognize it until 1862, during the Civil War, and only a tiny percentage of Black Americans ever settled there. The vast majority remained to struggle for freedom in America, a goal that their religious and political movements pursued relentlessly. Now and then the idea of a new self-governing, Black-nation homeland—sometimes compared with the objective of the Zionists—re-emerged, as it did in the early years of the Black Muslims, but never gained wide support with either Blacks or whites. It is interesting to speculate, if such a "Black Israel" had appeared, what effect it might have had on the theology of the Black churches, including their history of singing about a "promised land" that sometimes blended earth and heaven.

In April 3, 1968, on the night before his death, Martin Luther King stood in the pulpit of the Mason Temple in Memphis and told the congregation, "I have been to the mountaintop and I have *seen* the promised land." Once again, one of the oldest symbols in the Bible came alive. This "promised land" was a world, or at least an America, free of racism. In so many ways King embodied the essence of Black American Christianity. But why then, in hundreds of speeches, sermons, and books, did he almost never write or speak about "heaven"? The reason is that King's theology was about the reigning of God, something he called "the beloved community." He believed that this new era of peace and equality was beginning to take shape on earth but needed human struggle to bring it to completion. And he insisted that this human effort should be enacted in disruptive but nonviolent action against war and racism. He could quote passages from the Bible by heart, but they were always drawn from the verses in which Jesus and the prophets hail the coming of a day when "justice shall roll down like waters, and righteousness like an ever-flowing stream" (Amos 5:24). King's theology was a brilliant blend of what he learned in the Black church and in his formal education in graduate schools and seminaries steeped in the Social Gospel.

After his graduation from Morehouse College, from 1948 until 1951 King attended the largely white Crozer Seminary in Upland, Pennsylvania. But why? This school was scorned by conservative Baptists at the time for its liberalism in theology and politics. And this raises an intriguing question. For a young man with his background and family tradition of Black preachers, not the least of whom was "Daddy" King, Martin's imposing father, why did he go to Crozer, which was not a prominent school among white seminaries (it merged with Rochester in 1970). It seems an unlikely choice. Why did King not attend a Black seminary?

When I asked a prominent Black Baptist minister who had worked with King for years, he told me that it is probably precisely "Daddy" King's personality that motivated the young King to seek his education elsewhere. He wanted to put some distance between himself and both Daddy's conservative theology and Daddy's dominant parenting. It is also rumored that at that age (nineteen) he was notoriously not a serious student, and he looked forward to enjoying some of the extracurricular pleasures of postgraduate life. And Pennsylvania was a long way from Alabama, and Daddy King. Then he enrolled for doctoral studies in the Theological School of Boston University, known for its liberal theological "personalism." King wrote a doctoral dissertation comparing the ideas of God in the left-wing philosophical theologian Paul Tillich, who was then teaching at Union Theological Seminary in New York, and the University of Chicago religious humanist Henry Nelson Wieman. King's theological repertory contained an exceptional blend of elements. From the Black church he absorbed the long tradition of protest, but he also became aware of the lingering danger of the false promises of compensatory rewards for submission and docility. But instead of rejecting this disabling otherworldly devotion, he skillfully applied its powerful imagery to the earthly struggle. Rather than seeing heaven as a reward after death, he spoke of the "peaceable kingdom," a "beloved community" you could savor now while you fought for its coming on earth as it is in heaven.

Clearly, those who describe King as a product of the Black church are correct, but only partially. He represented a unique synthesis, one that enabled him to speak to a variety of audiences. Black preachers like Nat Turner and King and their followers appealed to the same sources to justify rebelling against their masters. But Turner had nothing to say to the white people except, "Let my people go." Historians have shown how slaves translated songs that spoke of heaven as "beyond Jordan," the promised land, and "over yonder" to mean beyond the "peculiar institution" and the states where it was legally enforced, to refer to the North. The same process went on during the civil rights movement when young Black marchers, freedom riders, and picketers chose hymns and spirituals in which references to heaven became references to freedom. The fluidity of the border between earthly and transcendental goals has become a hallmark of much of American religion.

During what some have termed "the King era" in America, another Black religious leader was creating a stir. Malcolm X was usually depicted in the media as King's antagonist, a man who dismissed nonviolence. But I worked with King in the Southern Christian Leadership Conference, and I know from personal conversations that King never saw Malcolm that way. He respected Malcolm, and the feeling was mutual. King sometimes told his friends that Malcolm "made his work easier" by posing an alternative approach. I believe that King increasingly admired the note of urgency in Malcolm's message.

One of King's most widely read books is *Why We Can't Wait* (1964). After Malcolm's murder, King moved to a more radical position. He came to believe that economic inequality lay at the basis of racial inequality, and he began organizing poor people across racial lines, as Malcolm had. He said that what we needed in America was "democratic socialism," but this remark is rarely mentioned in tributes to him. He completely lost favor with President Lyndon Johnson when he delivered his historic criticism of the Vietnam War in Riverside Church on April 4, 1967. The truth is that King and Malcolm were moving closer to each other before both were killed.

I only met Malcolm X once. When I was a graduate student at Harvard in March 1961, I noticed an announcement in *The Crimson* that Malcolm, who was then the best-known leader in the Black Muslim movement, would be speaking at the Harvard Law School Forum. He was then seen by many people, Black and white, as a dangerous radical, and I wanted to hear him; so I made my way through a parking lot, past the chemistry labs to the imposing Law Quadrangle with its stately library over whose doors is carved the Latin phrase *Non sub Homine sed sub Deo et Lege* ("not under man but under God and the law").

The hall was packed. Malcolm X was neatly dressed in suit and tie. He delivered a scalding denunciation of racism, but in a measured, eloquent style. After the talk he stood briefly at the door and shook hands with the students, including me, as we emerged. I was too overcome with awe to say anything but "Thank you." But as I wandered back through the Yard, I remembered an afternoon a few months earlier when I was chatting with a Black friend about Malcolm and he suddenly invited me to have a drink with him in a bar in Roxbury, the Black section of Boston, which Malcolm had once patronized. When we stepped through the swinging doors, I noticed that there were no other white people there. And as we bellied up to the bar, a tall, brawny, dark bartender spoke to my friend, "Stevens," he said, "why don't you and your *Caucasian* friend go find another bar?"

"Oh no, Big John," Stevens said, "you don't understand. This is Harvey, and he wants you to tell him about Malcolm."

"Aha," Big John answered, "so he wants to hear about the *man*! Well, all right then!" Big John then set a tall glass tumbler in front of me and filled it halfway with scotch. No ice. Then he began to describe how he and "Detroit Red" had worked together. The "Red" in Malcolm's nickname came from his red hair, which Malcolm hated because, he said, it was a reminder that one of his female ancestors had been raped by a red-headed white man. Big John said that he and Malcolm had staked out parties on Beacon Hill, pried open windows, and made off with furs and expensive coats. Malcolm was eventually arrested and imprisoned in the penitentiary in Boston that is now an upscale hotel and restaurant. Some years ago, while it was a prison, I visited it a few times with a group from my local church and assisted in leading services. I noticed even then that there were only two religious opportunities available to the inmates, Evangelical Christianity and Islam. A Catholic priest dropped in once a week and said Mass, but then left. Therefore, I was not surprised when I learned that in this prison Malcolm had met a member of the Nation of Islam and embraced the Muslim faith.

Malcolm's life from then on is one of the most absorbing of any in the history of the interaction of religion and politics. He began as a zealous follower of Elijah Muhammad, the leader of the Nation of Islam at the time. A stirring orator, Malcolm held the attention of audiences everywhere by his biting attacks on white institutions and white people in general. He sometimes ridiculed Martin Luther King and insisted that nonviolence was a nonstarter, a cruel hoax. He asserted that Black people in America had to win their freedom "by any means necessary." But he soon ran into differences with Elijah Muhammad and the Black separatism he advocated. Then, as a pious Muslim, he made the required hajj, a pilgrimage to Mecca, and, according to his own testimony, the experience changed his life. In Mecca, he said, he saw Black and white and brown and yellow devotees worshiping together in a peaceful celebration of the oneness of the one God and the underlying unity of all human beings. When he returned to America, Malcolm changed his name to El-Hajj Malik El-Shabazz. Then, in June 1964, he founded the Organization of Afro-American Unity, which identified racism, not white people as individuals, as the enemy of justice. At first, he concentrated on racial oppression, but then enlarged his attack to include the capitalist economic system, which brought him closer to King, whose thinking was moving in the same direction. Malcolm's organizing efforts were short lived because he was assassinated on February 21, 1965, in the Audubon Ballroom in Harlem. A neighborhood restaurant called X now stands a few yards from the spot.

Like Nat Turner; the revolutionary Baptist preacher Marcus Garvey; the Black nationalist church founder Sojourner Truth; Harriet Tubman, the rescuers of slaves; and many more, Malcolm X, the devout Muslim, occupies a permanent place in the gallery of Black Americans who, enlivened by faith, advanced the vision of the reigning of God. They differed from each other on some political and theological points, but they held one idea in common: whether enslaved, segregated, or oppressed in other ways, Black people should *not* merely wait to be welcomed into the pearly gates. In his speeches on street corners and in auditoriums, Malcolm lashed out at the Black people who had swallowed the "white lie" about a heavenly reward for those who "knew their place" and stayed in it. Heaven was not just a distant something to hope for in an unspecified future. Black people should claim the promises of Allah here and now. He enunciated what theologians have called a "realizing eschatology," but one that would not realize itself, one that with God's support, they would need to struggle for, as Malcolm liked to say, "by any means necessary."

There is another Christian movement, in some ways the most significant one spawned by African Americans, that must be mentioned here: Pentecostalism. In 1906 in Los Angeles, California, a small congregation of Black Christians was meeting in the rented second floor of what had recently been a stable on Azusa Street. Their pastor was a prayerful Black revivalist preacher named William J. Seymour, who had little formal education and was blind in one eye. He had recently arrived from Houston. As they prayed and sang, the congregation experienced what they felt was a descent of the Spirit. They had yearned and hoped for something like this for years. They had read the account of the first Pentecost, a Jewish holiday, in the Acts of the Apostles many times, and now it seemed to be happening again:

*When the day of Pentecost came, they were all together in one place. Suddenly a sound like the blowing of a violent wind came from heaven and filled the whole house where they were sitting. They saw what seemed to be tongues of fire that separated and came to rest on each of them. All of them were filled with the Holy Spirit and began to speak in other tongues as the Spirit enabled them.*

*Now there were staying in Jerusalem God-fearing Jews from every nation under heaven. When they heard this sound, a crowd came together in bewilderment, because each one heard their own language being spoken. Utterly amazed, they asked: "Aren't all these who are speaking Galileans? Then how is it that each of us hears them in our native language? Parthians, Medes and Elamites; residents of Mesopotamia, Judea and Cappadocia, Pontus and Asia, Phrygia and Pamphylia, Egypt and the parts of Libya near Cyrene; visitors from Rome (both Jews and converts to Judaism); Cretans and Arabs—we hear them declaring the wonders of God in our own tongues!" Amazed and perplexed, they asked one another, "What does this mean?"*

*Some, however, made fun of them and said, "They have had too much wine."*

The seekers, most of whom were Black, gathered in the old stable on Azusa Street, were shaken, and some were thrown to the floor. Others spoke in what they viewed as "strange tongues," languages they had never learned. Some were healed of illnesses. They concluded that a "second Pentecost" was now taking place in their midst. They were convinced that God was sending this new blessing because the end of the age was coming soon, and God wanted his people to be pure and holy, and the church cleansed of sins of denominational divisions, racial separation, and the inequality of women. They went on meeting every night, and the "signs," healings and speaking in tongues continued for a year. More seekers and skeptics flocked to Azusa Street. One white preacher from Alabama stayed for a week, and when he returned home he told his astonished flock that at Azusa Street he had seen "the color line washed away with the blood of the lamb."

Word got out, and people—Black and white, Mexican and Asian—began to crowd into the tiny space; most sought healing and a fresh relationship with God. But other people came as well. Reports of worshipers leaping in joy and rolling on the floor in ecstasy attracted scoffers and curiosity seekers. But some who came to laugh at the "Holy Rollers" were dismayed by seeing Black and white men and women hugging each other while they shouted and wept, and left in disgust. But there were others who "came to laugh and stayed to pray." All, however, saw something utterly remarkable going on. At the height of Jim Crow, the Azusa Street attic may have been the most integrated location in America. When they chose leaders for their growing congregation, they reflected this conviction. A photograph of the deacons at the time shows eight people, half Black and half white, half men and half women. But this was not the result of what we now call "social action." The Azusa Street "Pentecostals" (as they were thereafter called) believed that the Spirit of God was breaking down the sinful walls of racial separation, and that this breaking was a sure sign that the Second Coming was at hand. God was establishing a little beachhead of heaven in Los Angeles.

The Pentecostal movement grew rapidly in America, a living demonstration of the possibility, indeed necessity, of a racially inclusive church. But the pervasiveness of racism soon took its toll. As white Pentecostal preachers grew in number, they came to resent the Black leadership and began to organize groups of their own. Some of these white groups united in 1914 to form the

Assemblies of God, which has remained a largely white denomination. Still, Pentecostalism in a multitude of forms grew and spread rapidly around the world, especially in Africa, Latin America, and Asia. Today the largest congregation in South Korea is the Yoido Full Gospel Church in Seoul, with eight hundred thousand members. With its more than four hundred million members, Pentecostalism is the fastest growing religious movement in the world. But it was born, as Pentecostals love to remind people, in a Black congregation meeting in a setting like the one where Christ was born, a stable.

What do Pentecostals believe about heaven? The biblical text they refer to from the second chapter of the Acts of the Apostles is quoted above. The apostle Peter is quoting the prophet Joel to assure the people who were confused and upset about the "signs." In one of the funniest verses in the Bible, he insists that these folks, at three in the afternoon, were not drunk, but that what was happening was a "New Pentecost," and that God was making his dwelling place among human beings. Heaven had in effect come among them, and they were tasting its treasures. In some meetings, waves of uncontrollable joyful laughter broke out. While they had at first seen "speaking in tongues" as the ability to speak foreign languages, most now saw it as the Spirit of God praying within them. God was as close as their lungs and mouths. They did not give up on the conventional idea of a heaven after death, but it was not a keynote of Pentecostal preaching, and still is not. Pentecostals have retained the by-and-by, but they emphasize the here and now. Pentecostal teaching underlines the possibility of a blissful and rewarding life in the Spirit that can be lived here and now. It represents another kind of what we have called "realized eschatology," different in its own way from some of the other examples we have discussed.

One result of the tumultuous history of the faith of Black people in America, replete with its movements and counter-movements, from Nat Turner to Marcus Garvey to Malcolm X and Martin Luther King, is reflected in the distinctive ways these spokesmen understood heaven and the kingdom of God. But as varied as these references have been, there is one unambiguous idea they hold in common: they place the freedom and dignity of all the people God has created at the center. But beyond that there is little uniformity, and this is reflected in their music. From the earliest spirituals to gospel, reggae, freedom songs, and rap, the music fosters a luxuriant range of images. Opinions vary, including ideas about heaven. For years, a charismatic Black Baptist, Peter Gomes, was a professor at Harvard Divinity School and the preacher to the university at the Harvard Memorial Church. He once told the congregation that as a young boy he had asked his mother whether there would be any white people in heaven. She thought for a moment, then said that she supposed there would be, but "I do not plan to have anything to do with them."

There is no single Black American understanding of heaven. But even though they vary, all display one other feature in common: their concern with the relationship between the racial communities in the afterlife. This is understandable, since the source of so much suffering among Black people has been created by the ideas and institutions of white supremacy. How might this be corrected in heaven? There are roughly four possibilities:

1. Complete and amicable equality and integration, of which Father Divine's heaven and Martin Luther King's "dream" are the model.
2. Equality with some individual self-chosen integration and/ or some separation, for which the heaven of Peter Gomes's mother, and no doubt many other people, is the example.
3. Maximum separation with minimal relationship and only where necessary, as in Marcus Garvey's Back-to-Africa

movement and the African Orthodox Church and the Nation of Islam.

4. Radical inversion, with Blacks on top and others reduced to subservient status. This concept is not heard much today, but has been voiced in the past, sometimes by Blacks and white people who read the inversion passages literally; the first see it as rough justice, and the second see it as the culmination of their worst fears.

Any such listing of Black heavens, however, must be seen in the light of the defining themes of Black Christianity that we have underscored in this chapter. For the most part, Black Christians in America have managed to maintain both a personal-individual idea of heaven and a here-and-arriving reigning of God, which is already breaking down the Jericho walls of segregation.

As I conclude this chapter, a question remains. Why should Father Divine and his Peace Unity Mission, of which many Black spiritual leaders once voiced strenuous objections, be thought of as representative? I am aware that in some ways Father Divine's movement is not "representative" in the usual sense. It was not "typical." I know of no other group whose leader allowed, perhaps encouraged, his disciples to call him "God," or any group that housed many thousands of homeless people in cooperative communities, although here and there some sects like the Dunkers tried on a much smaller scale. Scholars who have tracked the Peace Unity Mission movement estimate that at the zenith of its life, it had two million members and a network of several hundred "heavens." Still, it was visibly and emphatically countercultural, insisting on racial integration in a period of Jim Crow, which was enforced by law and terror in the South and by custom in the North. During a depression, and in a culture of competitive capitalism, it promoted entrepreneurial cooperation. The innumerable Black men and women whose small businesses got started with a loan from his movement contributed a portion of their profits to a fund to help other would-be entrepreneurs. To his critics who attacked his organization as creeping socialism, Father Divine called his political and religious philosophy "Americanism."

But despite my reservations about Father Divine himself, I still consider his movement "representative" for our purpose here. During my years of teaching religious history, I have found that we can sometimes gain valuable insights about a faith by studying subgroups within it that have magnified one of its practices into defining tenets. Elements (or one element) that are present but usually not emphasized are escalated into prominence and high visibility. As I have shown earlier, the idea of building the kingdom of God on earth has, until it was recently undercut by "personal salvation," played a decisive role in American religion (see Richard Niebuhr, *The Kingdom of God in America*). Father Divine took what he called "God's administration" and made it his foundational motif. Further, he did so by eliminating the goal of "going to heaven," since heaven had now come to you. Any book on heaven that does not include this variant would be incomplete.

It is true that other branches of Christianity have seized upon parts of Christianity and transformed them into the essential message. One of the building bricks becomes the keystone. Baptists have done this with baptism; Catholics with apostolic succession; Quakers with the indwelling God; Pentecostals with the gifts of the Spirit. But in this book, we are chiefly concerned with the idea of heaven and the afterlife, what theologians have called "eschatology." And this was exactly the primary concern of Father Divine's movement. By understanding it, we can see more clearly, by comparison and contrast, how the ideas evident in his movement are presented in others. All Christian denominations teach that the kingdom of God or of heaven is "in the midst of us," or that God is present within every person. But while these ideas are often presented in ordinary small type, Father Divine pasted them on the wall and etched them in glaring, shiny capital letters.

Was Father Divine a heretic? His teachings, including his idea of heaven, were unconventional, but he did not invent them. They are transmuted versions of ideas that are familiar to many Christians. They force us to ask, if God is not within us in the way he interprets it, then just how is God present? And if heaven or God's kingdom is not in our midst as he explained it, then how and where is it present? After his death, the Peace Unity Mission declined rapidly; one by one the "heavens" closed, and the angels resumed worldly pursuits. And even though one historian names Father Divine the most significant figure in American Black religion between Marcus Garvey and Martin Luther King Jr., he has almost been forgotten. He deserves better.

A few years ago, I went back to Philadelphia for a class reunion at the University of Pennsylvania. After the speeches, handshakes, dinners, and drinks I strolled over to 40th and Chestnut to see what had happened to the "heaven." The building was still there, but it was no longer a heaven. The original name of the hotel had been restored. I stepped inside, but no choir of angels greeted me, and no sumptuous Communion feast had been laid. As Revelation says, "Heaven . . . had passed away." But I thought about Father Divine and his hope for a peaceful and racially integrated society, and I recognized that we are not in heaven yet, and in America we still had a long way to go.

# 14

# *Jerusalem as Heaven*

*Then I saw a new heaven and a new earth, for the first heaven and the first earth had passed away, and there was no longer any sea.*

*I saw the Holy City, the new Jerusalem, coming down out of heaven from God, prepared as a bride beautifully dressed for her husband.*

*And I heard a loud voice from the throne saying, "Now the dwelling of God is with men, and he will live with them. They will be his people, and God himself will be with them and be their God.*

*He will wipe every tear from their eyes. There will be no more death or mourning or crying or pain, for the old order of things has passed away." (Revelation 21:1–4 NIV)*

For centuries the city of Jerusalem has been a potent symbol for Jews, Muslims, and Christians. Every year at the close of the Passover Seder Jews repeat the words, "Next year in Jerusalem." Muslims reverence it as the second holiest city after Mecca. A favorite Protestant hymn I have often sung in church, "Jerusalem the Golden," explicitly equates the New Jerusalem with heaven:

*Jerusalem the Golden, with milk and honey blest,*
*Beneath thy contemplation sink heart and voice oppressed.*

*I know not, O I know not, what joys await us there,*
*What radiancy of Glory, what bliss beyond compare.*
*They stand, those halls of Sion,*
*All jubilant with song,*
*And bright with many an Angel*
*And all the Martyr throng.*

                    A. Ewing, based on a text by Bernard of Cluny

A later verse in the hymn says, "*There is the throne of David,*" thereby underlining the connection between the Jewish and Christian traditions. But the final lines, with their mention of "the home of God's elect" and all those dwelling in the city who are "clad in robes of white," clearly emphasize a traditional Christian hope for heaven. The final lines leave no doubt about the city's ultimate meaning:

*O sweet and blessed country*
*The home of God's elect!*
*O sweet and blessed country.*

As symbols of heaven go, Jerusalem is the Big Apple. In previous chapters I have pointed out how the idea of heaven can mean either a life after this one or a spiritual dimension alongside and intertwined with this one. In this chapter I will explore what endowing Jerusalem with such a degree of ultimacy reveals about the concept of an alternative or postmortal existence. And I will indicate how Jerusalem, as both earthly and heavenly, impinges on the tension between heaven and the kingdom of God, a recurrent theme in this book.

The words of "Jerusalem the Golden" invoke an otherworldly Jerusalem. But the metaphor of the city is so flexible that it can also invoke a social gospel Jerusalem-on-earth that we are summoned to build in the familiar anthem by William Blake, the official song of many English, and some American, secondary schools. And there is little doubt that the same congregations have sung both hymns without noting any contradiction.

JERUSALEM

*And did the countenance divine*
*Shine forth upon our clouded hills?*
*And was Jerusalem builded here*
*Among those dark satanic mills?*

*I will not cease from mental fight;*
*Nor shall my sword sleep in my hand*
*Till we have built Jerusalem*
*In England's green and pleasant land.*

William Blake (1757–1827)

The words of these two hymns focus the key question: Is Jerusalem something God brings down to earth as Revelation states? Or is it a supernal refuge our hearts long to enter as in "Jerusalem the Golden"? Or is it something, as Blake says, that God summons us to build in England's green and pleasant land, and presumably elsewhere as well?

Jerusalem has had so many meanings for so many people, and this is both its blessing and its curse. It is both a small earthly metropolis located on the eastern littoral of the Mediterranean Sea where the cross currents of empires have clashed. At the same time, it has been the Holy City of three faiths. It is both the symbol of a transcendent heaven and the goal of a gospel-mandated utopia to be built here on earth. Originally a Canaanite town, it was captured by King David in 1000 BCE and made his capital. It has been conquered and reconquered at least seven times. The biblical Book of Lamentations begins with an outcry for Jerusalem, like a woman who has been abandoned by all her lovers. But today, the reverse may be more accurate. Jerusalem may have too many "lovers"; and as one observer has said, some of them seem "willing to love her to death." Has the fusing of the earthly city with the heavenly one in so many minds made it more difficult to arrive at a reasonable settlement about its future?

The confusion in some people's minds of the material with the spiritual Jerusalem can sometimes produce comical results. Years ago, when we still placed phone calls through hotel switchboards, a friend told me that he had once tried to put in a person-to-person call to Jerusalem from Atlanta, but a sweet-voiced operator told him, "You can't call Jerusalem, honey. It's in the *Bible*." The fate of Jerusalem is that it *is* in the Bible, and you can *telephone* it. But the blending of the Jerusalem "up there" with the one "down here" has also resulted in consequences that are not so funny. It has had tragic consequences as armies have clashed not for its walls and streets but for its aura.

Were these grisly battles inevitable? Maybe not. When David made the city his capital, it was already inhabited by a Canaanite people known as Jebusites, for whom it was a sacred center of their own religion. Wisely, however, David did not banish the Jebusites or their priests. Rather, he invited them to stay in the city and continue to honor their gods on the same Mount Zion where he instituted the worship of Yahweh. Thus, contrary to an enduring belief about Jerusalem, the city did not begin its life as a bulwark of monotheism but as an "interfaith" capital with Jews and Jebusites offering their sacrifices side by side. But Jerusalem's controversial character began early. Even after David occupied the city and Solomon built the temple there to try to centralize (and better control) Jewish religious practice, there were large portions of the Jews who refused to accept its sacral supremacy. We find ample evidence of this Jewish anti-Jerusalem sentiment in the Gospels.

For example, in one of his most famous encounters, Jesus stops in a Samaritan village to get a drink of water from its public well. A local woman draws some for him, and a conversation starts. The woman wonders what Jesus is doing there since, as she reminds him, the Jews usually avoid contact with Samaritans. She underlines the division by pointing out that while her people worship at the local mountains, the Jews pray in Jerusalem. But Jesus refuses to go along with her divisive assumptions. He tells her that it doesn't matter where we pray, because "God is a Spirit, and those who worship him do so in spirit and in truth." Many people today fail to grasp how astonishing this statement was for a rabbi to make. His words undercut the assertion of the spiritual centrality of Jerusalem. If Christians had believed him, would they have dispatched armies with crosses on their shields to conquer it or to sing about it as a metaphor for heaven?

Have we made entirely too much of Jerusalem? Have we made it "matter" too much? The city's twofold ambiguity clearly continues to be what makes the city matter. The contradiction is portrayed graphically in a scene in the Hollywood film *The Holy Land*. After yet another fierce battle with the Crusaders in Jerusalem, the Muslim leader Saladin is pictured walking away from the city. He has made a deal with the "Franks," as the Arabs called the armies of the cross. Christians will be allowed to visit the city, but only so long as they arrive without weapons. The Crusaders have agreed. Now someone asks Saladin why both sides have made such a huge issue out of the city. Saladin stops and looks at the camera. "Jerusalem," he says, "it means nothing." Then he takes a few steps, pauses, and turns toward the camera again. "Jerusalem," he says, "it means everything."

Everything or nothing? Does Jerusalem "matter"? If so, why? For centuries it has never stopped mattering tremendously to a wide array of people, if for different reasons. Its unequaled symbolic and political importance has sparked hundreds of years of blood-drenched Crusades and jihads. And the spirit of the Crusades reached far beyond Palestine. The First Crusade started in

1096 CE. Four hundred years later, when Christopher Columbus set sail westward in 1492, he wore beneath his tunic the rough cloth garment of a Third Order Franciscan because, as he wrote in his diary, he wanted to use the wealth of "The Indies" to launch a new Crusade to liberate the Holy Land. When Spanish explorers encountered a resistant population in the southern islands of the Philippines, they called them *moros*—like the "Moors" driven out of Spain.

I confess that I am fond of the city of Jerusalem. I have visited it as a tourist and prayed there as a pilgrim. I have taught and lectured there and studied Torah there with one of its foremost scholar-rabbis. The city is fascinating, lovely in rain, sunlight, and lit by a full moon. It is packed with layers of history. *But it is not heaven.* Anyone who has lived there knows that its toilets, like toilets everywhere, can get clogged. It is noisy at rush hour, and, despite the Israeli tourist ads that describe it as "united," it is not united. It is a divided city, albeit not with walls or roadblocks today. It is divided into a Jewish city in the western half and an Arab city in the eastern. The people who reside in the two portions do not travel back and forth much. Not many visitors hear choirs of angels. And in the Church of the Holy Sepulcher there are sometimes scuffles between the Russian Orthodox, Roman Catholic, and Coptic contingents who share the sacred space. These three branches of Christianity, not fully trusting each other, eventually handed over the key to the site to a Palestinian Muslim family, which has performed its peacemaking duties among the quarrelsome followers of the Prince of Peace for generations. In a book that examines ideas about heaven, it might also be necessary to clarify the picture by identifying the "not heavens." But even so, the city's past and present open a window on the variegated scenarios of another life held by the faiths represented in it.

Many people today will think that nothing could be more appropriate for Christianity than a Jerusalem-oriented theology. But the history of Christianity suggests the contrary. For three hundred years after the life of Christ, Christians despised and avoided Jerusalem. They saw it not as a holy place but as accursed. It was where Jesus was betrayed and denied by his own followers, arrested, and tried by an alliance of Romans and the temple elite, humiliated, and tortured to death. There was nothing holy about it, and they stayed away from it.

But in the first decades of the fourth century this changed dramatically. After Constantine became emperor in 324 CE and made Christianity legal, his mother, Helena, became a devoted Christian. She decided to make a pilgrimage to Jerusalem, which lay within the Byzantine Empire her son ruled. She did go to Jerusalem, but this was no ordinary pilgrimage like the many thousands that would take place in subsequent centuries. She was, after all, the emperor's mother: no rustic hostels for her, no sleeping on straw mats. She traveled in regal style with an abundant entourage. Still, while in Jerusalem, she did something that countless pilgrims have done since. She fell victim to a local souvenir hawker and bought what she was solemnly assured was a piece of the wooden cross on which Christ had been nailed. Returning to Constantinople, she had a church built to house this most holy of relics. From then on, thousands of Christians have descended on Jerusalem and the Holy Land, providing a dependable revenue stream for generations of relic venders and inn keepers, coming home with who knows how many splinters of the true cross. Luther vainly tried to break this trade, seeing it as "popish." He advised people to forgo the arduous trek and to stay home and read their Bibles instead. But the flow has never abated, and the Crusades were a kind of armed pilgrimage. Today the largest percentage of pilgrim-

tourists are conservative Protestant Christians. If you meet a
gaggle of visitors shuffling along the Via Dolorosa, the chances
are it is a delegation from a Black or white Pentecostal or Baptist church in South Carolina or Alabama. Israelis welcome the
dollars these latter-day Helenas bring with them, and no self-
respecting TV evangelist can forgo presenting at least one program to the world from the Holy City, thus attracting even more
visitors. But for the pilgrims there is sometimes a surprise. They
soon learn that there have been Christians in Jerusalem since
the first century CE, and that these local sisters and brothers
think of themselves as Palestinians and do not share the visitors' ardent support for Israel. In any case, for good reasons and
bad, Jerusalem has long since ceased to be an abominable site.

In examining the Jewish-Christian link, it is essential to
remember that the central moment in the Passover celebration is the Seder, the traditional meal from which the Christian Communion is derived. There is no other symbol for the
reigning of God or of heaven than the feast, the messianic banquet. No book on images of heaven would be complete without
mentioning this. It says a lot. It is about a company of elated
people enjoying one another's company, and God's, and savor-
ing the fruits of the field and the vine. No one is excluded. In
the text used by Jews, the Haggadah, participants are explicitly instructed to invite everyone to the table. In Christian congregations the Communion has often been characterized by its
exclusiveness rather than its openness, a patent contradiction
of the inclusive intent of the Lord's Supper. This is ironic since
Jesus was often accused, rightly, of dining with sinners ("this
man dines with publicans and sinners"). The New Testament
scholar John Dominic Crossan says that Jesus's practice of dining publicly with those with whom he was not supposed to dine
(the "open table") was one of the most dramatically revelatory
elements of his message about the nature of the reigning of God.

(I am pleased to see that this "fencing" of the Communion table is now diminishing in many churches.)

One day, on Communion Sunday in the church I attend, there were two Communion tables instead of one. One was piled high with different varieties of bread: dark bread, cinnamon buns, fresh baked rolls, French loaves, raisin bread, and more. The other table had only two or three crusts. As the Communion liturgy began, the minster told us this was a graphic reminder of the unequal distribution of "our daily bread" in the world. She suggested that as we picked up a piece of bread from the heavily laden table for ourselves, we also move two pieces to the other table, which would be included in our weekly contribution to the local food bank. Luther contended that Communion, like preaching, is another way of proclaiming the gospel. I do not think that part of the message was lost on anyone. But there was another dimension. If the Communion table offers a foretaste of the messianic banquet, then it must feed everyone without regard to religious affiliation or their current moral condition.

I have no doubt that there will be more modifications of the Passover Seder, Communion, and other rituals in the future, but I hope in Passover, the mention of Jerusalem will remain one way or another. I have spent a lot of time visiting, studying, and teaching in that earthly city. Like any other modern city, it has traffic jams, pleasant and unpleasant neighborhoods, problems with too many or too few visitors, and challenges to governing itself. But it continues to remind us that unless the three disparate faiths that call it "holy" can share it, there is little chance that the many more peoples of the world can share our one and only holy earth. As the late Catholic theologian Hans Küng once said, "There can be no peace among the nations until there is peace among the religions."

Jerusalem is resilient, and I am confident that it will survive and flourish. Still, unlike some other cities, Jerusalem must cope with very particular stresses. One of these is what is called the "Jerusalem syndrome." This is a unique form of mental illness in which individuals fancy themselves, usually only temporarily, to be a personality drawn from the Bible or history. King David, Saul, Jeremiah, and, of course, Jesus Christ are among the favorites. The Hadassah Medical Center, the city's main hospital, has a small ward, which I once visited, to treat those who fall prey to this malady. The staff informed me that the condition usually lasted only a few days but was subject to reoccurrence. In other words, Jerusalem is a fully real brick and cement, glass and steel city where the garbage must be collected. But Jerusalem is much more than that. There is the aura, the heavenly Jerusalem. And I am also confident that its primal leitmotifs of peace, shared community, and liberation will endure to assure people that the freedom God intends for all creatures must have both a transcendent and an earthly component. "The kingdom of God is in the midst of you."

The history of Jerusalem and the history of the Jewish people mirror each other. A Canaanite city that King David made his capital in 1000 BCE, Jerusalem has changed rulers a dozen times in three thousand years. It was not a Jewish city when David moved in, and although there are those who claim that its name means "place of peace," with "salem" equivalent to "shalom," this is not accurate either. Jerusalem, often called the "City of David," bears the name of a Canaanite deity "Salem." Canaanites, Babylonians, Greeks, Romans, Muslims, Crusaders, Muslims again, a British Mandate, and then Jews again have succeeded each other, always leaving some trace of their presence. Some have tried to change its name but have only temporarily succeeded. In the second century CE, the Romans, who had incorporated it into their empire, renamed it Aelia Capitolina, and built a temple to Jupiter there. After its conquest by the Rashidun Caliphate in 636 its new rulers called it Al-Quds. To walk the streets of the Old City today is to be reminded of the layer upon layer of civilizations that have occupied and governed it. It has often been called the "city of three faiths," and this is borne out by three landmarks: (1) the Western Wall (once called the "wailing wall"); (2) the Mosque of Omar, built on top of the Temple Mount, known as the Al Aqsa Compound or Haram esh-Sharif in Islam, where the Prophet Muhammad is believed to have ascended to heaven; and (3) the Church of the Holy Sepulcher, which houses the tomb where Jesus was buried before his resurrection. I suppose I need to say "one of the tombs" (plural, because, not surprisingly, there are two locations that are claimed to be the real tomb by two Christian factions).

Visiting the holy places is hardly optional for anyone concerned with how the three faiths frame death, life after death, and heaven. Muslims do not claim that the Prophet rose from the dead, or that he will "come again." Although it surprises many people when they learn it, many Muslims say that when a "coming again" does take place, it will be Jesus who returns. For the Prophet himself, however, heaven is where he ascended to from the Temple Mount in Jerusalem. It is where he met with his prophetic predecessors who blessed his mission. Therefore, during the early years of Islam, believers prayed facing Jerusalem, until the Prophet himself told them to face Mecca; but he also said that Jerusalem would always be the second most holy city for Muslims, thus linking Islam spiritually to Judaism and Christianity.

Judaism itself does not "include" these other faiths, but it is beyond dispute that it has been touched and influenced, positively and negatively, by them. It can be said that Judaism is what it is today in some part because of its encounters with these two sister faiths. True, those encounters have often been violent and bloody, but in the years since World War II this hostile past is fading. During his visit to Jerusalem on January 4, 1964, the first in history by any pope, Pope Paul VI was greeted by a cheering crowd. When he made his way to the Old City and was photographed kneeling in prayer at the Western Wall, he sent out a resounding message that a new era in Christian-Jewish relations was beginning.

I tasted this new interfaith atmosphere when, in the summer of 2001, I taught in a remarkable interfaith seminar at something called the Elijah Institute in Jerusalem. We met daily in a guest house that had once been a Roman Catholic convent, with the warm permission of the sisters and of the local bishop. All of them were pleased that they could make this contribution to furthering the "peace of Jerusalem." The faculty consisted of Jewish, Christian, and Muslim teachers, and the student body also included young men and women from all three traditions. We did not avoid the issues we knew could be divisive, but we discussed them in an open and appreciative way. Interestingly, some of the most contentious exchanges occurred not between representatives of the major traditions, but between members of one of them. The two Jewish instructors enjoyed arguing with each other, sometimes about matters the others knew little about. I had some pointed interchange with the Jesuit scholar who, in a moment of impatience I once suggested, was still demonstrating an "infallibility complex." It was a tasteless remark, and I immediately regretted it (although it did contain a grain of truth). He accepted my apology and bought me a bourbon on the rocks that evening, after which we strolled around the city together, trying to one-up each other in recalling its complicated history and endeavoring to reassure each other that maybe those terrible times were now over. We ate, drank together, and parted friends. But I was reminded that, as previous ecumenical and interfaith meetings had taught me, often the hardest conversations are with your coreligionists. Although I am a Baptist by birth and conviction, I have often admitted that it is harder for me to maintain my equanimity in an exchange with a Baptist fundamentalist than with a Muslim or a Buddhist. Some have called this the "tyranny of small differences," but when voices are raised, it is not easy to dismiss the differences as small.

I was sorry to leave Jerusalem after that sampling of honest interfaith conversation. I knew I wanted to return whenever I could, and I began to wonder whether the city, given its complex history, might one day become a world center for such exchanges.

Other things have also enhanced the city's allure. Some Christians have begun to celebrate their own version of Passover, including the "next year in Jerusalem" benediction. They do this for a couple of reasons. Some want to highlight the continuity between the two faiths, striking a blow to the shameful history of Christian anti-Semitism. Some want to affirm their solidarity with Israel and the Jews. But Jews have not universally welcomed this paschal innovation. Some object to it as an unwarranted example of "cultural appropriation." But when I have asked Jewish leaders, both in America and in Israel, they have usually shrugged and said something like, "Well, it is better for them to be for us than against us. It is a rough world, and we need all the help we can get." Once again, the former Canaanite fertility festival, once transformed into a festival of freedom, has survived and flourished, albeit in new idioms. It is not clear at this point what effect, if any, these "Christian Passovers" have had on Christians' beliefs about death and the afterlife. But it must have some. After all, Passover is about being saved from death by smearing the doorframe with blood.

As with most other religious traditions, Judaism has survived external threats and internal divisions for a long time. Of course there are still alternative expressions of Judaism today: Orthodox (and Ultra-Orthodox), Conservative, Reformed, and Reconstructionist congregations may compete quietly, but rarely attack each other, except, ironically, in Israel, where Ultra-Orthodox leaders regularly attack the other branches. There are also congregations that identify themselves as Jewish, are led by rabbis, and observe most of the Jewish holidays, but accept Jesus as the promised messiah. Ordinarily they do not like to be called "Christian," which they consider a term that emerged only after Gentiles became a majority in the "Jesus movement." These Jews see themselves in direct continuity with the first followers of Jesus, all of whom were Jews. Unlike the denominations of Judaism named above, however, these "messianic Jews" are not recognized as "really Jews" by the other Jewish "denominations." Even with the remarkably flexible theology of modern Judaism, there are apparently limits.

But across all these subdivisions among Jews, and for century after century, there were two words that never failed to ring out: "return" and "Jerusalem." The consciousness of being in exile, which had begun as a geographic description, slowly became existential, seeped so deep into the Jewish soul that "exile" became not just political or geographical but religious and existential. No matter where on earth, including in Palestine (or later, Israel), you found yourself in exile. To be human was to be in exile, and "return" was now visualized as a full, unalienated life as persons (and for Jews, also as a people). When Jews in Topeka or Tokyo finish the Passover Seder meal, they say "next year in Jerusalem," but few if any believe that either the place or the time should be taken literally. "Jerusalem" is becoming a symbol for the fulfillment of humanity in the kingdom of God, and "next year" is beginning to mean when that kingdom comes "on earth as it is in heaven."

There were in the first years after the foundation of the state of Israel some Zionists who rejected any attempt to spiritualize or universalize exile and return. They viewed the dispersal of Jews all over the world as a real historical exile, and they saw

Jerusalem/Zion not as symbol of the redemption of the world, but as a haven on earth to which all Jews should aspire to return. The argument that arose from these different points of view was a vociferous one, but it has faded in importance. Now a majority of Jews celebrate Israel as a momentous accomplishment of the Jewish people. But few insist that all "real Jews" must live there. And the enthusiasts who touted the birth of Israel as the dawn of world redemption have modified their claims.

Meanwhile, studying the constant theme of "return" in Jewish faith reminded me that the same idea is also just as persistent in Christianity, in which it is expressed as "home" or "going home." I could cite numerous examples of this in hymns and prayers. One Protestant hymnbook I consulted listed in its topical index thirty-four hymns with some reference to "going home." On the face of it, this is a little peculiar. "Home" means a place you have been, are away from. Some people still refer to a baby as a "little bundle from heaven," but there is nothing in Christian theology to support the idea that we all came from heaven, although this is something that Mormons, like a range of non-Christian religions, teach. The idea that we *come* from heaven as well as that we are *going* there is a tenacious one and will not be going away soon.

Beliefs about "Jerusalem" and "return" are constant themes in Jewish history, but the meaning of the terms has changed while the terms themselves have survived. It is also important to note that much of conservative and fundamentalist Christian "end-time" theology has incorporated this Jerusalem-centered tradition. Many fundamentalists believe that when Jesus returns, which they say could be very soon, it will be to Jerusalem, which must, of course, be in Jewish hands. These interpreters would never consider the possibility of Jesus's returning to, for example, an internationally controlled city. This all adds up to the underlying reason for the unwavering financial and political support they give to Israel today. This theology also informs the widely read *Left Behind* series of fictional portrayals of the Second Coming of Christ. The title of these books alludes to a view of heaven that is popular among their readers that just before the Second Coming, all true (Christian) believers will be "raptured," taken directly to God's presence without having to die, while nonbelievers are "left behind" on earth. Here, "next year in Jerusalem" becomes "tomorrow, or the next day in Jerusalem," but only for a Christian elite. This current misrepresentation of the Christian idea of death and heaven represents only a minority, but an assertive one. I mention it here in part to show how much it draws on a long tradition of Jewish Jerusalem-centered belief, while distorting it almost beyond recognition.

There are two reasons why these themes in Jewish thought suggest the need to rethink the language we use in Christian theology. First, the fact that Jerusalem is both transcendental and this-worldly reminds us that the promise of God concerns both a new heaven and a new earth. God's redemption does not erase history. It includes history. Ultimately neither an otherworldly nor a this-worldly redemption suffices. Jerusalem's status as both prevents the ultimate hope from evaporating into an insubstantial haze or deteriorating into a romantic new technological Eden with no serpent.

Second, retaining the New Jerusalem as an integral aspect of human hope suggests that despite the painful separations that have troubled our history, Jews and Christians ultimately belong together, as St. Paul insists in the opening chapters of his Epistle to the Romans. The apostle is clear that the covenant God made with Israel cannot be broken. But he also argues that Gentiles can be welcomed into the covenant community through faith in Christ, which most Jews eventually rejected, leading to the schism between the two communities.

Understandably, Paul does not mention other religious communities such as Buddhism or Hinduism, which existed in his time but about which he was unaware. Nor does he refer to Islam, which had not yet appeared. But his words in the second chapter of Ephesians about how Christ has "broken down the dividing wall," which mentions Greeks and barbarians, reinforce his universal logic and strongly imply that he would believe these "outsiders" should be full participants in the covenant as well. Yes, there is something "golden" about Jerusalem. The preciousness of gold has been recognized since ancient times. Gold is a substance that people fight and kill for, as they have for the city. Why? Historians of finance agree that gold, other than as a component of decorative jewelry or currency, has little inherent value. Most also agree that in addition to these concrete values, part of the very appeal of gold is the mystery of its appeal. Here is what a historian of finance and currency says:

> *There is another characteristic of gold, which, though harder to pinpoint, is just as real: its mystery. In the world of finance and investing, we often like to tiptoe around the word "mystery." Yet, as is true with most disciplines, there is always a place for both science and art, and even mystery.*

Gold, this historian continues, "can stimulate a subjective personal experience," but gold can also be objectified if it's adopted as a system of exchange. Its value is what is called a "social construct." It is valuable because so many people believe it is valuable. Likewise, the "holiness" of Jerusalem is not inherent in its paving blocks and stone walls, not even in its inhabitants. Jerusalem is "holy" because, like the mystery of gold, generations of people have endowed it with holiness. In addition to its glitter, gold also has something "mysterious" about it, which one might call an "aura."

When I read these words, I remembered the words of Saladin in the film *Holy Land,* which I quoted above: "Jerusalem means nothing; Jerusalem means everything." In one sense Jerusalem is a mystery. It is not quite true that it means everything to some and nothing to others. Rather it means something different but important to countless people. If there is little agreement on what Jerusalem "means," there is also little agreement on what heaven is like. Various faith communities tend to create a Jerusalem of their own. But these symbolic cities must ultimately be grounded in the empirical one.

As we conclude these thoughts about Jerusalem, about its location, its history, even its holiness, it must never be forgotten that Jerusalem should not be equated with its walls and holy places. The living city of Jerusalem is made up of people, 874,186 of them at its last census. The Israeli poet Yehuda Amichai, a native Jerusalemite, has written that as he walks the streets of his hometown, he often overhears guides explaining the sights. Once he heard one pointing to a frieze on a wall. "See that man there with the basket of fruit? Well just above his head you can see an exquisite second-century frieze."

Amichai says that at that moment he hoped the day would come when the guide might say, "See that ancient frieze on the wall? Well just below it you can see a resident of Jerusalem carrying a basket of fruit home to his family."

# 15

# *The Transfiguration of Heaven*

*For lo!, the days are hastening on,*
*By prophet bards foretold,*
*When with the ever-circling years*
*Comes round the age of gold*
*When peace shall over all the earth*
*Its ancient splendors fling,*
*And the whole world give back the song*
*That now the angels sing.*

> Poem and Christmas carol written in 1849
> by Edmund Sears, pastor of the Unitarian
> Church in Wayland, Massachusetts

*And the One seated on the throne said, "Behold, I make*
*all things new." Then He said, "Write this down, for these*
*words are faithful and true." And He told me, "It is done! I*
*am the Alpha and the Omega, the Beginning and the End.*
*To the thirsty I will give freely from the spring of the water of*
*life. . . ."* (Revelation 21:5–6, Berean Study Bible)

An expedition like the one we have just taken through so many cultures, eras, and heavens can leave us tired and confused. But I hope our wanderings have not been aimless. Throughout the kaleidoscopic landscape, a single theme has run: that images of heaven both reflect the hopes and travails of a culture and, in turn, shape its way of life. Heavens are both aspirational and normative. Therefore, my continuous question has been: what does any given vision of heaven tell us about its earthly milieu? But that was only half of the project. The other half was theological. It was to employ what Paul Tillich called the "method of correlation." This meant first trying to uncover the concerns about the ultimate meaning of existence these representations of heaven were expressing, then to correlate this existential question with the appropriate symbols of faith.

It was important to me as I started this correlating process that when we think about concepts of heaven and the afterlife we try not to answer questions like, "But is this description true?" meaning, does it correspond to what is "really there"? I can understand why we voice such questions. But I did not intend to pursue them. I would like to think about heaven in a different way. Only cranks waste time investigating whether there ever was a "real" Mona Lisa or whether there was a "real" Don Quixote. The painting of the almost smiling lady and the tale of the knight of sad countenance are enough to stoke our imaginations.

Following this question-and-response method is not easy, but it sometimes reveals new dimensions you might otherwise have missed, and this is what happened to me. As I wrote, I found my thinking changing. I had started out convinced that the popular notion of "going to heaven" had largely displaced Jesus's message of the kingdom of God, and that this substitution was a ruinous distortion. The hope for the kingdom of God is for a vast transformation of history and of reality itself, a change that is fundamentally communitarian and in which nothing is lost. It is a transfiguration, defined as "a change that makes something better or more perfect."

However, it is worth recognizing that heaven is far from

dead nor has it passed away in either our high or popular culture. Heaven and hell have played a leading role in some of our greatest literature, from Homer to Dante to Milton's *Paradise Lost* and *Paradise Regained* to Marc Connelly's Pulitzer Prize–winning *The Green Pastures*, written in 1930, and produced with the first all-Black cast to appear on Broadway. In 1944, Jean-Paul Sartre's *No Exit* opened, with its notorious verdict that "hell is other people." Then there are films like *Black Orpheus*, which features a young man's search for his lover in the other world during Carnival in Brazil, and also *Flatliners* (1990 and 2017), in which a group of medical students experiment on each other with temporary deaths and short peeks into the next life. Belief and disbelief in heaven have contended with each other for a long time, and that dispute is far from over, something that randomly switching on a car radio any Sunday will amply demonstrate.

Heaven, however, in both colloquial and religious idiom in America today is unapologetically individualistic and minimalist. It is not a grand narrative, but a series of short stories. History, with all its achievements and catastrophes, is "left behind" (to use the language of the end-time novels in a different sense). Going to heaven is what some have aptly called an "extrication" salvation, meaning that it extricates human beings from whatever vexes or damages us, this "vale of tears," by simple removal. But it leaves the conditions that caused the pain unchanged so that they continue to plague those who have not yet been extricated. This makes it a severely egocentric view of salvation. I get saved, but *après moi le déluge.*

Since I started with a highly censorious perspective, the book was in danger of deteriorating into a relentless, and probably boring, tirade against conventional views of heaven. When I read the verse in Revelation, I had taken some cold comfort in seeing that St. John speaks of "heaven and earth" as having "passed away." My thought was, "Well, if that means heaven is dead or dying, good riddance." I almost entitled this book "The Death of Heaven." But that was impulsive and premature. I had not yet examined many heavens, and I had not read that verse in Revelation very carefully. At first glance, it had seemed to support what I thought was my justified disapproving stance toward "heaven talk," an attitude that was still firmly in place when I started to write. Christian theology, I thought, needed a thorough "de-heavening" to restore to Christianity the kingdom of God. But then two things intervened.

First, as I became more familiar with the vast variety of "heavens" we have encountered on this expedition, I also began to view them in a fresh way. I started to see them for what they are, fascinating and extraordinary creations of the human spirit. Like music, literature, and poetry, depictions of heaven are human inventions and an integral thread in the human story. It was not my purpose to affirm or deny the "reality" of any of the heavens, past or present, that we have visited in these pages. Even in uncovering the existential concern at the root of a vision of heaven, and then connecting it to a symbol of faith, I did not intend to defend either the validity of the underlying concern or the truth of the symbol. To attempt to do that would have carried me, as the saying goes, "Beyond my pay scale." I am not, however, ethically neutral about heavens or the roles they have played in the saga of humankind. It is undeniable that, like other such creations, images of heaven have often been misused in cruel and oppressive ways. One example is when their masters assured subjugated or enslaved people that they should bear up under present hardships because they would be rewarded in another life: there would be "pie in the sky by and by."

But heaven is not alone in its susceptibility to manipulation and exploitation. Virtually every human creation has also been abused. Writing has been seized upon and twisted into a vehicle for big and small lies. Scientific technology has been enlisted to devise ever more lethal weapons, capable of a scale of destruction unknown by previous generations. Films like Fellini's *La Strada* can awaken our sympathy for people looked upon as mentally challenged, but D. W. Griffith's *The Birth of a Nation* fanned racial discrimination. Even poetry has been twisted into barbs strung together into rhyming insults that deprecate the people they are flung at. But among all the inventions of the human spirit, music best illustrates this point. Melody, harmony, and rhythm have brought joy and comfort to young and old for centuries. But music has also been harnessed to thousands of causes and purposes, many of them heartless and destructive. In Germany, for example, where audiences thrilled to Beethoven's Fifth Symphony and Mozart's "The Magic Flute," mobs in the streets boomed the "Horst Wessel Song," the shrill Nazi hymn of hate.

There are whole albums of tender love songs, more than half of them lamenting a lost love. But there are also folders crammed with songs composed to fire up odium and stir people up to kill and maim other people in war. So many national anthems, like "La Marseillaise" or "The Star-Spangled Banner," reflect their birth in battles and summon hearers to press on with the bloody struggle. Protestants love to sing hymns, Catholics to intone Gregorian chants. Catchy tunes in a musical comedy spread quickly through the land. But not so long ago "minstrel shows" demeaned African Americans. And in fraternity houses and men's clubs, ditties that insult women are still belted out with gusto. Then there are lullabies that help children sleep, and work songs that strengthen men to fight exhaustion and boredom. And like heavens, music can convey the feel of varied regional and ethnic cultures. My point here is that although music has been put to multiple purposes, many of them hurtful, we do not refuse to welcome music into the catalog of human achievements. With few exceptions, this attitude of critical acceptance should be the rule. The fact that all these human handiworks I have listed can be misused should not banish the genre to which they belong. As the great Roman poet Terence said, "Nothing that is human is alien to me." Once we understand heavens not as divinely ordained, but as human creations, then they cannot be alien to us, and we owe them some sympathetic attention. It was at this point that I held my condemnatory purpose in check, at least until I learned more about what I was condemning.

The next thing that caused me to change my mind was that while reviewing the biblical references to "heaven," I went back to Revelation 21:1, which had pleased me so much earlier because it seemed to announce the death of heaven. But when I looked at it again, along with some commentaries, I was dismayed to discover that my interpretation had been hasty and uninformed, that is to say, "wrong." The text declares that in the ultimate victory of God, which has already begun, both heaven and earth will have "passed away," succeeded by a new heaven and a new earth. But this raises two related questions.

First, does the fact that the "new heaven" is still described as "a heaven" suggest *some element of continuity* between the old and the new heavens? For many years biblical scholars have suggested that it does. One of the classical commentators was one John Gill (1697–1771). Gill was an English Baptist who had learned Greek at eleven and later mastered Hebrew. His life ambition was to write a commentary on the whole Bible, which he actually succeeded in doing. It is still in use today, and in my opinion it can stand up to any more modern commentary. Here is what Gill says about the "passed away" mentioned in Revelation 21:

> not as to the substance of the heavens and earth, which will
> always remain, but as to the qualities of them, which will be

*altered: they will be renewed and refined, but not destroyed;*
*the bad qualities, or evil circumstances, which attend them*
*through the sin of man, will be removed and pass away, but*
*they themselves will continue in being.*

The Book of Revelation, like similar apocalyptic texts, is written in terms of a future triumph of God, but it is not just about the future. Biblical writers often use the future tense to say something about the present. And it is crucial to remember that for Jesus, this future is already occurring now. Thus, when Revelation describes a restored heaven and earth after their passing, it means that this change is already under way. It is happening, sometimes hidden, sometimes openly, "in the midst" of us if we open our eyes to see it. It is here "in part" now, and even though its ultimate fulfillment still lies ahead, we can taste its "first fruits" today.

But then there is the second part of Revelation 21:1, which I had been overlooking. It is about the "sea," which it says, "is no more." The "no more" here strikes a note of utter finality, even obliteration that "passed away" does not have. In the Bible, the "sea" (the word is sometimes translated as the "abyss") is the most recurrent symbol for the source of evil, chaos, and destruction. In Genesis, the sea had to be tamed and confined to certain limits to complete the creation. In Exodus it loomed as an impossible barrier during the Jews' escape from captivity until God made a path through it. One demonstration of the power God conferred on Jesus was that he could tame the waves and walk on the water. Thus, the verse in Revelation draws a stark contrast. While heaven and earth pass away and a transfigured version of them appears, the sea is gone forever. It is no more.

The destruction of the abyss and the transfiguration of heaven and earth are in keeping with other elements in biblical faith in which "regeneration," "renewal," and "return" figure so prominently. The promise of the transformation of heaven and earth, rather than their annihilation, is clearly voiced by the profound contrast just described between heaven on the one hand and the sea on the other. This does not diminish the seriousness of having "passed away" but emphasizes the power of a God who can take even a heaven that has passed away and make it into a "new heaven."

The archetype of this kind of change is the resurrection of Christ. The disciples' confidence that he was alive after his crucifixion was not based on the idea that he had never really died (against the antagonists of Christianity who claimed he had merely been in a coma). For the disciples, their master had indeed been dead, really dead, but God had raised him. And his followers also insisted that the Jesus who had risen was the same Jesus they had known as they wandered through Galilee before his arrest. And, to forestall any lingering doubts they may have harbored about this, Jesus used several actions to demonstrate the continuity between his life before and after his crucifixion. He talked with them, had them touch his wounds, and ate a breakfast of broiled fish with them. This continuity between the pre- and post-Easter Jesus is the same continuity promised between the old and the new heaven and earth.

The sweeping promise of the resurrection, first of Christ and then of all things, is that, ultimately, nothing is lost. "All things are made new" (2 Corinthians 5:17). Empires and civilizations rise and fall. People are born and die, but God will be faithful to his promise, a promise infinitely more far-reaching than the wish for a heaven populated by disembodied essences uprooted from history with all its successes and failures. What then about the myriad depictions of heaven that have been part of human life since it became human? Might they also be "made new"?

If we set aside the literalist readings of the descriptions of heaven we have found, and look at them as creations of the spiritual imagination, then—like all other such creations—we can recognize and value them as integral to the whole human and cosmic saga, the history that God is redeeming. Empirically "true" or not, these pictures of the hereafter have had untold influence on countless people. To leave them out would be to present a truncated account.

During this long trip we have added a lot of stamp marks in our passports. Was all that travel necessary? Not necessary, perhaps, but invaluable and deeply enriching. The Christian doctrine of the incarnation asserts that in sharing our humanity in one person, God shares it with all humans, and if "nothing human is foreign to us," then the more we know about what is human, the more human we become. Karl Marx once wrote that religion is the "sigh of the oppressed creature, the heart of a heartless world, and the soul of soulless conditions. . . ." If, then, the gospel of Christ impels us to ameliorate the oppression, soften the heartlessness, and enliven the soullessness, then we have to know how those who suffer under these conditions experience them, and what we can do to change them.

The transformation promised by the coming of the kingdom of God is repeatedly described in the Bible as a form of healing. But one of the first questions a doctor asks when starting to treat a patient is, "Where is the pain?" Marx was primarily a diagnostician, concerned with locating the pain. Famously, he also added the words "opium of the people" to his description of religion. But, as some of his interpreters have said, Marx was saying that under the heartless and soulless conditions he recognized, religion provided a way to survive. Marx's answer, however, was not to increase the dosage of the opium but to change the repressive structures that made it necessary.

Ideas about heaven have often been dismissed as pipe dreams or wishful thinking. Undoubtedly, there is an element of truth in these denunciations, but if they enable us to know more about

the hope and hurt of distressed or even not so distressed creatures, what is it that causes the distress? This is not to suggest
that all these causes can be eradicated, but realizing that does
not mean that none of them can. It is true that insisting on the
perfect can be the enemy of the good, but recognizing that some
things cannot be changed does mean that we should not try to
change the things that can be changed. A skilled and sympathetic therapist helps people to distinguish the changeable from
the unchangeable, but that insight can also come from learning
to be aware of our own habitual ways of thinking.

It is said that "travel is broadening," and our tour through
so many heavens should add to that enlargement. A given culture's idea of heaven is an important clue to its anxieties and
aspirations. Just as we might explore a prehistoric cave habita-
tion and ask what kinds of people lived here, we can ask the
same questions of a civilization's visualizations of the afterlife.
We can ask similar questions when we visit the places where
people lived a thousand years or many thousands of years ago.
Similar queries are inspired by works of art, the layout of towns,
burial customs, poetry, and songs. What was running through
the imaginations of those sculptures and painters? The flaccid
idea that we should not waste our time on such fantasizing since
we "can never really know" should be ignored. The speculation
I am discussing here amplifies our mental universe, places us in
a wider cultural world, and can suggest possibilities we might
never have thought of.

As we end this expedition it is vital to remember that the
symbol of ultimate fulfillment that most frequently appears is
a *feast*. As a ritual, feasting is present in a wide assortment of
forms in nearly every religion. In Christianity, from its outset,
gathering around food, usually including bread and wine, has
been the defining action. This food sharing can range from "two
or three" grouped together to the thousands who assemble in

St. Peter's for a midnight Christmas Mass. Generations of Christians have seen the Communion meal, the Lord's Supper, as a sign of the kingdom, the heavenly feast. This gastronomic custom has weathered many storms. Despite their bitter disputes with the Catholics, the reformers kept it. Even Unitarians and Quakers, the most thoroughgoing of ecclesiastical downsizers, still observe a form of Communion. When Sister Mary Corita Kent, the Catholic pop artist, looked for a symbol that would cross denominational lines and even the lines between religious and nonreligious people, she chose bread. She liked to caricature commercial products, and one of her favorite slogans, this one delighting in the Eucharist, was, "Have you tried wonder bread lately?" When she presided over an antiwar rally in Boston decades ago, with an ingenious bit of wordplay, she called the event "A Peace of Bread."

Communion is a powerful and enduring symbol. But it has also been the victim of confusing labeling and disingenuous characterizations. It was often called "the medicine of immortality," but this designation is highly misleading. The concept of immortality, although it has persisted in much of popular piety, and even in some official liturgies, is not the same as resurrection, and it is not a Christian teaching. Also, the likening of mortality to a sickness for which we need a spiritual medication runs counter to the biblical concept of what it means to be mortal, which is to be finite and to have only a limited span of years.

In the creation story in Genesis, Eve is tempted by the wiles of the serpent to lure her into eating the fruit of the forbidden tree, to "be like God," and not having to die. In other words, it is Satan who is dangling a medicine of immortality. The reason she and Adam succumb to the tempter is that they were not content with being merely human but yearned to be "like God." Being mortal is neither a sin nor a disease. The biblical understanding is that our alienation from God and others, which we know as sin, is not the result of our mortality or our finitude, but of our refusal to accept our finitude. Being mortal is not a sin, not something we need to be cured of.

The Communion meal, the Lord's Supper, is not a prescription remedy; it is an enactment of the fulfillment of God's purpose and a taste of what is to come. The elements used are not nectar and ambrosia, the delicacies of the gods; they are not even manna that falls from the skies. They are the most ordinary of ordinary things: bread and wine. And these ingredients are the products of human labor in planting, cultivating, harvesting, baking, or bottling, shipping, and distributing: a complete economy. Those who partake of the feast include (or should include) persons of "all sorts and conditions." No one should be excluded. Most significantly, everyone at the Communion table receives an equal portion. No one gets any more than anyone else. It is the model of a radically distributive society. Thus, with the aspirational/normative pattern described above, the Communion meal is not only pointing to what lies ahead but is demonstrating what could be going on here and now.

Even though I was raised in a tradition that does not make Communion central (we observed it once a month), I have come to realize how potent it can be. It was at a Communion service that I had one of the most memorable spiritual experiences of my life. Our whole family used to spend part of each summer on beautiful Martha's Vineyard. In addition to swimming and sailing there, on Sunday we also attended a small Episcopal church in the town of Vineyard Haven. Down the street from that church was a camp for what we now call special-needs children. It was named Camp Jabber Wacky. On Sunday mornings, the camp counselors escorted twenty or so of the children, ages ten to fourteen, to attend a service in the church. The rector welcomed them, even though they could occasionally be unintentionally disruptive. They loved to sing, although what they sang was not always what the congregation was singing; and when the hymn ended, they sometimes continued to sing until a counselor discreetly quieted them. But no one in the congregation ever objected.

Once during a Communion service, I found myself kneeling at the altar rail with children from Camp Jabber Wacky on both sides of me. Then when the minister distributed the "bread of heaven" and wine, I noticed that the children took it along with everyone else. It was at that moment that I had my epiphany. "Yes," I thought, "*this* is what it is *all about*, a foretaste of the kingdom of God!"

I recognized that, short of a miraculous new medical breakthrough, probably none of these children would ever "succeed" as our society measures success. They would not be admitted to elite colleges, or maybe any college. They would not become celebrated musicians or head profitable corporations. They would probably never write any books. But in God's sight, they were just as welcome as I was to this sign of the coming new reality. And I also realized that since the first fruits of that new era were appearing among us, I should be treating what Jesus called "these little ones" as fellow citizens of our shared kingdom.

Now, years later, and after surveying dozens of "heavens," it is this image of "the ultimate" that remains with me, a beloved community in which everyone is welcomed and special-needs children sing for as long and as loud as they want to.

# Index

abduction, extraterrestrial, 193-99.
  *See also* Mack, John
abolitionist movement, and kingdom
  of God, 85
Achilles, in Hades, 118, 119
Aelia Capitolina (Jerusalem), 256
Aeneas, visit to Hades, 117, 120, 121
*Aeneid* (Virgil), 117, 120, 121
African Orthodox Church, 232–44
afterlife
  alternative visions of, 154, 161,
    162
  beliefs of early followers of Jesus,
    54, 56
  of children, in Swedenborg, 142,
    144
  depictions of, 116–31
  Greek vision of, 118–23
  for Homer, 123
  Jewish interest in, 92–96, 99,
    102–4
  lack of consensus on, among
    first-century Jews, 53
  Mormon beliefs about, 213, 214
  for Plato, 123
  in Swedenborg's writings, 141–45
  for Virgil, 123
  *See also* heaven; hell, kingdom of
    God; reigning of God
Ahlstrom, Sidney, 216
Al-Quds (Jerusalem), 256
alien abductions. *See* abduction,
  extraterrestrial
alienation, and original sin, 179

*aliyah*, 100
America, as City on a Hill, 83
American Colonization Society, 233
American Revolutionary War, and
  kingdom of God, 84
Americanism, of Father Divine, 245
Amichai, Yehuda, 264
Amish, 202
Anabaptists, baptism by immersion,
  18
ancestors
  accessibility to, among Native
    peoples, 200
  invoking of, 157, 158, 160, 162
angelology, 184
angels
  in art and poetry, 187, 188
  belief in, 188, 189, 199, 200
  in the Bible, 183, 184
  depictions of, 182, 187
  disappearance of, 191
  divinity of, 186
  fallen, 185
  of Father Divine, 222–24
  hierarchies of, 185, 186
  as messengers and agents of
    God, 183, 184
  origin as humans, in Swedenborg,
    143
  role in ruling nations, 184, 185
  Sadducean disbelief in, 51
  in Swedenborg's visions and
    auditory experiences, 140–45
  in theological discourse, 189, 190

279

"spiritual but not religious," 218–20
Southern Christian Leadership
  Conference, 236
speaking in tongues, and Pentecostalism, 240, 241, 242
Spinoza, Baruch, excommunication
  from synagogue, 137, 138
spiritual bodies, of angels, 186, 187
spiritual eyes (Swedenborg), 142
Spiritualism, 191, 216–18
spiritualist churches, 191
Spiritualists, and unity with God, 226
Sree Padmanabhaswamy (Hindu)
  Temple (South India), 8
Stein, Gertrude, xiii, xiv
Sunday, Billy, 210
Swedenborg, Emanuel
  and angels, 140–45
  on dying, 142
  as heretic, 136, 137
  intellectual followers of, 132
  on problem of evil, 142
  as scientist, 136
  and spiritual meaning of
    Scripture, 140, 150
  visions/auditions of, 139–41
symbolic language, 11
*Symbolic Wounds* (Bruno Bettelheim), 16
symbols/symbolism
  Communion as, 275–77
  death and rebirth, 23–25
  feasting and ultimate fulfillment,
    274
  Jerusalem, as, 247, 248
  and literalism, 148–51
  messianic banquet as, 254
  significance of, 11

Tartarus, 120, 122
Teresa of Avila, Saint
  and unity with God, 225
  visions of, 138

Tetzel, Johannes, and sale of
  indulgences, 167
theology of the people, 173
Thomas Aquinas, Saint
  on angels, 186, 187
  on reincarnation, 96
threshold syndrome, and purgatory,
  173, 174
*Tibetan Book of the Dead*, 174, 214
Tillich, Paul
  and hermeneutic of culture, 173,
    176, 177
  and method of correlation, xiii,
    xiv, 266
  and quest for meaning, xv, xvi
  on religious language, 148–50
Toplady, Augustus Montague, 180
Tostesen, Daniel, 196
transfiguration, of heaven and earth,
  267–77
transmigration of souls, 96
*Treatise on Purgatory* (Catherine of
  Genoa), 179
trinitarian theology, and angels,
  184
true church, 63, 64, 68, 70, 80
true cross relic, 253
Tubman, Harriet, 239
Turner, Nat
  slave revolt of, 229–32
  visions and heavenly messages of,
    230, 231
Twelve Steps (Alcoholics Anonymous), 175

ultimate human destiny, 3–9
*Unam Sanctam*, and papal authority
  and power, 66
Uncle Frank (funeral director), xi,
  31–34, 36–37, 39–44, 46
Universal Negro Improvement
  Association, 232
Unleavened Bread, Feast of, 106